Teacher's Guide

Studio 3 VERT

www.pearsonschools.co.uk
✓ Free online support
✓ Useful weblinks
✓ 24 hour online ordering

0845 630 33 33

Tracy Traynor

ALWAYS LEARNING PEARSON

Published by Pearson Education Limited, Edinburgh Gate, Harlow, Essex, CM20 2JE.

www.pearsonschoolsandfecolleges.co.uk

Text and ActiveTeach platform © Pearson Education Limited 2013

Edited by Sara McKenna
Designed by Emily Hunter-Higgins
Typeset by Kamae Design, Oxford
Original illustrations © Pearson Education Limited 2013
Illustrated by Caron at KJA Artists
Cover design by Emily Hunter-Higgins
Cover photos © Main picture: Studio Natacha Nicaise/Natacha Nicaise; Mountain: Shutterstock/M.M.G.; Skateboarder: Getty Images/PhotoDisc; Parkour: Corbis/Cardinal; Eiffel Tower: Shutterstock/Ints Vikmanis; La Défense square arch: Shutterstock/Alexander Mul

First published 2013

17 16 15
10 9 8 7 6 5 4 3

British Library Cataloguing in Publication Data
A catalogue record for this book is available from the British Library

ISBN 978 1 44796029 4

Copyright notice

The material in this publication is copyright. Pages may be freely downloaded, edited and/or photocopied for use exclusively by and within the purchasing institution. Under no circumstances may copies of the material be offered for sale. If you or anyone else wish to use the material in any way other than that specified you or they must apply in writing to the publishers.

This product is accompanied by downloadable editable Word files. Pearson Education Limited is not responsible for the quality, accuracy or fitness for purpose of the materials contained in the Word files once edited. To revert to the original Word files, redownload them from the given URL.

Printed in the UK by Henry Ling Ltd.

Acknowledgements

Every effort has been made to contact copyright holders of material reproduced in this book. Any omissions will be rectified in subsequent printings if notice is given to the publishers.

Contents

Introduction 4

Module 1	**Ma vie sociale d'ado**	15
Module 2	**Bien dans sa peau**	48
Module 3	**À l'horizon**	76
Module 4	**Spécial vacances**	105
Module 5	**Moi dans le monde**	135

Introduction

Course description

Studio is a fully differentiated 11–14 French course in three stages – *Studio 1* for Year 7, *Studio 2* for Year 8 and *Studio 3* for Year 9. The Year 7 resources also include a separate short book, *Accès Studio*, which enables flexibility in teaching the language according to pupils' prior experience of learning French at Key Stage 2. In *Studio 3 Vert* pupils can be assessed at National Curriculum levels 1 to 5.

The course has been written to reflect the world pupils live in, using contexts familiar to them in their everyday lives and teaching them the vocabulary that they need to communicate with young French people of their own age on topics that interest and stimulate them. They are introduced to young French people and given insight into the everyday life and culture of France and other French-speaking countries, encouraging intercultural understanding.

At the same time, *Studio* ensures that pupils are taught the language learning skills and strategies that they need to become independent language learners. The elements of the 2014 Programme of Study for Key Stage 3 Modern Languages (grammar and vocabulary, and linguistic competence) are fully integrated into the course. In addition, pupils have the chance to experience cross-curricular studies and are given regular opportunities to develop and practise the personal, learning and thinking skills required to operate as independent enquirers, creative thinkers, reflective learners, team workers, self-managers and effective participators.

Studio ActiveTeach (see details on pp. 5–6) provides easy-to-use and exciting technology designed to add dynamism and fun to whole-class teaching. For individual pupil use, *Studio ActiveLearn* provides a wealth of exciting differentiated material for pupils to access individually via computers or mobile devices, in class or for homework.

Differentiation

Studio 3 Vert is written for those pupils who will progress at a moderate or slow pace through the National Curriculum levels in Year 9. Pupils who are able enough can reach Level 5 by the end of the book. Clearly, pupils will work at different levels and at different paces, and every module caters for the given range of National Curriculum levels in the following ways:

- There are differentiated activities within the target range of NC Levels in listening, speaking, reading and writing throughout the Pupil Book.
- Ideas are given in the Teacher's Guide for simplifying and extending the Pupil Book activities.
- *En plus* units at the end of every module contain longer reading and listening passages to provide opportunities for extension work.
- The *À toi* section at the back of the Pupil Book provides extra reading and writing activities at reinforcement and extension levels.
- The *Studio 3 Vert* workbook provides further reading and writing activities at reinforcement and extension levels.

Studio 3 Vert

Pupil Book

- Full coverage of the 2014 Programmes of Study for Key Stage 3 MFL
- Assessment right from the start
- Exciting video introducing pupils to the lives of young people in France
- Fully integrated grammar explanations and practice ensuring logical and rigorous progression
- Opportunities for cross-curricular topics and emphasis on language learning skills
- Fully integrated opportunities for PLTS

The Pupil Book consists of five core subdivided as follows:

- Five double-page core units – these contain the core material that must be taught to ensure that all the key language and grammar is covered in Year 9.
- *Bilan* – this is a checklist of 'I can' statements, allowing pupils to check their progress as part of Assessment for Learning.
- *Révisions* – optional revision activities that can be used as a 'mock' test preceding the end of module *Contrôle* in the Assessment Pack.
- *En plus* – an optional unit in which no new core language is introduced. The unit can therefore be missed out if you are short of time. However, these units contain lots of useful activities and tips for developing language learning skills, including longer reading and listening passages and opportunities for oral presentations.
- *Je parle* and/or *J'écris* – an extra challenge to develop speaking or writing skills.
- *Studio Grammaire* – two pages where the key grammar points introduced in the module are explained fully and accompanied by practice activities.
- *Vocabulaire* – two pages of module word lists for vocabulary learning and revision, plus a *Stratégie* tip box to help pupils acquire the skills they need to learn vocabulary and structure and understand texts more effectively.

© Pearson Education Ltd 2013. Copying permitted for purchasing institution only. This material is not copyright free.

At the back of the Pupil Book there are four further sections:
- *À toi* – self-access differentiated reading and writing activities. *À toi A* contains reinforcement activities for lower-ability pupils, and *À toi B* contains extension activities for higher-ability pupils. These are ideal for use as homework.
- Verb tables.
- *Speaking and writing skills* – one page of tips on how to improve speaking and writing skills.
- *Mini-dictionnaire* – a comprehensive French-English glossary, organised alphabetically and containing all the vocabulary encountered in *Studio 3 Vert*. There is also a list of the French rubrics used in the Pupil Book.

Teacher's Guide

The Teacher's Guide contains all the support required to help teachers use *Studio 3 Vert* effectively in the classroom:
- Clear and concise teaching notes, including lesson starters, plenaries and PLTS references for every unit.
- Full cross-referencing to the 2014 National Curriculum Programme of Study
- Cross-referencing to the Foundation Certificate of Secondary Education in French (Revised specification with first testing in 2014).
- Overview grids for each module highlighting grammar content and skills coverage.
- Answers to all the activities.
- The complete audioscript for all the listening activities in the *Studio 3 Vert* Pupil Book.
- Guidance on using the course with the full ability range.

With the Teacher's Guide there is an accompanying customisable scheme of work offering complete help with planning, and showing how the course covers the National Curriculum Programme of Study.

The Teacher's Guide is available as a printed, spiral-bound book (scheme of work supplied as downloadable Word files with instructions on how to access them inside the front cover). Alternatively both the complete Teacher's Guide content and scheme of work can be purchased and accessed as Word files online (via the *ActiveTeach* Library). From there they can be downloaded and printed off as necessary.

ActiveTeach

ActiveTeach is a powerful and motivating resource combining the 'book on screen' and a wealth of supporting materials – providing you with the perfect tool for whole-class teaching.
- Use the on-screen Pupil Book with all the listening activities included.
- Zoom in on areas of text and activities to facilitate whole-class teaching.
- Build your own lessons and add in your own resources to help personalise learning.
- Use fun and motivating electronic flashcards to teach new vocabulary.
- Consolidate language using the whole-class interactive games.
- Use the video clips to introduce your pupils to the lives of young French people.
- Teach and revise grammar using PowerPoint® presentations, followed by interactive grammar activities on key grammar points.
- Download and print off a variety of extra worksheets for starters, plenaries, consolidation of grammar, thinking skills, language-learning skills, development of the four skills (reading, writing, speaking and listening), self assessment and vocab lists. These are ideal for follow-up work, cover lessons and homework.
- You can also download and print off worksheets with a current topical and cultural focus. These are updated half-termly, and, once up online, will remain there to be accessed or downloaded at any time.

The wide variety of worksheets in *ActiveTeach* (mentioned above) can be used to consolidate and extend pupils' learning as follows:

Module 1

Learning skills	Learning vocabulary
Listening skills	Transcription
Grammar skills	The present tense
Thinking skills	Logic puzzle
Grammar skills	The perfect tense
Learning skills	Using spider diagrams
Grammar skills	Using two tenses
Assignment	Mon blog (with NC assessment)

Module 2

Reading skills	Reading unfamiliar texts
Thinking skills	Odd one out!
Grammar skills	Using negatives
Grammar skills	The near future
Thinking skills	Making connections
Grammar skills	Using three tenses together
Assignment	Le sport et le fitness (with NC assessment)

Module 3

Thinking skills	Cracking the code
Grammar skills	Irregular verbs and asking questions
Learning skills	Looking up nouns in a dictionary
Grammar skills	The near future and *je voudrais*
Learning skills	Using different tenses
Thinking skills	Making logical connections
Reading skills	Reading a poem
Assignment	Mon CV (with NC assessment)

© Pearson Education Ltd 2013. Copying permitted for purchasing institution only. This material is not copyright free.

Module 4

Grammar skills	Asking questions using question words
Listening skills	Listening for gist and detail
Learning skills	Learning by heart
Thinking skills	Logic puzzle
Grammar skills	Using the perfect tense
Thinking skills	Drawing from text
Reading skills	Reading complicated texts
Assignment	Le centre de vacances (with NC assessment)

Module 5

Thinking skills	Unravelling texts
Grammar skills	Using three tenses
Learning skills	Interpreting texts
Thinking skills	Fact or opinion?
Learning skills	Recognising patterns
Grammar skills	Infinitives
Assignment	Le bonheur (with NC assessment)

Assignment (Défi)

The worksheets include a collaborative assignment or challenge (Défi) to be carried out in pairs or groups.

The assignments consist of two worksheets, one containing the instructions for the task, the other providing preparation tasks and language to help the pupils.

The focus of the assignments is to help the pupils develop further their extended speaking and writing skills in cross-curricular contexts while fostering PLTS.

Audio

The audio files for the course contain all the recorded material for the listening activities in the Pupil Book. These audio files are also contained on ActiveTeach so only teachers who do not purchase ActiveTeach will need to buy the Audio Files. The different types of activities can be used for presentation of new language, comprehension and pronunciation practice. The material includes dialogues, interviews and songs recorded by native speakers.

After purchasing the audio files for Studio, you can access and download them online from the ActiveTeach Library. From there they can be saved onto your computer or network for future use.

Please note: the audio files and ActiveTeach do not contain the listening material for the end of module tests and end of year test. This material can be found in the Assessment Pack (see right).

Workbooks

The Studio 3 Vert workbook contains one or two pages of activities for each double-page unit in the Pupil Book. It fulfils a number of functions:

- It provides self-access reading and writing activities designed to offer the pupils enjoyable ways of consolidating and practising the language they have learned in each unit.
- It gives extra practice in grammar and thinking skills, with integrated activities throughout.
- Revision pages at the end of each module (Révisions) help pupils revise what they have learned during the module.
- Module word lists (Vocabulaire) with English translations are invaluable for language learning homework.
- The J'avance pages at the end of each module allow pupils to record their National Curriculum level in listening, speaking, reading and writing and set themselves improvement targets for the next module.
- NC level descriptors in pupil-friendly language at the back of the workbook allow pupils to see what they must do to progress through the NC levels in all four skills.

The Workbooks are available as print books sold in packs of 8 or can be downloaded as PDFs from the ActiveTeach Library.

Assessment Pack

The Assessment Pack contains all the assessment material required to assess pupils in Year 8 in all four skills, as well as self-assessment sheets.

- End of module tests in all four skills – listening, speaking, reading and writing.
- End of year test in all four skills.
- Covers levels 4 to 7.
- Target setting sheets.

The assessment pages and the audio can be downloaded online from the ActiveTeach Library. There you will find Word files and PDF versions of the test sheets, alongside the sound files for the listening tests.

Grammar coverage

Grammar is fully integrated into the teaching sequence in Studio to ensure that pupils have the opportunity to learn thoroughly the underlying structures of the French language. All units have a grammar objective so that pupils can see clearly which grammar structures they are learning. The key grammar points are presented in the Studio Grammaire boxes on the Pupil Book pages and fuller explanations and practice are provided in the Studio Grammaire pages at the end of each module. In addition, there are grammar PowerPoint® presentations in ActiveTeach for presenting new grammar concepts to classes, followed by interactive practice activities that can be used with whole classes or for individual practice. Worksheets focusing on the key grammar topics taught in *Studio 3 Vert* are also provided in *ActiveTeach* and can be printed off for individual pupil use.

Grammar points explained and practised in *Studio 3 Vert*:
- present tense of regular *–er* verbs
- present tense of *aller, avoir, être, faire, prendre*
- perfect tense of regular verbs
- perfect tense of irregular verbs
- perfect tense with *être*
- the near future (*aller* + infinitive)
- using three tenses together
- *je voudrais* + infinitive
- reflexive verbs
- modal verbs (*vouloir, pouvoir, devoir*) + infinitive
- forming questions (using rising intonation, *est-ce que* and question words)
- negatives (*ne ... pas, ne ... jamais*)
- adjective agreement
- possessive adjectives
- *à* + the definite article
- the partitive article
- *il faut* + infinitive
- expressions with *avoir*

Coverage of the Programmes of Study in *Studio 3 Vert*

In *Studio* the 2014 National Curriculum Programme of Study is covered comprehensively. The Programme of Study is as follows:

1 Grammar and vocabulary

Pupils should be taught to:
- identify and use tenses or other structures which convey the present, past, and future as appropriate to the language being studied
- use and manipulate a variety of key grammatical structures and patterns, including voices and moods, as appropriate
- develop and use a wide-ranging and deepening vocabulary that goes beyond their immediate needs and interests, allowing them to give and justify opinions and take part in discussion about wider issues
- use accurate grammar, spelling and punctuation

2 Linguistic competence

Pupils should be taught to:
- listen to a variety of forms of spoken language to obtain information and respond appropriately
- transcribe words and short sentences that they hear with increasing accuracy

- initiate and develop conversations, coping with unfamiliar language and unexpected responses, making use of important social conventions such as formal modes of address
- express and develop ideas clearly and with increasing accuracy, both orally and in writing
- speak coherently and confidently, with increasingly accurate pronunciation and intonation
- read and show comprehension of original and adapted materials from a range of different sources, understanding the purpose, important ideas and details, and provide an accurate English translation of short, suitable material
- read literary texts in the language, such as stories, songs, poems and letters, to stimulate ideas, develop creative expression and expand understanding of the language and culture
- write prose using an increasingly wide range of grammar and vocabulary, write creatively to express their own ideas and opinions, and translate short written text accurately into the foreign language.

The table below outlines the points from the Programme of Study in short form, and shows where they are covered in *Studio 3 Vert*. The content of the course is also matched to the Programme of Study unit by unit throughout this Teacher's Guide.

1 Grammar and vocabulary (GV)	
GV1 Tenses	M1 U1, M1 U2, M1 U3, M1 U4, M1 U5, M2 U4, M2 U5, M3 U1, M3 U3, M4 U4, M4 U5, M5 U3
GV2 Grammatical structures	M2 U1, M2 U2, M2 U3, M3 U2, M3 U4, M3 U5, M4 U1, M4 U2, M4 U3, M4 U5, M5 U1, M5 U2, M5 U4
GV3 Developing vocabulary	M1 U2, M2 U1, M2 U3, M2 U4, M3 U4, M3 *En plus*, M4 U1, M4 U3, M5 U2
Opinions and discussions	M1 U3, M1 U4, M2 U2, M3 U2, M3 U5, M4 U2
GV4 Accuracy	M1 U2, M1 U5

© Pearson Education Ltd 2013. Copying permitted for purchasing institution only. This material is not copyright free.

2 Linguistic competence (LC)	
LC1 Listening and responding	M1 U1, M1 U3, M2 U3, M2 U4, M2 *En plus*, M3 U1, M3 U5, M3 *En plus*, M4 U3, M4 U4, M4 *En plus*, M5 U2, M5 U3, M5 U4
LC2 Transcription	Worksheet 1.2
LC3 Conversation	M1 U3, M1 *En plus*, M2 U2, M2 U5, M2 *En plus*, M3 U3, M3 U5, M4 U2, M4 U4, M5 U1, M5 U2, M5 *En plus*
Conversation (dealing with the unexpected)	M4 U1
Conversation (using modes of address)	*Studio* 1
LC4 Expressing ideas (speaking)	M1 U1, M2 U5
Expressing ideas (writing)	M1 U4, M1 *En plus*, M3 U1, M3 U4, M4 U1, M5 U1, M5 U3, M5 *En plus*
LC5 Speaking coherently and confidently	M1 U5, M2 U5, M4 U5
Accurate pronunciation and intonation	M1 U1, M1 U4, M1 U5, M2 U1, M3 U3, M4 U2, M4 U3, M5 U3
LC6 Reading comprehension	M1 U2, M1 *En plus*, M2 U1, M2 U2, M2 U3, M2 U4, M2 *En plus*, M3 U1, M3 U2, M3 U3, M3 *En plus*, M4 U4, M4 U5 (authentic), M4 *En plus*, M5 U1, M5 U4, M5 *En plus* (adapted from authentic)
Translation into English	M1 *En plus*, M3 U4, M4 *En plus*, M5 U4
LC7 Literary texts	Worksheet 3.7

LC8 Writing creatively	M3 U2, M4 U5, M4 *En plus*, M5 *En plus*
Translation into French	M3 U3

National Curriculum Levels in *Studio*

The 2014 National Curriculum no longer includes Level Descriptors for Levels 1–8 and exceptional performance. In order to ensure sound progression, as well as to aid progress tracking and reporting, *Studio* keeps the levels in place, using the level descriptors as they were in the previous Curriculum. In the course they feature in the following ways:

- All activities in the course are levelled (in the teacher's notes) from Levels 1–7
- End of Module Assessments for *Studio* have been written using the National Curriculum Levels to indicate the level of challenge
- Workbooks contain self assessment and target setting pages based around the old National Curriculum Levels.

As the new National Programmes of Study become established in schools from 2014, their use in Studio, as well as the use of the older NC Level descriptors, will be reviewed to make sure that the course provides the most valid and up to date account of how achievement is measured and progress is tracked.

Coverage of Personal Learning and Thinking Skills in *Studio 3 Vert*

Activities supporting PLTS development are included throughout the course. Key examples are highlighted in the Teacher's Guide using the PLTS icon PLTS : one PLTS is identified in each unit, with Modules 1–5 all featuring the full range of PLTS. A selection of these is listed below, with details of how they meet the curriculum requirements.

Personal Learning and Thinking Skills	
I Independent enquirers	Pupil Book activities throughout the course (e.g. M3 U1 ex. 6); ICT-/other research-based activities (e.g. M2 U2 suggestion after ex. 7, M4 U2 ex. 7)
C Creative thinkers	Regular activities developing skills strategies (how to improve listening/speaking, etc.) (e.g. M5 U4 ex. 8); activities requiring pupils to identify patterns and work out rules (e.g. M1 U3 Starter 2, M4 U5 ex. 6); activities requiring creative production of language (M2 U1 ex. 9 and all *Je parle/J'écris* sections)
R Reflective learners	Ongoing opportunities to assess work and identify areas for improvement (e.g. M2 En plus ex. 3, M1 U4 ex. 7), including all *Bilans* and Plenaries (e.g. M5 U3 Plenary) and all *Je parle/J'écris* sections
T Team workers	Regular pair- and team-work activities (e.g. M5 U1 ex. 3), including many Starters (e.g. M3 U5 Starter 2); regular peer assessment (e.g. M4 U3 Starter 2 and all *Je parle* sections); links with partner schools (e.g. M1 U2 ex. 8 suggestion)
S Self-managers	Ongoing advice on managing learning (e.g. M2 U3 Plenary), including strategies to improve learning (e.g. M4 U4 ex. 5)
E Effective participators	Opportunities throughout the course for pupils to contribute (e.g. M3 U2 Starter 1), including discussions based on module openers, presentations (e.g. M2 U5 ex. 6 and all *Je parle* sections) and all Plenaries (e.g. M5 U2 Plenary)

Pupils may find the following short forms useful as a reference in class:

I am a/an …	Today I …		
Independent enquirer	PLTS	**I**	worked on my own to find out something new
Creative thinker	PLTS	**C**	used what I know to work out or create something new
Reflective learner	PLTS	**R**	thought about what I've learned and how I can improve
Team worker	PLTS	**T**	worked well with other people
Self-manager	PLTS	**S**	took responsibility for improving my learning
Effective participator	PLTS	**E**	took part in the lesson in a positive way

© Pearson Education Ltd 2013. Copying permitted for purchasing institution only. This material is not copyright free.

Coverage of the Foundation Certificate of Secondary Education in French in *Studio 3 Vert*

Studio can be used to teach the Key Stage 3 FCSE qualification from AQA. The following table shows where each of the FCSE units and sub-topics for the Revised Specification (2014) can be taught using *Studio 3 Vert*. Many of the FCSE units and subtopics that do not appear in the *Studio 3 Rouge* or *Vert* grid are covered in *Studio 1* or *Studio 2 Rouge/Vert*. A separate leaflet is also available showing the FCSE Revised Specification coverage across all three stages of *Studio* (*Studio 1*, *Studio 2 Rouge/Vert*, *Studio 3 Rouge/Vert*).

Unit 1 – Relationships, family and friends

Sub-topics	Where in *Studio 3 Vert*
Reading and listening	
Family and step family	
Personal details about family	
Mini biography of family	
Rank in family	
Personal details about friends	
Girlfriend, boyfriend	Module 1, Unit 4
Relationships and reasons for good and bad relations within family and friends	Module 5, Unit 1
Issues	Module 5, Unit 1
Taking sides in an argument	Module 5, Unit 1
Pets	
Clothes	
Family celebrations	
Prepositions	
Numbers	
Speaking and writing	
Personal information	Module 1, Unit 1
Family/friends	
Meeting up with friends/activities	Module 1, Unit 3 / Module 1, Unit 4
Descriptions	Module 1, Unit 1
Hobbies/free-time activities	Module 1, Unit 3 / Module 1, Unit 4

Unit 2 – Education and future plans

Sub-topics	Where in *Studio 3 Vert*
Reading and listening	
Education School: teachers, problems, transport, timetable, uniform, facilities, type of school, location, subjects, rules, school clubs, sport, progress report, items in school bag	Module 4, *En plus*
Future plans	
Plans for after school	Module 3, Unit 1
Plans for jobs and careers	Module 3, Unit 1 / Module 3, Unit 5
Plans for future study	Module 3, Unit 1
Advantages and disadvantages of jobs	Module 3, Unit 3
Advantages and disadvantages of staying on at school	
Time	
Prepositions of place	
Alphabet	
Numbers	
Sequence	Module 2, Unit 4
Speaking and writing	
Physical description of school	
School activities	
Opinions	
Uniform	
Future plans	Module 3, Unit 1 / Module 3, Unit 5

© Pearson Education Ltd 2013. Copying permitted for purchasing institution only. This material is not copyright free.

Unit 3 – Holidays and travel

Sub-topics	Where in *Studio 3 Vert*
Reading and listening	
Holidays	Module 4, Unit 1
Types of holiday	Module 4, Unit 2
Camping	Module 4, Unit 2
Activities	Module 4, Unit 1 Module 4, Unit 2 Module 4, Unit 3
Travel	
Accommodation	Module 4, Unit 1
Weather on holiday	
Problems on holiday	Module 4, Unit 4
Holiday experiences	Module 4, Unit 4
Speaking and writing	
Destination	Module 4, Unit 1
Travel	
Accommodation	Module 4, Unit 1
Activities	Module 4, Unit 1 Module 4, Unit 2 Module 4, Unit 3

Unit 4 – Leisure

Sub-topics	Where in *Studio 3 Vert*
Reading and listening	
Hobbies	Module 1, Unit 3 Module 1, Unit 4
Free time/hobbies	Module 1, Unit 3 Module 1, Unit 4
Television	
Films	
Cinema	
Music	Module 1, Unit 5 Module 1, *En plus*
Gardening	
Going out	Module 1, Unit 3 Module 1, Unit 4
Theatre visit	
Clubs	
Around town	
Leisure centre	

Sub-topics	Where in *Studio 3 Vert*
Speaking and writing	
Hobbies/activities	Module 1, Unit 3 Module 1, Unit 4
Preferences	Module 1, Unit 3 Module 1, Unit 4
Going out	Module 1, Unit 3 Module 1, Unit 4
Pocket money	

Unit 5 – Healthy lifestyle

Sub-topics	Where in *Studio 3 Vert*
Reading and listening	
Healthy living	Module 2, Unit 4
Food/drink	Module 2, Unit 3
Healthy/unhealthy eating	Module 2, Unit 3 Module 2, Unit 4
Fast food	Module 2, Unit 3 Module 2, Unit 4
Exercise	Module 2, Unit 4 Module 2, Unit 5 Module 2, *En plus*
Life as a footballer	
Sports	Module 2, Unit 1 Module 2, Unit 4
Leisure centres	
Alcohol	
Smoking	
Illness	
Chemist's	
Stress	
Exam pressure	
Health farms	Module 2, Unit 4
Speaking and writing	
State of health	Module 2, *En plus*
Activities	Module 2, Unit 4 Module 2, Unit 5 Module 2, *En plus*
Eating and drinking	Module 2, Unit 3 Module 2, Unit 4
Opinions	Module 2, Unit 2

© Pearson Education Ltd 2013. Copying permitted for purchasing institution only. This material is not copyright free.

Unit 6 – Food and drink

Sub-topics	Where in *Studio 3 Vert*
Reading and listening	
Food/drink vocabulary items	Module 2, Unit 3
Eating out	
Opinions about food and drink	Module 2, Unit 3
Shopping for food	
Unhealthy/healthy food choices	Module 2, Unit 3 Module 2, Unit 4
Speaking and writing	
Food and drink habits	Module 2, Unit 3 Module 2, Unit 4
Eating out	
Opinions about food and drink	Module 2, Unit 3

Unit 7 – Local area and environment

Sub-topics	Where in *Studio 3 Vert*
Reading and listening	
Facilities	
Locations	Module 4, Unit 1
Preferences	Module 5, Unit 2 Module 5, Unit 3
Environment	Module 5, Unit 2
Recycling	Module 5, Unit 2
Weather	
Speaking and writing	
Local area	
Activities	
Environment	Module 5, Unit 2

Unit 8 – Celebrations

Sub-topics	Where in *Studio 3 Vert*
Reading and listening	
Birthdays	
Various festivals	Module 1, *En plus*
Parties	
Celebrating	
Engagements and weddings	
Celebrating success	
Carnival	Module 1, *En plus*
End of exams	
Speaking and writing	
Parties	
Opinions	
Special celebrations	Module 1, *En plus*

Games and other teaching suggestions

Reading aloud

There are many reading activities in the Pupil Book which give scope for further activities.

1 You can use the texts to practise reading aloud. As an incentive, award five points to a pupil who can read a text without any errors. Points could also be given to teams, depending on seating arrangements – tables, rows, sides of the room.
2 Set a challenge – 'I bet no one can read this without a single mistake' or ask a volunteer pupil to predict how many mistakes he/she will make before having a go, then seeing if he/she can do better than predicted.
3 Texts could be read round the class with pupils simply reading up to a full stop and then passing it on to someone else in the room. They enjoy this activity if it is fast. Alternatively, pupils can read as much or as little as they want before passing it on.
4 You can also read a text, pause, and have the pupils say the next word.

Reading follow-up

Motivation and participation can be enhanced by dividing the class into two teams and awarding points. Once they know a text very well, pupils should be able to complete a sentence from memory, hearing just the beginning. Move from a word to a phrase to a sentence: i.e. you say a word, the pupils give the word in a short context and then in a longer context.

1. You read aloud and stop (or insert the word 'beep') for pupils to complete the word or sentence.
2. You read aloud and make a deliberate mistake (either pronunciation or saying the wrong word). Pupils put up their hand as soon as they spot a mistake.
3. *Hot potato*: Pupils read a bit and pass it on quickly to someone who may not be expecting it.
4. *Marathon*: A pupil reads aloud until he/she makes a mistake. Pupils have to put up their hand as soon as they hear a mistake. A second pupil then takes over, starting at the beginning again and trying to get further than the previous pupil.
5. *Random reading*: You read a phrase at random and the pupils have to say the next bit.
6. You can play music and get the pupils to pass an object round the class. When the music stops, the person with the object has a turn. Let a pupil control the music, facing away from the class.

Mime activities

Mimes are a motivating way to help pupils to learn words.

1. You say a word, for example a job, sport or hobby, or an adjective, and the pupils mime it. This can be done silently with the whole class responding. Alternatively, it can be done as a knock out game starting with six volunteers at the front who mime to the class as you say each word. Any pupil who does the wrong mime or who is slow to react is knocked out. Impose a two-minute time limit.
2. Pupils say a word or phrase and you mime it – but only if the pupils say it correctly. This really puts you on the spot and gets the pupils trying very hard. You could also insist that the pupils say it from memory.
3. You mime and pupils say the word or phrase.
4. Send five or six pupils out of the room. They each have to decide on an adjective which sums up their character. They return to the room individually or together, each one miming their character adjective. The remaining pupils then guess the adjective. Get them to use a sentence, e.g. *Daniel est intelligent*.
5. *Envoyé spécial*: One person goes out of the room. The rest of the class decides on a character adjective to mime. The volunteer comes back into the room and has to guess the adjective that the class is miming. Again, encourage the use of whole sentences.
6. *Class knock-down*: As *Envoyé spécial*, but this time everyone in the class can choose different qualities to mime. The volunteer returns to the room with everyone doing his/her own mime. The volunteer points to each pupil and names the character adjective. If the volunteer is correct, the pupil sits down. This works well as a timed or team activity. The aim is to sit your team down as quickly as possible.
7. A version of charades is a good activity at the end of the lesson. Organise two teams, A and B. Have all the adjectives written down on separate cards, masculine forms only. Put the cards in a pile at the front. A volunteer from Team A comes to the front, picks up the first card and mimes it. The rest of the team must not see the word on the card. Anyone from Team A can put up his/her hand and is then invited by the volunteer to say the word. If correct, the volunteer picks up the next card and mimes it. The aim is to get through the whole list as quickly as possible. Note down the time for Team A. Team B then tries to beat that time.

Exploiting the songs

1. Pupils sing along. Fade out certain bits while they continue. When most of them know the song quite well you can pause the audio to let them give you the next line by heart. Then try the whole chorus, followed by a few verses completely from memory.
2. You could try the 'pick up a song' game: you fade the song after a few lines, the pupils continue singing, and then you fade the song up again towards the end and they see whether they have kept pace with the recording.

Translation follow-up

Motivation and participation can be enhanced by dividing the class into two teams and awarding points. Once they know the text very well, you should be able to say any word, phrase or sentence from the text at random for the pupils to translate into English without viewing the text.

1. You translate the text and stop (or insert the word 'beep') for pupils to complete the word or sentence.
2. You translate, making a deliberate mistake. Pupils put up their hand as soon as they spot a mistake.
3. *Hot potato*: A pupil translates a bit and passes it on quickly to someone who may not be expecting it.

4 *Marathon*: A pupil translates until he/she makes a mistake. Pupils have to put up their hand as soon as they hear a mistake. A second pupil then takes over, starting from the beginning again and trying to get further than the previous pupil.
5 *Random translation*: You read a phrase in French at random and the pupils have to translate it.
6 One half of the class has their books open, the other half has them closed. The half with their books open reads a sentence in French at random. The other side has to translate. Do about five then swap round.
7 You can play music and get the pupils to pass an object round. When the music stops, the person with the object has a turn. Let a pupil control the music, facing away from the class.

Writing follow-up (text dissection)

Whiteboards are a useful tool. They do not need to be issued to every pupil. Pupils can work in pairs or groups or they can pass the whiteboards on. You could also divide the class into teams, with one whiteboard per team.

After reading a text in some detail:

1 Display some anagrams of key words from the text and ask pupils to write them correctly. You will need to prepare these in advance and check carefully. Award points for correct answers on each board.
2 Display some jumbled phrases from the text, e.g. *foot au je dimanche joue le*. Pupils rewrite the phrase correctly in their exercise books or on the board. They could work in teams, producing one answer per team on paper.
3 Display an incorrect word or phrase in French and ask pupils to spot the mistake and correct it. This can also be done as 'spot the missing word' or 'spot the word that is in the wrong place'.
4 Ask pupils to spell certain words from memory. Differentiate by first reading out a few words in French and then giving a few in English for them also to write out in French.
5 *Mini-dictée*: Read four or five short sentences in French for pupils to write out. Again, this could be a group exercise.
6 Give pupils phrases in English to write out in French.

Comprehension follow-up

1 Ask questions in English about the text.
2 Ask questions in French about the text.
3 True or false?
4 Who … ?

Vocabulary treasure hunt

1 Find the word for …
2 Find (three) opinions.

Grammar treasure hunt

1 Find (three) adjectives.
2 Find (two) feminine adjectives.
3 Find a verb in the *nous* form.
4 Find a plural noun.
5 Find a negative.

A variation on pairwork

Musical pass the mobile phone: One pupil controls the music, facing away from the class. While the music is playing, a toy or old mobile phone is passed from pupil to pupil. As soon as the music stops, the music operator (who is ideally also equipped with a phone) says the first statement of a dialogue. The other pupil who has ended up with the phone replies. They can, if they like, disguise their voice. The music operator tries to guess who is speaking. The game then continues.

Symbols used in these teaching notes

➕ extension material/suggestion for extending an activity

Ⓡ reinforcement material/suggestion for reinforcing language

PLTS example of an activity which supports personal learning and thinking skills development

💭 thinking skills activity (workbooks only)

Module 1: Ma vie sociale d'ado

(Pupil Book pp. 6–29)

Unit & Learning objectives	Programme of Study references	Key language	Grammar and other language features
1 Je suis comme ça! (pp. 8–9) Describing yourself Using the verbs *avoir* and *être*	**GV1** Tenses (present: *avoir* and *être*) **LC1** Listening and responding **LC4** Expressing ideas (speaking) **LC5** Accurate pronunciation and intonation	*J'ai les cheveux blonds/noirs*, etc. *J'ai les yeux bleus/marron*, etc. *Je suis beau/belle. Je suis drôle/gentil(le)/intelligent(e)*, etc.	**G** *avoir* and *être* (present tense singular) **G** adjective agreement
2 Planète Facebook (pp. 10–11) Talking about Facebook Using present tense verbs	**GV1** Tenses (present) **GV3** Developing vocabulary **GV4** Accuracy (spelling) **LC6** Reading comprehension	*Je poste des messages à mes copains. Je modifie mes préférences. Je commente des photos*, etc.	**G** regular *–er* verbs and *faire* (present tense singular) – developing techniques for checking accuracy – developing writing skills
3 Tu veux y aller? (pp. 12–13) Inviting someone out Using the verb *aller*	**GV1** Tenses (present: *aller*) **GV3** Opinions and discussions **LC1** Listening and responding **LC3** Conversation	*Je vais … au centre commercial/à la patinoire*, etc. *Tu veux aller … … au cinéma /à la piscine? ce soir/demain (matin)*, etc. *Génial!/Pourquoi pas?*, etc. *Non, merci./Tu rigoles!*, etc.	**G** *aller* (present tense singular)
4 Qu'est-ce que tu as fait samedi? (pp. 14–15) Describing a date Using the perfect tense	**GV1** Tenses (perfect) **GV3** Opinions and discussions **LC5** Accurate pronunciation and intonation **LC4** Expressing ideas (writing)	*J'ai dansé avec … Je suis allé(e) à une fête avec …* etc. *C'était … romantique/sympa*, etc. *nul/un désastre*, etc.	**G** the perfect tense (*je/tu/il/elle*) – developing techniques for checking accuracy
5 Fou de musique! (pp. 16–17) Describing a music event Using *on* in the perfect tense	**GV1** Tenses (using *on* in the perfect tense) **GV4** Accuracy (spelling) **LC5** Speaking coherently and confidently **LC5** Accurate pronunciation and intonation	*On a écouté toutes sortes de musiques. On a chanté. On a dansé toute la soirée. On a mangé de la pizza. On a regardé le concert sur des écrans géants. On a bien rigolé.*	**G** the perfect tense (*on*) – developing techniques for checking accuracy

© Pearson Education Ltd 2013. Copying permitted for purchasing institution only. This material is not copyright free.

1 Ma vie sociale d'ado

Unit & Learning objectives	Programme of Study references	Key language	Grammar and other language features
Bilan et Révisions (pp. 18–19) Pupils' checklist and practice exercises			
En plus: La Fête de la Musique (pp. 20–21) Finding out about music festivals around the world	**LC3** Conversation **LC4** Expressing ideas (writing) **LC6** Reading comprehension **LC6** Translation into English	Review of language from the module	– developing reading skills – developing writing skills
Je parle (pp. 22–23) Extended speaking practice	**GV1** Tenses (past, present and future) **LC4** Expressing ideas (speaking) **LC5** Speaking coherently and confidently	Review of language from the module	– developing speaking skills – checking your work
J'écris (pp. 24–25) Extended writing practice	**GV3** Developing vocabulary **GV4** Accuracy (grammar; spelling; punctuation) **LC4** Expressing ideas (writing) **LC8** Writing creatively	Review of language from the module	– developing writing skills – checking your work
Studio Grammaire (pp. 26–27) Detailed grammar summary and practice exercises			**G** adjectives **G** the present tense: • regular –er verbs • irregular verbs: aller, avoir, être and faire **G** the perfect tense with avoir **G** the perfect tense with être
À toi (pp. 116–117) Self-access reading and writing at two levels			

© Pearson Education Ltd 2013. Copying permitted for purchasing institution only. This material is not copyright free.

(Pupil Book pp. 8–9)

1 Je suis comme ça!

Learning objectives
- Describing yourself
- Using the verbs *avoir* and *être*

Programme of Study references
GV1 Tenses (present: *avoir* and *être*)
LC1 Listening and responding
LC4 Expressing ideas (speaking)
LC5 Accurate pronunciation and intonation

FCSE links
Unit 1: Relationships, family and friends (Personal information; Descriptions)

Grammar
- *avoir* and *être* (present tense singular)
- adjective agreement

Key language
Je m'appelle …
J'ai … ans.
J'ai les cheveux …
blonds
noirs
bruns
roux
J'ai les yeux …
bleus
marron
gris
verts
Je suis beau/belle.
Je suis …
très/assez/un peu
drôle
gentil(le)
intelligent(e)
lunatique
sportif/sportive
timide

PLTS
S Self managers

Cross-curricular
All subjects: keeping a Skills Notebook

Resources
Audio files:
01_Module1_Unit1_Ex1.mp3
02_Module1_Unit1_Ex4.mp3
Workbooks:
Cahier d'exercices Vert, page 3
ActiveTeach:
Starter 2 resource
p.008 Flashcards (a)
p.008 Flashcards (b)
p.008 Grammar
p.008 Grammar practice
p.009 Grammar
p.009 Grammar practice
p.009 Learning skills
ActiveLearn:
Listening, Reading
Grammar, Vocabulary

Starter 1
Aim

To introduce language for person descriptions; To review adjective agreement

Write up the following. Give pupils three minutes working in pairs to write the name of an appropriate person for each sentence (someone in the class or a famous person).
J'ai les cheveux blonds et les yeux bleus.
J'ai les cheveux bruns et les yeux marron.
J'ai les cheveux noirs et les yeux verts.

Ask pupils to translate the sentences into English and hear answers. Ask the class what is unusual about the way you talk about hair in French (*les cheveux* is plural). Remind pupils that adjectives agree with nouns. Ask which colour adjective used in the sentences doesn't change form (*marron*).

Alternative Starter 1:
Use ActiveTeach p.008 Flashcards (a) to review hair and eye colour.

1 Écoute et lis. Qui parle? Écris la bonne lettre. (1–6) (Listening L2)

Listening. Pupils listen to six people introducing themselves, and read the text at the same time. They identify who's speaking each time by writing the correct letter. Draw pupils' attention to the tip box on the false friend *lunatique*

Audioscript Track 1

1 Je m'appelle Noah. J'ai quatorze ans. J'ai les cheveux bruns. Je suis sportif.
2 Je m'appelle Laura. J'ai treize ans. J'ai les cheveux blonds. Je suis drôle.
3 Je m'appelle Abdel. J'ai douze ans. J'ai les cheveux noirs. Je suis gentil.
4 Je m'appelle Manon. J'ai quinze ans. J'ai les yeux marron. Je suis intelligente.
5 Je m'appelle Hugo. J'ai onze ans. J'ai les yeux bleus. Je suis lunatique.
6 Je m'appelle Olivia. J'ai seize ans. J'ai les yeux gris. Je suis timide.

Answers
1 f 2 e 3 d 4 a 5 b 6 c

Studio Grammaire: *avoir* and *être* (present tense singular)

Use the *Studio Grammaire* box to review *avoir* and *être* in the present tense (singular). There is more information and further practice on Pupil Book p. 26.

© Pearson Education Ltd 2013. Copying permitted for purchasing institution only. This material is not copyright free.

1 Ma vie sociale d'ado 1 Je suis comme ça!

2 Trouve et copie les phrases de l'exercice 1. (Reading L2)

Reading. Pupils identify and write out the French versions of the English sentences listed in the exercise 1 text. Draw pupils' attention to the tip box on the use of *brun/marron*. Ask them when each is used (*brun* with hair, *marron* with eyes).

Answers
1. J'ai quatorze ans.
2. J'ai les yeux bleus.
3. J'ai les yeux marron.
4. J'ai les cheveux bruns.
5. Je suis sportif.
6. Je suis timide.
7. Je suis drôle.
8. Je suis lunatique.

3 En tandem. Jeu de mémoire. Tu dis deux phrases de l'exercice 1. Ton/Ta camarade dit si c'est vrai ou faux. (Speaking L3)

Speaking. In pairs: pupils play a memory game. They take it in turn to choose a character from exercise 1: they say who they are and describe themselves. Their partner says whether the description is true or false. A sample exchange is given. Some vocabulary is glossed for support.

Starter 2

Aim

To review adjectives for describing people

Write up the following. Give pupils three minutes working in pairs to write out the adjectives correctly, supplying the missing letters. They then identify whether each adjective is masculine or feminine, or could apply to both.

1. _nt_ll_g_nt
2. sp_rt_v_
3. g_nt_ll_
4. l_n_t_q_ _
5. dr_l_
6. t_m_d_

Check answers. (**Answers:** 1 *intelligent* – M, 2 *sportive* – F, 3 *gentille* – F, 4 *lunatique* – both, 5 *drôle* – both, 6 *timide* – both)

Alternative Starter 2:

Use ActiveTeach p.008 Flashcards (b) to review adjectives for describing people or ActiveTeach p.009 Grammar practice to practise adjectives.

4 Écoute. Copie et complète le tableau. (1–5) (Listening L3)

Listening. Read together through the key language box on qualifiers. Pupils then copy out the grid. They listen to five people describing themselves and complete the grid with the details.

Audioscript Track 2

1. Je m'appelle Émilie. J'ai treize ans. J'ai les cheveux bruns et les yeux gris. Je suis très gentille.
2. Je m'appelle Karim. J'ai quatorze ans. J'ai les cheveux noirs et les yeux marron. Je suis un peu timide.
3. Je m'appelle Marion. J'ai douze ans. J'ai les cheveux blonds et les yeux verts. Je suis très sportive.
4. Je m'appelle Lucas. J'ai seize ans. J'ai les cheveux bruns et les yeux marron. Je suis assez intelligent et très beau!
5. Je m'appelle Clara. J'ai quinze ans. J'ai les cheveux roux et les yeux bleus. Je suis assez belle, mais un peu lunatique!

Answers

	name	age	hair colour	eye colour	personality
1	Émilie	13	**brown**	grey	very kind
2	Karim	14	black	brown	a bit **shy**
3	Marion	12	**blond**	green	very **sporty**
4	Lucas	16	brown	**brown**	quite **intelligent**, very good-looking
5	Clara	15	red	blue	quite good-looking, a bit **moody**

Pupils choose a person from the grid and write a description of him/her in French, using the details supplied and the appropriate verb forms.

Studio Grammaire: adjective agreement

Use the *Studio Grammaire* box to review adjective agreement. There is more information and further practice on Pupil Book p. 26.

5 Lis le texte. Copie et complète la fiche pour chaque personne. (Reading L3–4)

Reading. Pupils read the text, then copy and fill in the profile for each person. Draw pupils' attention to the tip box on *ne … pas*. Some vocabulary is glossed for support.

© Pearson Education Ltd 2013. Copying permitted for purchasing institution only. This material is not copyright free.

1 Je suis comme ça! Ma vie sociale d'ado

Answers

Name: Cassandra
Age: 14
Physical appearance: (long) black hair, brown eyes
Personality: (quite) sporty, (very) sociable
Any other details: likes football and tennis

Name: Maxime
Age: 15
Physical appearance: blue eyes, (short) blond hair
Personality: (very) funny and nice
Any other details: (thinks he's) (quite) good-looking and (very) modest

Name: Quentin
Age: 13
Physical appearance: red hair, green eyes
Personality: (a bit) shy, (very) kind and sincere
Any other details: not sporty, but loves cinema

Name: Chloé
Age: 16
Physical appearance: brown hair, grey eyes
Personality: (quite) intelligent, but (a bit) moody
Any other details: likes swimming

6 En tandem. Présente-toi! Ton/Ta camarade commente ta prononciation. (Speaking L3)

Speaking. In pairs: pupils introduce themselves to each other. They comment on each other's pronunciation. A list of comments that they can use to do this is supplied.

➕ **PLTS** S

Encourage pupils to keep a Skills Notebook (in addition to a separate Vocabulary/Language Notebook). This can be used to note down tips on developing skills and strategies that will help the pupils improve their performance. It could include the following:

− any tips that come up in the Pupil Book or in the course of a class
− details of any areas of weakness pupils identify in their own work when they check it
− suggestions for improvement arising from feedback by you, a partner or the class
− information about how to aim for a higher level.

Point out that if pupils get into the habit of noting this kind of information and reviewing it regularly, it will make them much more effective learners. This approach can then be used in other subjects.

7 Écris un e-mail avec une description de toi à trouvedesamis.fr. (Writing L3)

Writing. Pupils write an email to trouvedesamis.fr about themselves, using the key language box to give details of their name, age, hair and eye colour and their character, along the lines of the entries in exercise 5.

Give them time to memorise their text, then tell the class about themselves. Suggest techniques for memorising, e.g. write out the sentences, each on a separate piece of paper; shuffle them, then practise putting them in order; cover all but the first two words of a sentence as a prompt, etc.

Plenary

Review hair and eye colour by choosing pupils at random to describe themselves using *J'ai les cheveux ...* and *J'ai les yeux ...*

Repeat, this time eliciting descriptions of character. Encourage pupils to include qualifiers.

Alternative Plenary:

Use ActiveTeach p.008 Grammar practice to review and practise *avoir* and *être*.

Workbook, page 3

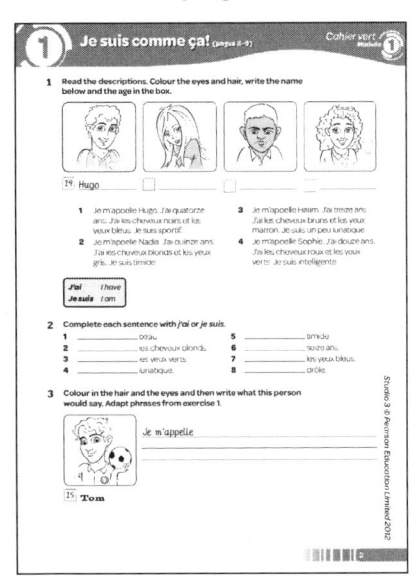

© Pearson Education Ltd 2013. Copying permitted for purchasing institution only. This material is not copyright free.

1 Ma vie sociale d'ado 1 Je suis comme ça!

Answers

1. 1 Name: Hugo; age: 14; hair should be coloured black and eyes blue.
   2 Name: Nadia; age: 15; hair should be coloured blond and eyes grey.
   3 Name: Halim; age: 13; hair should be coloured brown and eyes brown.
   4 Name: Sophie; age: 12; hair should be coloured red and eyes green.

2. 1 Je suis 2 J'ai 3 J'ai 4 Je suis 5 Je suis 6 J'ai 7 J'ai 8 Je suis

3. Je m'appelle Tom. J'ai quinze ans. J'ai les cheveux (answers will vary) et les yeux (answers will vary). Je suis sportif.

Worksheet 1.1 Learning vocabulary

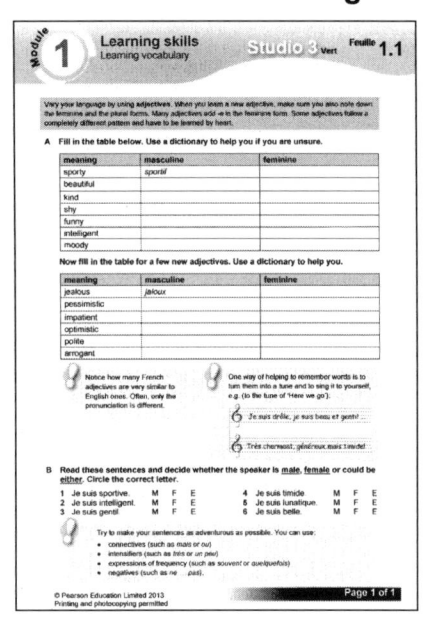

Answers
A

meaning	masculine	feminine
sporty	*sportif*	sportive
beautiful	beau	belle
kind	gentil	gentille
shy	timide	timide
funny	drôle	drôle
intelligent	intelligent	intelligente
moody	lunatique	lunatique

meaning	masculine	feminine
jealous	*jaloux*	jalouse
pessimistic	pessimiste	pessimiste
impatient	impatient	impatiente
optimistic	optimiste	optimiste
polite	poli	polie
arrogant	arrogant	arrogante

B 1 F 2 M 3 M 4 E 5 E 6 F

2 Planète Facebook

(Pupil Book pp. 10–11)

Learning objectives
- Talking about Facebook
- Using present tense verbs

Programme of Study references
GV1 Tenses (present)
GV3 Developing vocabulary
GV4 Accuracy (spelling)
LC6 Reading comprehension

Grammar
- regular –er verbs and *faire* (present tense singular)

Key language
Qu'est-ce que tu fais sur Facebook?
Je poste des messages à mes copains.
Je modifie mes préférences.
Je regarde les photos de mes copains.
Je commente des photos.
J'invite mes copains à sortir.
Je fais des quiz.
quelquefois
souvent
tous les jours
tous les soirs
tous les weekends
une fois/deux fois par semaine

PLTS
T Team workers

Cross-curricular
ICT: making contact on social networks

Resources
Audio files:
03_Module1_Unit2_Ex1.mp3
04_Module1_Unit2_Ex5.mp3
Workbooks:
Cahier d'exercices Vert, page 4
ActiveTeach:
Starter 1 resource
Starter 2 resource
p.010 Grammar
p.010 Grammar practice
p.010 Grammar
p.011 Listening skills
p.011 Grammar skills
ActiveLearn:
Listening, Reading
Grammar, Vocabulary

Starter 1

Aim

To introduce key verbs in the topic

Write up the following. Give pupils two minutes to find the French versions of the verbs in the texts in exercise 1.

1 I invite	4 I do
2 I post	5 I look at
3 I comment on	6 I update

(Answers: **1** j'invite, **2** je poste, **3** je commente, **4** je fais, **5** je regarde, **6** je modifie)

Alternative Starter 1:

Use ActiveTeach p.010 Grammar practice to review and practise the present tense of –er verbs.

1 Écoute et écris les lettres dans le bon ordre. (1–6) (Listening L2)

Listening. Pupils listen to six conversations and note the letter of the correct picture for each. *Je modifie mes préférences* is glossed for support.

Audioscript Track 3

1 – Salut! Qu'est-ce que tu fais sur Facebook?
  – Je regarde les photos de mes copains.
2 – Et toi, qu'est-ce que tu fais sur Facebook?
  – Moi, j'invite mes copains à sortir.
3 – Pardon. Qu'est-ce que tu fais sur Facebook?
  – Euh … Je poste des messages à mes copains.
4 – Et toi, qu'est-ce que tu fais?
  – Alors … je fais des quiz. C'est cool!
5 – Et toi, qu'est-ce que tu fais sur Facebook?
  – Je commente des photos! J'adore ça!
6 – Pardon. Qu'est-ce que tu fais sur Facebook?
  – Je modifie mes préférences.

Answers
1 c **2** e **3** a **4** f **5** d **6** b

Studio Grammaire: regular –er verbs and *faire* (present tense singular)

Use the *Studio Grammaire* box to review *regarder* and *faire* in the present tense (singular). There is more information and further practice on Pupil Book p. 26.

2 En tandem. Fais des conversations. Utilise les renseignements d'en bas. (Speaking L3)

Speaking. In pairs: pupils make up conversations, using the details supplied (the letters refer to the pictures in exercise 1). A sample exchange is given.

3 Copie les phrases. Écris correctement les mots en rouge. (Writing L2-3)

Writing. Pupils unscramble the jumbled words and copy out the complete sentences. Draw pupils' attention to the tip box on how best to tackle the activity.

© Pearson Education Ltd 2013. Copying permitted for purchasing institution only. This material is not copyright free.

1 Ma vie sociale d'ado 2 Planète Facebook

Answers
1 Je **fais** des quiz.
2 Je **regarde** les photos de mes copains.
3 J'**invite** mes copains à sortir.
4 Je **poste** des messages à mes copains.
5 Je **modifie** mes préférences.
6 Je **commente** des photos.

R Pupils work in pairs. One pupil prompts with the start of a sentence, e.g. *J'invite …* The other (with Pupil Book closed) gives the whole sentence.

Starter 2
Aim
To review the language for Facebook activities
Write up the following. Give pupils three minutes working in pairs to identify which of the activities you would do on Facebook.
1 *Je commente des photos.*
2 *Je modifie mes préférences.*
3 *J'achète des souvenirs.*
4 *Je vais à la crêperie.*
5 *Je fais des quiz.*
6 *Je poste des messages à mes copains.*
7 *J'invite mes copains à sortir.*
8 *Je mange un kilo de bananes.*
9 *Je regarde les photos de mes copains.*
Check answers, asking pupils to translate each sentence into English.
(**Answers:** 1, 2, 5, 6, 7, 9)

4 Fais correspondre le français et l'anglais. (Reading L1)

Reading. Pupils match the French and the English versions of the frequency expressions. Encourage them to use reading strategies (cognates, grammatical knowledge, context, etc.).

Answers
1 d 2 f 3 b 4 e 5 a 6 c

5 Écoute. Copie et complète le tableau en anglais. (1–5) (Listening L4)

Listening. Pupils copy out the grid. They then listen to five conversations about how teenagers use Facebook and complete the grid with the details in English. *Tu fais ça souvent?* is glossed for support.

Audioscript Track 4
1 – Qu'est-ce que tu fais sur Facebook?
   – Je poste des messages à mes copains.
   – Tu fais ça souvent?
   – Ah, oui! Je fais ça tous les jours!
2 – Qu'est-ce que tu fais sur Facebook?
   – Je modifie mes préférences.
   – Tu fais ça souvent?
   – Non. Je fais ça une fois par semaine.
3 – Qu'est-ce que tu fais sur Facebook?
   – Je fais des quiz.
   – Tu fais ça souvent?
   – Ben, quelquefois. Je fais ça quelquefois.
4 – Qu'est-ce que tu fais sur Facebook?
   – J'invite mes copains à sortir.
   – Tu fais ça souvent?
   – Oui, je fais ça tous les weekends.
5 – Qu'est-ce que tu fais sur Facebook?
   – Je regarde et je commente les photos de mes copains.
   – Tu fais ça souvent?
   – Alors, oui. Je fais ça tous les soirs.

Answers

	what?	how often?
1	posts messages	every day
2	updates likes	once a week
3	does quizzes	sometimes
4	invites friends out	every weekend
5	looks at and comments on (friends') photos	every evening

6 Lis les textes et réponds aux questions. (Speaking L3)

Speaking. Pupils read the texts and answer the questions by identifying who is being described each time. Some vocabulary is glossed for support.

Answers
1 Mina 2 Léa 3 Antoine 4 Léa 5 Antoine
6 Mina

© Pearson Education Ltd 2013. Copying permitted for purchasing institution only. This material is not copyright free.

7 Qu'est-ce que tu fais sur Facebook? Tu fais ça souvent? Écris un paragraphe. Invente, si tu veux!
(Writing L4)

Writing. Pupils write a paragraph saying what they do on Facebook and how often they do it. They can invent the details if they prefer. A sample opening is supplied. Draw pupils' attention to the tip box on improving their writing.

PLTS T

If you have connections with a partner school, pupils could make friends on a social networking site with their French peers.

Plenary
Ask the class to list all the things you can do on Facebook. Take a class vote on who does each activity and identify the two most popular activities.

Workbook, page 4

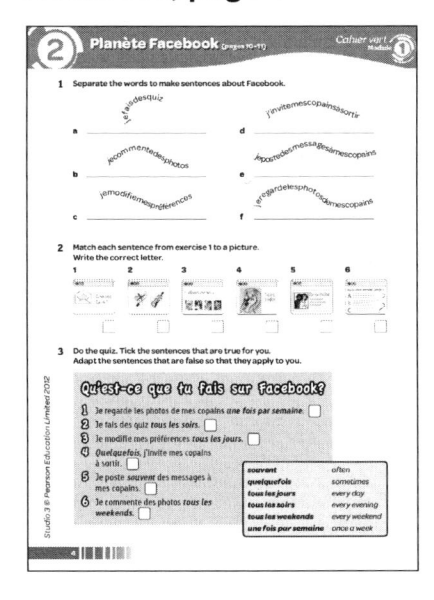

Answers
1. a Je fais des quiz.
   b Je commente des photos.
   c Je modifie mes préférences.
   d J'invite mes copains à sortir.
   e Je poste des messages à mes copains.
   f Je regarde les photos de mes copains.
2. 1 e 2 c 3 f 4 b 5 d 6 a
3. (Answers will vary.)

Worksheet 1.2 Transcription

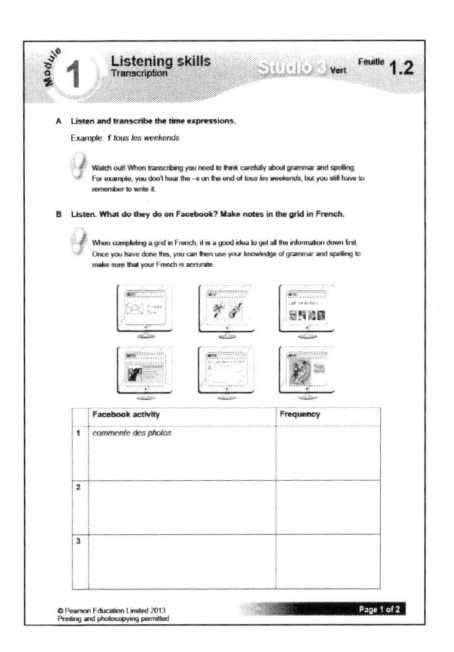

Answers
A
1. tous les weekends
2. souvent
3. tous les jours
4. une fois par semaine
5. quelquefois
6. tous les soirs

1 Ma vie sociale d'ado 2 Planète Facebook

B & C

	Facebook activity	Frequency
1	Elle commente des photos. Elle fait des quiz.	tous les soirs quelquefois
2	Il regarde ses messages. Il joue à des jeux.	tous les jours tous les weekends
3	Elle invite ses copains à sortir. Elle modifie ses préférences.	une fois par semaine souvent

Worksheet 1.3 The present tense

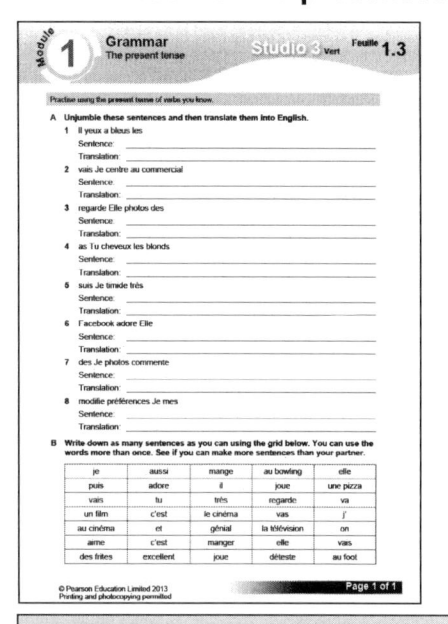

Answers

A 1 Il a les yeux bleus. He has blue eyes.

   2 Je vais au centre commercial. I'm going to the shopping centre.

   3 Elle regarde des photos. She looks at photos.

   4 Tu as les cheveux blonds. You have blonde hair.

   5 Je suis très timide. I am very shy.

   6 Elle adore Facebook. She loves Facebook.

   7 Je commente des photos. I comment on photos.

   8 Je modifie mes préférences. I update my likes.

B (Answers will vary.)

3 Tu veux y aller?

(Pupil Book pp. 12–13)

Learning objectives
- Inviting someone out
- Using the verb *aller*

Programme of Study references
GV1 Tenses (present: *aller*)
GV3 Opinions and discussions
LC1 Listening and responding
LC3 Conversation

FCSE links
Unit 1: Relationships, family and friends (Meeting up; Free-time activities)
Unit 4: Leisure (Hobbies; Free time; Going out; Preferences)

Grammar
- *aller* (present tense singular)

Key language
Où vas-tu le weekend?
Je vais …
au centre commercial
au centre de loisirs
au cinéma
au fastfood
à la patinoire
à la piscine
Tu veux aller …
au cinéma/à la piscine?
ce matin
cet après-midi
ce soir
demain (matin)
samedi (après-midi/soir)
Oui, je veux bien.
D'accord.
Génial!
Pourquoi pas?
Non, merci.
Tu rigoles!
J'ai horreur de ça!
Désolé(e), je ne peux pas.

PLTS
C Creative thinkers

Resources
Audio files:
05_Module1_Unit3_Ex1.mp3
06_Module1_Unit3_Ex5.mp3
07_Module1_Unit3_Ex6.mp3
Workbooks:
Cahier d'exercices Vert, page 5
ActiveTeach:
Starter 1 resource
Starter 2 resource
p.012 Grammar
p.012 Grammar practice
p.013 Video 1
p.013 Video worksheet 1
p.013 Class activity
p.013 Thinking skills
ActiveLearn:
Listening, Reading
Grammar, Vocabulary

Starter 1
Aim
To introduce language for talking about where you go at the weekend

Write up the following. Give pupils three minutes to choose three places that they go to at the weekend and write a sentence for each of them.

Le weekend, je vais …
  au cinéma.
  au fastfood.
  au centre commercial.
  au centre de loisirs.
  à la piscine.
  à la patinoire.

Hear answers, asking pupils to translate their sentences into English.

Alternative Starter 1:
Use ActiveTeach p.012 Grammar practice to review and practise *aller* and *faire*.

1 Écoute et regarde les photos. Qui parle? (1–6) (Listening L2)

Listening. Pupils listen to six people talking about where they go at the weekend and use the pictures to identify who's speaking each time.

Audioscript Track 5
1 – Bonjour. Où vas-tu le weekend?
  – Euh … Je vais au cinéma.
2 – Et toi? Où vas-tu le weekend?
  – Je vais au fastfood.
3 – Pardon. Où vas-tu le weekend?
  – Alors, je vais au centre commercial.
4 – Salut! Où vas-tu le weekend?
  – Je vais au centre de loisirs.
5 – Et toi? Où vas-tu le weekend?
  – Moi, je vais à la piscine.
6 – Pardon. Où vas-tu le weekend?
  – Ben … Je vais à la patinoire.

Answers
1 *Guillaume* 2 Flavie 3 Baptiste 4 Yasmine
5 Najim 6 Amina

Pupils work in pairs. They write a label for each of the places pictured in exercise 1, using the correct form of à + the definite article, e.g. *à la piscine*. Review the different forms first.

2 En tandem. Jeu de mime. (Speaking L3)

Speaking. In pairs: pupils play a mime game, taking it in turn to ask/guess and to mime/answer. A sample exchange is given.

© Pearson Education Ltd 2013. Copying permitted for purchasing institution only. This material is not copyright free.

1 Ma vie sociale d'ado 3 Tu veux y aller?

> **Studio Grammaire: *aller* (present tense singular)**
>
> Use the *Studio Grammaire* box to review *aller* in the present tense (singular). There is more information and further practice on Pupil Book p. 26.

R As a class, chant the singular forms of *aller* several times. Repeat, this time replacing *je vais* with two hand claps. Continue in this way until all singular forms are replaced with hand claps. Then reintroduce the verb forms one by one until the class is chanting the whole verb again.

3 Copie et complète le texte. (Writing L3)

Writing. Pupils copy and complete the gap-fill text, using the picture prompts. Some vocabulary is glossed for support.

> **Answers**
>
> Je m'appelle Julie. Tous les weekends, je vais au **centre commercial** avec mes copains. Souvent, je vais aussi au **fastfood**. Quelquefois, je vais au **cinéma** ou à la **patinoire**. Mais je ne vais pas à la **piscine** parce que je n'aime pas ça.

> **Starter 2**
>
> **PLTS** C
>
> **Aim**
>
> To review time expressions
>
> Write up the following. Give pupils two minutes to translate the English expressions 1–6 into French, using the language supplied below to help them.
>
> dimanche – Sunday
> ce matin – this morning
> demain soir – tomorrow evening
> samedi après-midi – Saturday afternoon
>
> 1 tomorrow morning   4 this evening
> 2 Saturday evening   5 Saturday morning
> 3 Sunday afternoon   6 tomorrow afternoon
>
> (**Answers: 1** demain matin, **2** samedi soir, **3** dimanche après-midi, **4** ce soir, **5** samedi matin, **6** demain après-midi)
>
> ***Alternative Starter 2:***
>
> Use ActiveTeach p.013 Class activity to practise language for talking about social life.

4 Complète les phrases pour toi. (Writing L3)

Writing. Pupils complete the gap-fill sentences, giving details about themselves.

5 Écoute. Qu'est-ce que tu entends? Choisis la bonne réponse. (1–5) (Listening L4)

Listening. Pupils listen to five conversations. They complete the sentences by choosing the correct option from the two given each time (**a** or **b**). Draw pupils' attention to the language box on time expressions.

> **Audioscript Track 6**
>
> 1 – Allô, oui?
>   – Salut, c'est Rémi! Tu veux aller au cinéma, ce soir?
>   – Ce soir? Oui, je veux bien, merci.
> 2 – Salut, Alexandra!
>   – Salut. Tu veux aller à la piscine, demain?
>   – Demain? Ah, non, je suis désolée, je ne peux pas.
> 3 – Allô?
>   – Salut, Sarah. C'est Mina. Tu veux aller au fastfood, cet après-midi?
>   – Au fastfood, cet après-midi? Ah, oui! Génial!
> 4 – Allô, oui?
>   – Coucou, c'est moi!
>   – Salut, Mathieu!
>   – Tu veux aller au centre commercial, samedi matin?
>   – Samedi matin? D'accord. Pourquoi pas?
> 5 – Salut, Karima.
>   – Salut, Tariq. Tu veux aller à la patinoire, demain soir?
>   – Pardon?
>   – Tu veux aller à la patinoire, demain soir?
>   – Tu rigoles! J'ai horreur de ça!

> **Answers**
>
> 1 a 2 a 3 b 4 a 5 b

6 Écoute à nouveau. La réaction est positive ☺ ou négative ☹ ? (1–5) (Listening L4)

Listening. Pupils listen again to the exercise 5 recording. This time they note whether the response in each conversation is positive (drawing a smiley face) or negative (drawing a sad face). Use the key language box to check comprehension of useful expressions before they start.

© Pearson Education Ltd 2013. Copying permitted for purchasing institution only. This material is not copyright free.

3 Tu veux y aller? Ma vie sociale d'ado

Audioscript Track 7

As exercise 5.

Answers

1 ☺ 2 ☹ 3 ☺ 4 ☺ 5 ☹

7 En tandem. Lis la conversation à voix haute, puis change les mots soulignés. Utilise les idées A, B et C. (Speaking L4)

Speaking. In pairs: pupils read the sample conversation aloud, then change the underlined words (using the prompts A, B and C) to make three conversations of their own. They take it in turn to ask and answer. Encourage them to read expressively.

8 Écris trois invitations par e-mail. Invente les renseignements. (Writing L3)

Writing. Pupils write three emails inviting a friend out. They should invent the places and times. A sample is given.

Plenary

Challenge the class to come up with as many different time expressions as they can (*demain soir, quelquefois, samedi après-midi*, etc.). If they can name more than 12 correctly, they win; if they can't, you win.

Workbook, page 5

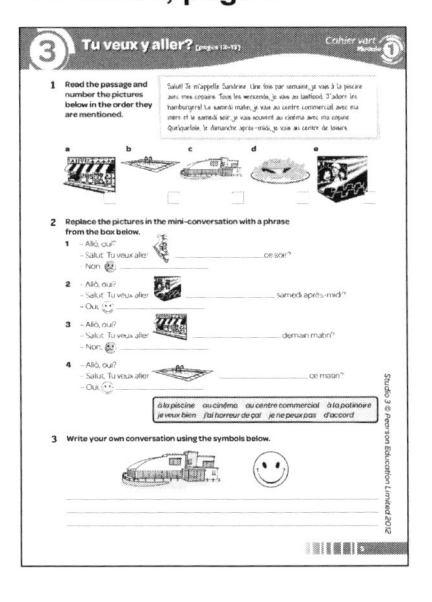

Answers

1 a 2 b 3 c 5 d 1 e 4

2 1 Tu veux aller **à la patinoire** ce soir? – Non, **j'ai horreur de ça!/je ne peux pas.**

  2 u veux aller **au cinéma** samedi après-midi? – Oui, **je veux bien/d'accord.**

  3 Tu veux aller **au centre commercial** demain matin? – Non, **je ne peux pas./j'ai horreur de ça!**

  4 Tu veux aller **à la piscine** ce matin? – Oui, **d'accord/je veux bien.**

3 (Example answer:)
  – Allô, oui?
  – Salut. Tu veux aller **au centre de loisirs** samedi après-midi?
  – Oui, **je veux bien.**

Worksheet 1.4 Logic puzzle

© Pearson Education Ltd 2013. Copying permitted for purchasing institution only. This material is not copyright free.

1 Ma vie sociale d'ado 3 Tu veux y aller?

Answers

A 1
- every evening: looks at messages
- every day: looks at friends' photos and comments on them
- sometimes: plays games and does quizzes
- often: watches videos on YouTube

2
- intelligent: Noah
- beautiful: his friend Hélène
- fun: watching videos
- boring: updating his likes

3 updating his likes.

B 1 The invitation is for Saturday but the reply is 'Yes, I'd like to. See you on Sunday!'

2 The reply is that the person can't come, but still says 'See you tomorrow!'

3 The person says no and doesn't want to go to the cinema, but then says he/she loves it!

C 1 Oui, je veux bien. À samedi!

2 Oui, je veux bien. À demain!/Désolé, je ne peux pas.

3 Non merci, je n'aime pas le cinéma./Oui, je veux bien. J'adore le cinéma!

D (Answers will vary.)

Video

The video component provides opportunities for speaking activities in a plausible and stimulating context. The StudioFR team, whom pupils met in Studio 1 and 2 – Marielle, Samira, Hugo, Alex and Mehdi – make video reports on a range of topics to send to StudioGB, their counterpart in the UK. Each video is around three minutes long.

Episode 1: Le speed dating

Marielle decides to take the team speed dating, where Samira and Hugo emerge as StudioFR's first couple. Video worksheet 1 can be used in conjunction with this episode.

Answers to video worksheet (ActiveTeach)

1 A – Marielle (as she's so sociable and full of romantic ideas).
– Questions like *Qu'est-ce que tu aimes faire?*

2 A She is looking at an advert for speed dating on her home page (*page perso*).

B Yes, they seem very enthusiastic.

3 A She goes shopping.

B Shopping and fashion.

C He plays games and quizzes and goes on his home page.

D To show what the people really think of each other.

E They don't really like each other. She thinks he's a pain (*pénible*) and loves his computer too much and he thinks she is pretty but selfish (*belle mais trop égoïste*).

4 A Go for a picnic.

B Horror films.

C She thinks he's shy.

D He thinks she's nice.

E The boy, because he likes her but she doesn't really like him.

5 A Go to a concert.

B He's very arrogant.

C No, she would never go out with him.

6 A No. (Too shy; funny but arrogant.)

B No. (A pain; generous but jealous.)

C Because they realise they get on better with each other.

D On the Studio home page.

E Because he's been brushed off again!

F Samira and Hugo are their first speed-dating couple.

© Pearson Education Ltd 2013. Copying permitted for purchasing institution only. This material is not copyright free.

4 Qu'est-ce que tu as fait samedi?

(Pupil Book pp. 14–15)

Learning objectives
- Describing a date
- Using the perfect tense

Programme of Study references
GV1 Tenses (perfect)
GV3 Opinions and discussions
LC5 Accurate pronunciation and intonation
LC4 Expressing ideas (writing)

FCSE links
Unit 1: Relationships, family and friends (Girlfriend, boyfriend; Meeting up; Free-time activities)
Unit 4: Leisure (Hobbies; Free time; Going out; Preferences)

Grammar
- the perfect tense (je/tu/il/elle)

Key language
Qu'est-ce que tu as fait samedi?
J'ai dansé avec …
J'ai joué au bowling avec …
J'ai mangé un hamburger avec …
J'ai regardé un DVD avec …
Je suis allé(e) au cinéma avec …
Je suis allé(e) en ville avec …
Je suis allé(e) à une fête avec …
C'était …
génial
romantique
sympa
ennuyeux
nul
un désastre

PLTS
R Reflective learners

Resources
Audio files:
08_Module1_Unit4_Ex1.mp3
09_Module1_Unit4_Ex4.mp3
Workbooks:
Cahier d'exercices Vert, page 6
ActiveTeach:
Starter 1 resource
Starter 2 resource
p.014 Flashcards
p.014 Grammar
p.014 Grammar practice
p.015 Flashcards
p.015 Video 2
p.015 Video worksheet 2
p.015 Grammar skills
ActiveLearn:
Listening, Reading
Grammar, Vocabulary

Starter 1
Aim
To review the perfect tense

Write up the following. Give pupils two minutes working in pairs to write out the *je* form of the perfect tense for all the infinitives listed, using the model supplied.

visiter	–	j'ai visité
1 danser	–	j'ai _____
2 jouer	–	_____
3 manger	–	_____
4 regarder	–	_____

Check answers, asking pupils to translate the perfect tense verbs. Ask them to summarise how the perfect tense is formed. Remind them that although most verbs use *avoir* in the perfect tense, a few don't do so. Ask if they can remember any verbs that don't use *avoir*, reminding them as necessary of *aller: je suis allé(e)*.

Alternative Starter 1:
Use ActiveTeach p.014 Flashcards to introduce language for describing a date in the past.

1 Écoute et mets les images dans le bon ordre. (1–6) (Listening L5)
Listening. Pupils listen to six conversations and identify the correct picture for each one.

Audioscript Track 8
1 – Qu'est-ce que tu as fait samedi?
 – J'ai regardé un DVD avec Max.
2 – Qu'est-ce que tu as fait samedi?
 – Je suis allé au cinéma avec Chloé.
3 – Qu'est-ce que tu as fait samedi?
 – J'ai joué au bowling avec Enzo.
4 – Qu'est-ce que tu as fait samedi?
 – J'ai dansé avec Emma!
5 – Qu'est-ce que tu as fait samedi?
 – e suis allée en ville avec Seb.
6 – Qu'est-ce que tu as fait samedi?
 – J'ai mangé un hamburger avec Zoë.

Answers
1 d **2** e **3** b **4** a **5** f **6** c

Studio Grammaire: the perfect tense (*je*)
Use the *Studio Grammaire* box to review the *je* form of the perfect tense (verbs taking *avoir*, and the verb *aller* with *être*). There is more information and further practice on Pupil Book p. 27.

R Pupils translate the following sentences into French.

1 I danced with Sam. 3 I ate a hamburger.
2 I went into town. 4 I watched a DVD.

© Pearson Education Ltd 2013. Copying permitted for purchasing institution only. This material is not copyright free.

1 Ma vie sociale d'ado 4 Qu'est-ce que tu as fait samedi?

(**Answers: 1** J'ai dansé avec Sam. **2** Je suis allé(e) en ville. **3** J'ai mangé un hamburger. **4** J'ai regardé un DVD.)

2 Écris correctement les phrases. (Writing L3)

Writing. Pupils write out each jumbled sentence correctly. Draw their attention to the tip box on the spelling and pronunciation of past participles.

Answers
1 J'ai mangé un hamburger avec Lucas.
2 J'ai joué au bowling avec Claire.
3 J'ai dansé avec Nathan.
4 J'ai regardé un DVD avec Natasha.
5 Je suis allé en ville avec Anna.
6 Je suis allée au cinéma avec Frank.

3 En tandem. Imagine que tu es sorti(e) avec des célébrités! (Speaking L5)

Speaking. In pairs. Pupils imagine that they've been out with some celebrities. They take it in turn to ask and answer about what they did. A sample exchange is given. Some vocabulary is glossed for support.

Starter 2

Aim

To review the perfect tense

Write up the following, replacing each underlined word with a line, for pupils to write in the missing word. Give pupils three minutes to write out the complete sentences.

ai mangé allé joué suis regardé

1 Je suis <u>allé</u> au cinéma.
2 J'ai <u>regardé</u> un DVD.
3 J'ai <u>joué</u> au bowling.
4 Je <u>suis</u> allée à une fête!
5 J'<u>ai</u> dansé avec Alex.
6 J'ai <u>mangé</u> un hamburger.

Alternative Starter 2:

Use ActiveTeach p.015 Flashcards to introduce language for saying what something was like in the past, or use ActiveTeach p.014 Grammar practice to practise the perfect tense.

4 Écoute. C'était comment? Note l'activité et la lettre de la bonne opinion. (1–5) (Listening L5)

Listening. Pupils listen to five conversations about what people did on Saturday. For each they note the activity in English and the letter of the picture showing the correct opinion. *Je suis allé(e) à une fête* is glossed for support.

Audioscript Track 9

1 – *Qu'est-ce que tu as fait samedi?*
  – *Je suis allé au cinéma avec Marion.*
  – *Et alors? C'était comment?*
  – *Ben … C'était sympa.*
  – *C'était sympa? D'accord!*
2 – *Qu'est-ce que tu as fait samedi soir?*
  – *J'ai regardé un DVD avec Louis.*
  – *C'était comment?*
  – *C'était ennuyeux! En-nuyeux!*
  – *Pourquoi c'était ennuyeux?*
  – *Parce que je déteste les films de science-fiction!*
3 – *Qu'est-ce que tu as fait samedi après-midi?*
  – *J'ai joué au bowling avec Léa.*
  – *C'était comment? C'était romantique?*
  – *Tu rigoles! C'était nul, complètement nul.*
  – *Ah, bon? Pourquoi?*
  – *Elle est pénible, Léa!*
4 – *Qu'est-ce que tu as fait samedi soir?*
  – *Je suis allée à une fête! Et j'ai dansé avec –*
  – *Qui? Tu as dansé avec qui?*
  – *Avec Alex!*
  – *C'est pas vrai! C'était comment?*
  – *C'était romantique. Très romantique!*
5 – *Alors, qu'est-ce que tu as fait samedi?*
  – *Bof … Je suis allé au fastfood avec Julie. J'ai mangé un hamburger, mais …*
  – *Mais quoi?*
  – *C'était un désastre!*
  – *Un désastre? Pourquoi?*
  – *Parce que Julie ne mange pas de hamburgers: elle est végétarienne!*
  – *Dur, mon vieux.*

Answers
1 cinema, a 2 DVD, c 3 bowling, d
4 party/dancing, b
5 fast-food restaurant/burger, e

5 En tandem. Fais trois conversations. Utilise les phrases de l'exercice 1 et invente les prénoms. (Speaking L5)

Speaking. In pairs: pupils make up three conversations, choosing from the phrases in exercise 1 and making up the names of the people involved. A framework is supplied.

6 Lis les textes et complète le tableau. (Reading L5)

Reading. Pupils read the texts, then copy and complete the grid.

4 Qu'est-ce que tu as fait samedi? Ma vie sociale d'ado

Answers

	where?	good date?	bad date?	why?
1	town		✓	Yasmine talked on mobile phone for two hours – boring.
2	park	✓		Gabriel sang and played guitar – romantic.
3	party	✓		Met a beautiful girl, danced and chatted – nice.
4	cinema		✓	Dylan ate a burger, two ice creams and a huge packet of popcorn – horrible.

Studio Grammaire: the perfect tense (il/elle)

Use the *Studio Grammaire* box to review the *il/elle* form of the perfect tense (verbs taking *avoir*, and the verb *aller* with *être*). There is more information and further practice on Pupil Book p. 27.

7 Écris ton blog imaginaire! (Writing L5)

PLTS R

Writing. Pupils write a blog, making up the details. Encourage them to be as inventive as possible. A framework is given.

When they have finished, pupils check their work for accuracy. Ask them to identify two areas in which they think they can improve next time they do an extended writing task. Encourage them to note these in their Skills Notebook.

Plenary

Ask the class when the perfect tense is used and how it is formed, giving you examples from the unit.

Give phrases from the unit using the infinitive, e.g. *regarder un DVD*. Pupils make up a sentence using the perfect tense, e.g. *J'ai regardé un DVD*.

Workbook, page 6

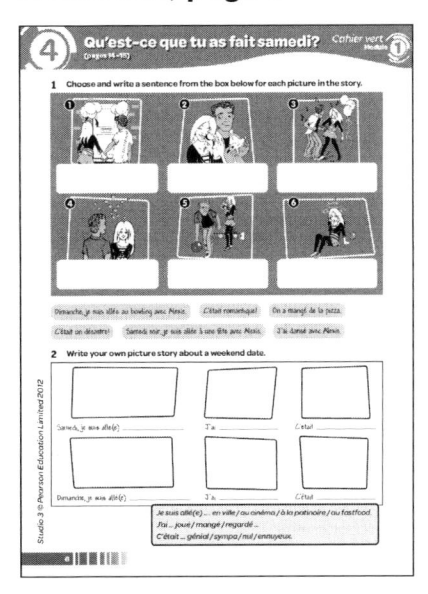

Answers

1 1 Samedi soir, je suis allée à une fête avec Alexis.
   2 On a mangé de la pizza.
   3 J'ai dansé avec Alexis.
   4 C'était romantique!
   5 Dimanche, je suis allée au bowling avec Alexis.
   6 C'était un désastre!

2 (Answers will vary.)

Worksheet 1.5 The perfect tense

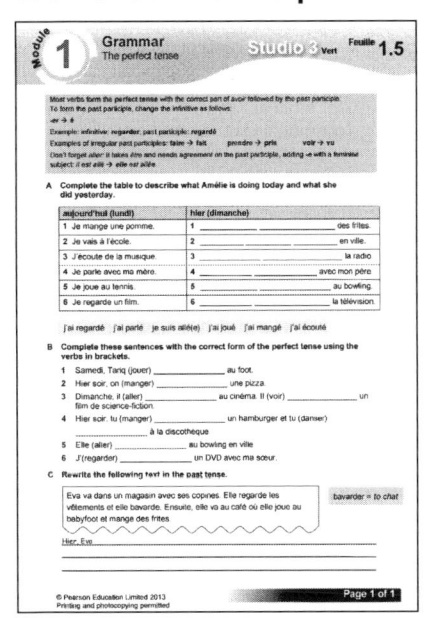

© Pearson Education Ltd 2013. Copying permitted for purchasing institution only. This material is not copyright free.

1 Ma vie sociale d'ado 4 Qu'est-ce que tu as fait samedi?

> **Answers**
> **A** 1 J'ai mangé 2 Je suis allé(e) 3 J'ai écouté
>   4 J'ai parlé 5 J'ai joué 6 J'ai regardé
> **B** 1 a joué 2 a mangé 3 est allé; a vu
>   4 as mangé; as dansé 5 est allée
>   6 ai regardé
> **C** Hier, Eva est allée dans un magasin avec ses copines. Elle a regardé les vêtements et elle a bavardé. Ensuite, elle est allée au café où elle a joué au babyfoot et a mangé des frites.

Video

Episode 2 Le rendez-vous

Samira and Hugo go on a secret first date... followed closely by the rest of the team. Video worksheet 2 can be used in conjunction with this episode.

> **Answers to video worksheet (ActiveTeach)**
> 1 **A** Probably well. They are both level-headed and pleasant.
>   – (Answers will vary.)
>   – They are likely to be surprised, mildly jealous but generally pleased and certainly curious.
> 2 **A** If she would like to go into town with him.
>   **B** Eavesdropping!
>   **C** Don't say anything to the others. He doesn't want them to know he and Samira are going out.
>   **D** She says she's going into town to buy bread for her mother (*Je vais acheter du pain pour ma mère*).
>   **E** Hugo says he's going home (*Je vais à la maison*).
>   **F** They don't want the others to know about their date and follow them.
> 3 **A** At a café.
>   **B** They are following them to see what happens.
>   **C** They are eating chocolate cake and he loves it.
>   **D** She's afraid Hugo and Samira might see them.
>   **E** For a walk in the park.
>   **F** To the cinema.
>   **G** Yes, they agree on everything, including what film to see.
> 4 **A** Hugo says he went for a walk in the park (*J'ai fait une promenade au parc*).
>   **B** They find out that the others have been following them and taking pictures.
>   **C** Yes. They got on well and were holding hands.
>   **D** Speed dating works!

© Pearson Education Ltd 2013. Copying permitted for purchasing institution only. This material is not copyright free.

(Pupil Book pp. 16–17)

1.5 Fou de musique!

Learning objectives
- Describing a music event
- Using *on* in the perfect tense

Programme of Study references
GV1 Tenses (using *on* in the perfect tense)
GV4 Accuracy (spelling)
LC5 Speaking coherently and confidently
LC5 Accurate pronunciation and intonation

FCSE links
Unit 4: Leisure (Music)

Grammar
- the perfect tense (*on*)

Key language
On a écouté toutes sortes de musiques.
On a chanté.
On a dansé toute la soirée.
On a mangé de la pizza.
On a regardé le concert sur des écrans géants.
On a bien rigolé.

PLTS
E Effective participators

Resources
Audio files:
10_Module1_Unit5_Ex2.mp3
11_Module1_Unit5_Ex3.mp3
Workbooks:
Cahier d'exercices Vert, page 7
ActiveTeach:
Starter 1 resource
Starter 2 resource
p.016 Class activity
p.017 Learning skills
p.017 Grammar skills
ActiveLearn:
Listening, Reading
Grammar

Starter 1
Aim
To review the topic of music
Write up the following. Give pupils three minutes to come up with a music artist in each category.

le R&B
le hip-hop
le reggae
le jazz
le pop
le rock
la techno

Hear answers. Take a vote by a show of hands on the most popular choice in each category.

Alternative Starter 1:
Use ActiveTeach p.016 Class activity to practise the perfect tense.

1 Lis et trouve le bon texte pour chaque image. (1–6) (Reading L5)

Reading. Pupils read the sentences and match them to the correct pictures.

Answers
See audioscript for exercise 2: pupils listen to the exercise 2 recording to check their answers.

2 Écoute et vérifie. (1–6) (Listening L5)

Listening. Pupils read the sentences and match them to the correct pictures.

Audioscript Track 10

Je m'appelle Nathan. Le weekend dernier, je suis allé à un festival de musique avec mes copains.

1 On a écouté toutes sortes de musiques.
2 On a dansé toute la soirée.
3 On a aussi chanté!
4 On a mangé de la pizza.
5 On a regardé le concert sur des écrans géants.
6 a bien rigolé. C'était génial!

Answers
1 f 2 e 3 b 4 a 5 c 6 d

Studio Grammaire: the perfect tense (*on*)

Use the *Studio Grammaire* box to review the *on* form of the perfect tense (verbs taking *avoir* and the verb *aller* with *être*). There is more information and further practice on Pupil Book p. 27.

R Pupils work in pairs. They take it in turn to prompt with an infinitive (e.g. *regarder*) and to respond with the *on* form of the perfect tense (*on a regardé*).

3 Écoute Marielle et choisis la bonne réponse. (1–7) (Listening L5)

Listening. Pupils listen to Marielle talking about her trip to a concert. They complete the sentences by choosing the correct option (**a**, **b** or **c**) from the two or three given each time.

© Pearson Education Ltd 2013. Copying permitted for purchasing institution only. This material is not copyright free.

1 Ma vie sociale d'ado 5 Fou de musique!

Audioscript Track 11

1. *Je m'appelle Marielle et j'adore le R&B.*
2. *Samedi dernier, je suis allée à un concert avec mes copines.*
3. *On a vu un de mes chanteurs préférés, qui s'appelle Freddy.*
4. *On a dansé toute la soirée.*
5. *C'était super!*
6. *Après le concert, on est allées en ville, …*
7. *… où on a mangé des glaces.*

Answers

1 b 2 a 3 a 4 b 5 a 6 a 7 a

Starter 2

Aim

To review language for talking about a trip to a music event

Write up the following, jumbling the order of the words in each sentence. Give pupils three minutes working in pairs to choose three of the sentences and write them out correctly.

1. *Ma passion, c'est le rap.*
2. *Je suis allé à un concert avec mes amis.*
3. *On a écouté un de mes groupes préférés.*
4. *On a dansé et c'était génial!*
5. *Après le concert, on est allés au fastfood.*

Check answers.

4 Prépare un exposé oral. Utilise les images et adapte les phrases de l'exercice 3. (Speaking L5)

Speaking. Pupils prepare a presentation, using the pictures supplied and adapting the sentences from exercise 3. A sample opening is given.

5 En tandem. Fais ton exposé oral. Ton/Ta camarade commente ta prononciation. (Speaking L5)

PLTS E

Speaking. In pairs: pupils give their presentation. They comment on each other's pronunciation. A list of comments that they can use to do this is supplied.

6 Lis le texte et complète les phrases. (Reading L5)

Reading. Pupils read the text and complete the gap-fill sentences. Some vocabulary is glossed for support. Draw pupils' attention to *Stratégie 1* on Pupil Book p. 29 on understanding exactly what verbs mean.

Answers

1. Last weekend, Alyzée went to **a (world music) concert** with **her brother**.
2. They listened to **all sorts of music: a salsa group, a reggae singer, a (great) pop-rock duo**.
3. There were lots of people, and they watched **the concert on giant screens**.
4. The atmosphere was **fantastic** and they sang and **danced (all night)**.
5. After the concert, they **went to a restaurant,** where they **ate pizza.**

7 Imagine que tu es allé(e) à un concert ou un festival. Écris ton blog. (Writing L5)

Writing. Pupils imagine that they've been to a concert or festival and write a blog entry about it. A list of features to include is supplied, along with a framework. Draw pupils' attention to the tip box on checking spelling.

Plenary

Ask some pupils to read out their blog entry to the class. Ask the rest of the class to give constructive feedback.

Workbook, page 7

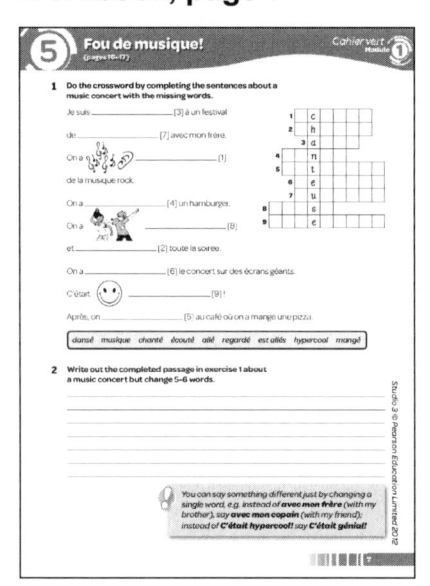

Answers

1. 1 écouté 2 chanté 3 allé 4 mangé
5 est allés 6 regardé 7 musique 8 dansé
9 hypercool

2 (Answers will vary.)

© Pearson Education Ltd 2013. Copying permitted for purchasing institution only. This material is not copyright free.

Worksheet 1.6 Using spider diagrams

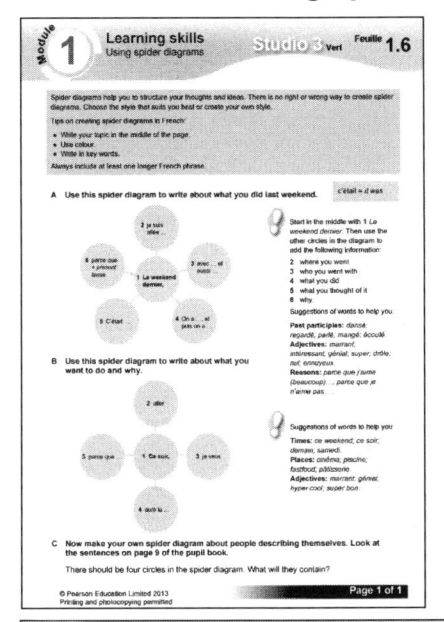

Answers
(Answers will vary.)

Worksheet 1.7 Using two tenses

Answers

A Paul
Ma passion, c'est la musique. J'écoute la radio tous les jours et je joue souvent de la guitare. Le weekend dernier, je suis allé à un concert de rap. Le rap, c'est hyper cool.

Chloé
Moi, je suis très sportive. Samedi, je suis allée au centre sportif et j'ai joué au tennis de table. C'était génial. Quelquefois, je joue au basket mais c'est difficile. Je n'aime pas ça.

Samira
J'adore aller sur Facebook. Je fais des quiz et je regarde les photos de mes copines. Hier, j'ai modifié mes préférences et puis j'ai posté un message à mon copain Omar. Il est très gentil!

B 1 suis allé 2 vais 3 regarde 4 ai mangé
5 joue 6 mange

C Paul
My passion is music. I listen to the radio every day and I often play the guitar. Last weekend, I went to a rap concert. Rap is really cool.

Chloé
I'm very sporty. On Saturday, I went to the sports centre and I played table tennis. It was great fun. Sometimes I play basketball but it's difficult. I don't like it.

Samira
I love going on Facebook. I do quizzes and I look at photos of my friends. Yesterday I updated my likes and then I posted a message to my friend Omar. He is very nice!

(Pupil Book pp. 18–19)

1 Bilan et Révisions

Bilan

Pupils use this checklist to review language covered in the module, working on it in pairs in class or on their own at home. Encourage them to follow up any areas of weakness they identify. There are Target Setting Sheets included in the Assessment Pack, and an opportunity for pupils to record their own levels and targets on the *J'avance* page in the Workbook, p. 12. You can also use the *Bilan* checklist as an end-of-module plenary option.

Révisions

These revision exercises can be used for assessment purposes or for pupils to practise before tackling the assessment tasks in the Assessment Pack.

Resources
Audio files:
12_Module1_Rev_Ex1.mp3
13_Module1_Rev_Ex2.mp3
Workbooks:
Cahier d'exercices Vert, pages 8 & 9

1 Écoute et note la lettre de la bonne activité sur Facebook. (1–6) (Listening L3)

Listening. Pupils listen to six conversations and for each note the letter of the correct picture.

Audioscript Track 12

1 – Qu'est-ce que tu fais sur Facebook?
   – Je poste des messages à mes copains.
   – Tu fais ça souvent?
   – Je fais ça tous les jours.
2 – Qu'est-ce que tu fais sur Facebook?
   – Je fais des quiz.
   – Tu fais ça souvent?
   – Je fais ça quelquefois.
3 – Qu'est-ce que tu fais sur Facebook?
   – Je modifie mes préférences.
   – Tu fais ça souvent?
   – Je fais ça une fois par semaine.
4 – Qu'est-ce que tu fais sur Facebook?
   – J'invite mes copains à sortir.
   – Tu fais ça souvent?
   – Je fais ça tous les weekends.
5 – Qu'est-ce que tu fais sur Facebook?
   – Je regarde les photos de mes copains.
   – Tu fais ça souvent?
   – Je fais ça tous les soirs.
6 – Qu'est-ce que tu fais sur Facebook?
   – Je commente des photos.
   – Tu fais ça souvent?
   – Je fais ça deux fois par semaine.

Answers
1 d 2 f 3 e 4 c 5 a 6 b

2 Écoute à nouveau et note la fréquence de chaque activité. (1–6) (Listening L4)

Listening. Pupils listen again to the exercise 1 recording and note the frequency of each activity.

Audioscript Track 13

As exercise 1.

Answers
1 b *(every day)* 2 a (sometimes)
3 e (once a week) 4 d (every weekend)
5 c (every evening) 6 f (twice a week)

3 En tandem. Fais quatre conversations téléphoniques. Change les mots soulignés. (Speaking L3)

Speaking. In pairs: using the prompts A to D, pupils change the underlined words in the model telephone conversation supplied to make up four new conversations. They take it in turn to give the invitation and to respond.

4 Lis l'e-mail. C'est vrai (V) ou faux (F)? (Reading L5)

Reading. Pupils read the email, then decide whether each sentence is true (writing V) or false (writing F).

Answers
1 V 2 V 3 F 4 V 5 F 6 F

5 Qu'est-ce que tu as fait samedi? Écris des phrases. (Writing L5)

Writing. Pupils write sentences saying what they did on Saturday, using the picture prompts supplied.

Answers

1 Samedi matin, j'ai mangé un hamburger avec Julie/Tariq. C'était sympa.
2 Samedi après-midi, j'ai regardé un DVD avec Anna/Max. C'était ennuyeux.
3 Samedi soir, je suis allé(e) au cinéma avec Chloé/Hugo. C'était génial/super/cool!

© Pearson Education Ltd 2013. Copying permitted for purchasing institution only. This material is not copyright free.

Bilan et Révisions Ma vie sociale d'ado 1

Workbook, pages 8 and 9

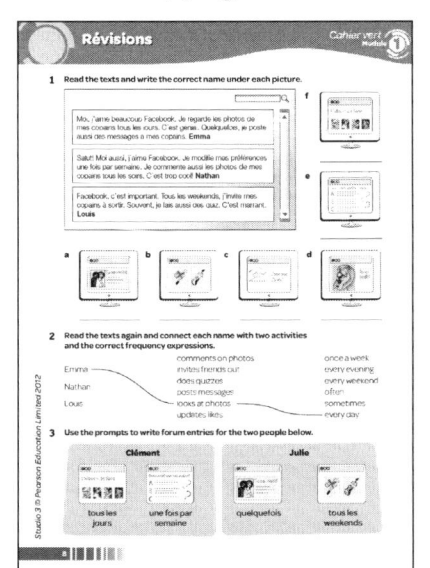

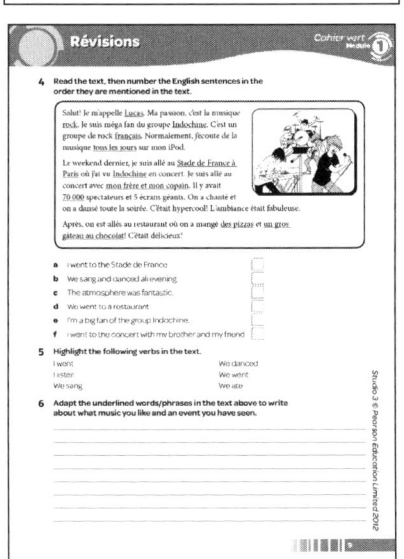

Answers

1. a Louis b Nathan c Emma d Nathan
   e Louis f Emma

2. Emma looks at photos every day.
   Emma posts messages sometimes.
   Nathan updates likes once a week.
   Nathan comments on photos every evening.
   Louis invites friends out every weekend.
   Louis often does quizzes.

3. (Example answers:)

   Clément: Moi, j'aime beaucoup Facebook. Je regarde les photos de mes copains tous les jours. C'est génial. Je fais aussi des quiz une fois par semaine. C'est marrant.

   Julie: Salut! Moi aussi, j'aime Facebook. J'invite quelquefois mes copains à sortir. Je modifie mes préférences tous les weekends.

4. 1 e 2 a 3 f 4 b 5 c 6 d

5. I went: Je suis allé
   I listen: j'écoute
   We sang: on a chanté
   We danced: on a dansé
   We went: on est allés
   We ate: on a mangé

6. (Answers will vary.)

© Pearson Education Ltd 2013. Copying permitted for purchasing institution only. This material is not copyright free.

En plus: La Fête de la Musique

(Pupil Book pp. 20–21)

Learning objectives
- Finding out about music festivals around the world

Programme of Study references
LC3 Conversation
LC4 Expressing ideas (writing)
LC6 Reading comprehension
LC6 Translation into English

FCSE links
Unit 4: Leisure (Music)
Unit 8: Celebrations (Various festivals; Carnival; Special celebrations)

Key language
Review of language from the module

PLTS
l Independent enquirers

Cross-curricular
Music: international music festivals
ICT: internet research

Resources
Audio files:
14_Module1_EnPlus_Ex1.mp3
15_Module1_EnPlus_Ex5.mp3
ActiveTeach:
p.021 Assignment 1
p.021 Assignment 1: prep

Starter

Aim

To introduce the topic

Ask the class about their experience of music festivals. Have they ever been to one? What kind of music did they hear? What else did they do there? What was it like? Tell them that exercise 1 is about music festivals and ask them to predict the kind of vocabulary that will come up.

1 Écoute et lis. (Listening L5)

Listening. Pupils listen to two teenagers talking about music festivals, and read the texts at the same time. Draw pupils' attention to the tip box on reading skills.

Audioscript Track 14

– Le 21 juin, c'est la Fête de la Musique. Deux jeunes parlent de la Fête de la Musique dans leur pays.
– Je m'appelle Ousmane. J'ai 14 ans et j'habite à Tunis, la capitale de la Tunisie. Ici, le soir de la Fête de la Musique, on se retrouve au centre-ville, où il y a un stand avec des écrans géants. D'abord, le DJ joue un peu de techno ou un peu de hip-hop et on danse. Après, c'est la musique «live»! L'année dernière, j'ai vu un excellent trio de rappeurs tunisiens. Ensuite, il y avait Cheb Khaled, qui est un de mes chanteurs préférés. C'est un chanteur tunisien qui chante du raï. Le raï, c'est un style de musique pop chanté en arabe et en français. La musique a continué jusqu'à minuit! C'était super!
– Je m'appelle Lola. J'ai 13 ans. J'habite à Pointe-à-Pitre, la capitale de la Guadeloupe. Ici, la Fête de la Musique, c'est un carnaval caribéen où on peut écouter toutes sortes de musiques. Par exemple, il y a du reggae, du jazz, du calypso et du zouk, qui est un style de musique et de danse traditionnel. Normalement, il fait beau et on danse dans la rue. L'année dernière, j'ai écouté un groupe de cent musiciens! C'était un groupe de tambouristes. Le tambour, c'est un instrument traditionnel de la Guadeloupe. C'était génial!

2 Relis les textes. Qui dit ça? Ousmane ou Lola? Écris O ou L (Reading L5)

Reading. Pupils read the texts in exercise 1 again. They then identify who said each of the sentences in English, Ousmane (writing O) or Lola (writing L).

Answers
1 O 2 L 3 L 4 O 5 L 6 O 7 O 8 L

3 Qu'est-ce que c'est en anglais? Regarde les textes et utilise tes réponses à l'exercice 2. (Reading L5)

Reading. Pupils use the exercise 1 texts and their answers to exercise 2 to work out the English for the French expressions listed.

Answers
1 we meet (up)
2 in the town centre
3 until midnight
4 a Caribbean carnival
5 in the street
6 a hundred musicians
7 a group of drummers

4 Relis les textes. Choisis la bonne réponse et écris la phrase complète. (Reading L5)

Reading. Pupils read the exercise 1 texts again. They complete the sentences by choosing the correct option from the two given each time.

© Pearson Education Ltd 2013. Copying permitted for purchasing institution only. This material is not copyright free.

En plus: La Fête de la Musique Ma vie sociale d'ado 1

Answers

1 Tunis, c'est **la capitale de la Tunisie.**
2 Cheb Khaled, c'est **un chanteur tunisien.**
3 Le raï, c'est **un style de musique.**
4 Pointe-à-Pitre, c'est la capitale de **la Guadeloupe.**
5 Le zouk, c'est **un style de musique.**
6 Le tambour, c'est **un instrument de musique.**

5 Écoute. On parle de la Fête de la Musique en Tunisie ou en Guadeloupe? Écris T ou G. (1–4) (Listening L5)

Listening. Pupils listen to four conversations about the two music festivals described in exercise 1. They identify whether each conversation is about the festival in Tunisia (writing T) or Guadeloupe (writing G).

Audioscript Track 15

1 – *Tu as écouté quelle sorte de musique à la Fête de la Musique?*
– *J'ai écouté toutes sortes de musiques: du reggae, du jazz, du calypso, du zouk …*
– *Est-ce que tu as dansé, aussi?*
– *Ah oui, on a dansé dans la rue! C'était génial!*

2 – *Tu es allée à la Fête de la Musique?*
– *Oui! Je suis allée au centre-ville avec ma famille.*
– *Il y avait beaucoup de monde?*
– *Oui, mais on a regardé le concert sur des écrans géants. Et la musique a continué jusqu'à minuit!*

3 – *C'était comment, la Fête de la Musique?*
– *C'était super. D'abord, le DJ a joué du hip-hop et on a dansé.*
– *Il y avait aussi de la musique traditionnelle?*
– *Oui, j'ai écouté un de mes chanteurs préférés: Cheb Khaled.*
– *Tu aimes le raï, alors?*
– *Ah oui, j'adore le raï!*

4 – *Tu es allée à la Fête de la Musique?*
– *Oui. Il y avait un groupe de cent tambouristes!*
– *Tu rigoles! Cent tambouristes? Quel bruit!*
– *Ah oui, c'était impressionnant!*
– *Et il a fait beau?*
– *Ah oui, bien sûr! Il fait toujours beau pour la Fête de la Musique!*

Answers

1 G 2 T 3 T 4 G

6 En tandem. Interviewe Ousmane ou Lola. Utilise les questions suivantes. (Speaking L5)

Speaking. In pairs: pupils make up interviews, taking it in turn to play the role of Ousmane/Lola and to ask the questions. A framework is supplied.

7 Imagine que tu habites à Paris. Décris la Fête de la Musique dans ta ville. Mentionne les renseignements suivants. (Writing L5)

Writing. Pupils imagine that they live in Paris and write a description of the music festival that takes place there. A list of features to include is supplied, along with a framework. Draw pupils' attention to the tip box on improving their writing by using extended sentences.

Pupils could research French music festivals on the internet and summarise the details in English.

Plenary

Ask some pupils to read out their descriptions of music festivals. Ask the class which of these festivals they would be most interested in visiting.

Worksheet 1.8 Mon blog. Assignment 1: writing

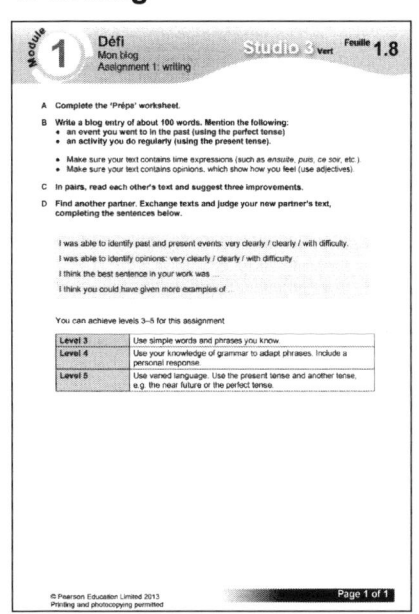

© Pearson Education Ltd 2013. Copying permitted for purchasing institution only. This material is not copyright free.

1 Ma vie sociale d'ado **En plus: La Fête de la Musique**

Worksheet 1.9 Mon blog: Prépa

Answers

A 1 Last weekend, Sarah went to a motorbike race.

2 Sarah is not interested in motorbikes, but Valentin loves them.

3 At the race, the atmosphere was pleasant but not very romantic.

4 Afterwards, Sarah and Valentin went to a very nice little restaurant.

5 Sarah thinks Valentin is funny and extremely nice.

6 Sarah has bought tickets for a Beyoncé concert.

7 Beyoncé is Sarah's favourite singer.

8 Valentin thinks Beyoncé is very beautiful.

B gentil; ne m'intéresse pas; adore; sympa; romantique; délicieuse; amusant; bien; je préfère; préférée; aime; trouve; belle.

C **Present:** j'ai; il s'appelle; il est; m'intéresse; adore; préfère; aime; trouve.
Perfect: je suis allée; était; on a mangé; j'ai acheté.
Time expressions: le weekend dernier; après; ensuite.

① Je parle

(Pupil Book pp. 22–23)

The challenge
- Giving a 3-minute presentation: taking part in a 'blind date' speed-dating event in French

Overview
Explain how this section works.
- Pupils read the context and what they need to do to complete the challenge.
- They then read the list of suggested details to include. Explain that they should use this both to help structure their content and as a checklist as part of their final preparations.
- Explain that the exercises which follow in this section are structured to help them prepare for their presentation.
- Before starting, pupils read the POSM feature: this will help them to improve their performance. Encourage them to use this approach routinely in speaking tasks.

Programme of Study references
GV1 Tenses (past, present and future)
LC4 Expressing ideas (speaking)
LC5 Speaking coherently and confidently

Resources
Audio files:
16_Module1_Jeparle_Ex1.mp3
17_Module1_Jeparle_Ex4.mp3
18_Module1_Jeparle_Ex5.mp3

1 Listen to Florian say these sentences. Which of them could he use in his speed-dating presentation? There are two 'red herrings'. (1–8)

Pupils listen to Florian talking about himself, and read the text at the same time. They identify the six sentences that he could use in his speed-dating presentation (the other two sentences would not be useful).

Audioscript Track 16

1 Je m'appelle Florian.
2 J'ai quatorze ans.
3 Je voudrais un coca.
4 J'ai les cheveux blonds et les yeux bleus.
5 Ma passion, c'est le sport!
6 Le weekend, je vais au centre de loisirs.
7 Mon tee-shirt est dans le frigo.
8 Je suis gentil et intelligent.

Answers
1 ✓ 2 ✓ 3 ✗ 4 ✓ 5 ✓ 6 ✓ 7 ✗ 8 ✓

2 Adapt the six correct sentences from exercise 1 so that they refer to you.

Pupils rewrite the sentences in exercise 1 using their own details.

3 Look back over the module and find connectives, qualifiers and frequency words that you could use in your presentation to join sentences together or make them longer. Make three lists in French and English.

Pupils copy and complete the table using connectives, qualifiers and frequency words they find by looking back through the module. Point out to pupils that they can improve their writing by including examples of these types of words.

Answers

connectives	qualifiers	time/frequency phrases
et (and) mais (but) ou (or) où (where) qui (who) aussi (also) avec (with) parce que (because)	très (very) assez (quite) un peu (a bit)	souvent (often) quelquefois (sometimes) tous les jours (every day) tous les soirs (every evening) tous les weekends (every weekend) une fois par semaine (once a week) deux fois par semaine (twice a week)

4 Listen to Élodie and fill in the gaps, using the words provided. Add any extra connectives, qualifiers or frequency words that she uses to your lists.

Pupils listen to Élodie and complete the gap-fill text, using the words supplied. They then identify any connectives, qualifiers and frequency words she uses which they did not note in exercise 3 and add them to the lists they compiled. *le cours de danse* is glossed for support.

© Pearson Education Ltd 2013. Copying permitted for purchasing institution only. This material is not copyright free.

1 Ma vie sociale d'ado Je parle

Audioscript Track 17

Je m'appelle Élodie et j'ai treize ans. J'ai les cheveux noirs assez longs et les yeux marron. Ma passion, c'est la danse, mais j'aime aussi le cinéma. Tous les weekends, je vais à mon cours de danse ou je vais à la patinoire avec mes copains. Je ne vais pas à la piscine, parce que je n'aime pas ça. Je suis très drôle, mais quelquefois, je suis un peu lunatique.

Answers
1 assez 2 mais 3 weekends 4 ou
5 parce que 6 quelquefois 7 un peu

5 Listen to these people talking about their memorable experiences. Note down the correct ending for each sentence. (1–5)

Pupils listen and match the sentence halves. Draw pupils' attention to the tip box on using a range of tenses. Some vocabulary is glossed for support.

Audioscript Track 18

1 Je suis allé à un match de football et j'ai rencontré David Beckham.
2 J'ai participé à un concours de judo et j'ai gagné!
3 J'ai joué de la guitare à un concert à la télé.
4 J'ai chanté et dansé dans un concours de talent.
5 Je suis allée à New York et j'ai rencontré Ben Stiller.

Answers
1 b 2 c 3 a 4 e 5 d

6 Unscramble these opinions about past events. Use the English translations to help you.

Pupils write out the opinions, unscrambling the jumbled words. The English translations of the opinions are supplied for support.

Answers
1 C'était génial!
2 C'était sympa.
3 C'était super!
4 C'était drôle.
5 C'était hypercool!

7 Write a sentence about a memorable experience for your presentation and say what it was like. It doesn't have to be true!

Pupils write a sentence about a memorable experience in the past. An example is given. They can make up the details.

8 Wow your audience with some extended sentences! Write two sentences for your presentation, using these ideas.

Pupils focus on writing a further two sentences, using the ideas supplied to enhance the content of their presentation.

9 Prepare what you are going to say for the speed-dating challenge.

Pupils prepare their presentation. They can write it out in full first, then memorise it. Draw their attention to the tips on p. 128 of the Pupil Book and encourage them to follow the advice here. They should then check the accuracy and sense of what they have written, correcting and redrafting as necessary.

10 Now memorise your presentation and rehearse it!

Pupils memorise and practise their presentation, using the information on Pupil Book p. 128 to help them.

Pupils then give their presentation. They should ask their audience to give constructive feedback. Pupils use this to identify areas for improvement in the next extended speaking task they do.

(Pupil Book pp. 24–25)

J'écris 1

The challenge
- Writing a 100-word blog entry on a music festival for a music magazine

Overview

Explain how this section works.
- Pupils read the context and what they need to do to complete the challenge.
- They then read the list of suggested details to include. Explain that they should use this both to help structure their content and as a checklist as part of their final preparations.
- Explain that the exercises which follow in this section are structured to help them prepare for the extended writing task.
- Before starting, pupils read the POSM feature: this will help them to improve their performance. Encourage them to use this approach routinely in writing tasks.

Programme of Study references
GV3 Developing vocabulary
GV4 Accuracy (grammar; spelling; punctuation)
LC4 Expressing ideas (writing)
LC8 Writing creatively

1 Look at these sentences. They are correct, but if you used them all in your blog, it would sound a bit repetitive. Rewrite them, using some of the alternatives in the box.

Pupils rewrite the sentences to make them as varied as possible, using the alternative structures supplied.

Example answers
1 *Ma passion, c'est le rap.*
2 *J'aime écouter du hip-hop et du R&B.*
3 *Je suis méga fan de Dizzee Rascal.*
4 *J'adore la musique de Lady Gaga.*
5 *de mes groupes préférés, c'est JLS.*

2 Giving reasons will earn you extra marks. Find the French equivalent of each English phrase in the music from the mp3 player and copy it out correctly.

Remind pupils that including reasons in their writing will earn them extra marks. Pupils find the French versions of the English reasons listed in the wordsnake. *parce que* is glossed for support.

Answers
1 *parce que j'aime les mélodies*
2 *parce que j'aime la rythmique*
3 *parce que j'aime les paroles*
4 *parce que ça me donne envie de danser*

3 Complete these sentences about what you did at the festival. Use your own ideas and remember that you are a music journalist! Then put the sentences into whatever order you like, using the sequencing words in the box.

Pupils complete the sentences on what they did at the festival, using their own ideas and ordering the sentences as they wish, using the sequencing words supplied.

Example answer
D'abord, j'ai interviewé Rihanna. Ensuite, je suis allé à un concert de Elbow. Puis j'ai rencontré Justin Bieber. Après, j'ai mangé un poulet-frites.

4 Write three sentences saying what something was like, which you could use with some of your sentences from exercise 3. Look back at the module for ideas.

Pupils write three opinions using *C'était …*, looking back through the module for ideas.

Example answer
C'était génial/super/fantastique/hypercool/ sympa/intéressant/ennuyeux/nul/un désastre.

5 Read the text and fill in the gaps, using the words from the box.

Pupils complete the gap-fill text using the words supplied. *hier* is glossed for support.

Answers
1 musiques 2 passion 3 rythmique
4 chanteurs 5 génial 6 ville
7 hamburger-frites

6 Now write your blog from the music festival. Use your answers to the exercises above and borrow ideas from the text in exercise 5.

Pupils write their blog entry on the music festival, using the language they have developed in the lesson and developing ideas from exercise 5. Draw pupils' attention to the tip box on improving their writing by including special phrases. Encourage them to identify other phrases in the module they could use. Draw their attention to the writing tips

© Pearson Education Ltd 2013. Copying permitted for purchasing institution only. This material is not copyright free.

1 Ma vie sociale d'ado J'écris

on Pupil Book p. 128 and encourage them to follow the advice here.

7 Check what you have written carefully, or ask a friend to check it. Use the checklist below. Redraft your blog entry, correcting any mistakes.

Pupils check their work or swap with a partner and check each other's work. A checklist is supplied. They then do a second draft, correcting any mistakes.

(Pupil Book pp. 26–27)

Studio Grammaire

The *Studio Grammaire* section provides a more detailed summary of the key grammar covered in the module, along with further exercises to practise these points. The activities on ActiveTeach pages 26 and 27 are repeated from elsewhere in the module.

Grammar topics
- adjectives
- the present tense
  – regular –*er* verbs
  – irregular verbs: *aller, avoir, être* and *faire*
- the perfect tense with *avoir*
- the perfect tense with *être*

Adjectives

1 Translate these sentences into French, once for a boy, once for a girl.

Pupils translate the sentences into French, making the adjectives agree.

Answers
1 Je suis intelligent. Je suis intelligente.
2 Je suis gentil. Je suis gentille.
3 Je suis sportif. Je suis sportive.
4 Je suis drôle. Je suis drôle.
5 Je suis timide. Je suis timide.

The present tense
Regular –er verbs

2 Copy out the two verbs below and fill in the gaps. Follow the pattern of *regarder*, above.

Pupils copy and complete the verbs, using the model of *regarder* to work out the missing verb forms.

Answers	
inviter (to invite)	**commenter** (to comment on)
j'**invite**	je **commente**
tu **invites**	tu **commentes**
il/elle **invite**	il/elle **commente**
on **invite**	on **commente**.

3 Copy out these sentences, putting the correct ending on to the verbs in brackets.

Pupils copy out the sentences, replacing the infinitive prompts with the correct verb forms.

Answers
1 Je **modifie** souvent mes préférences.
2 Je **poste** des messages à mes copains.
3 Tu **invites** tes copains à sortir.
4 Il **regarde** les photos de ses copains.
5 Elle **commente** des photos.
6 On **adore** Facebook!

Irregular verbs: *aller, avoir, être* and *faire*

4 Copy out the sentences, choosing the correct form of the verb. Then match each sentence to the correct translation. Look at the verb tables on page 126 if you need help.

Pupils copy out the sentences, choosing the correct verb form from the two options given each time. They then match each sentence to the correct translation.

Answers	
1	Je **vais** au centre commercial. – c
2	Tu **as** les yeux bleus. – f
3	Il **est** un peu timide. – d
4	On **fait** des quiz. – g
5	Je **suis** très intelligent. – a
6	Elle **a** les cheveux noirs. – b
7	On **va** à la piscine. – e

© Pearson Education Ltd 2013. Copying permitted for purchasing institution only. This material is not copyright free.

1 Ma vie sociale d'ado Studio Grammaire

The perfect tense with *avoir*

5 Complete the following sentences with the past participles on the right.

Pupils copy out the sentences, choosing from the past participles given to fill in the gaps. They then translate the sentences into English.

Answers

1 J'ai **mangé** de la pizza. – I ate some pizza.
2 Tu as **regardé** la télé. – You watched television.
3 Elle a **écouté** de la musique. – She listened to music.
4 On a **dansé** à la discothèque. – We danced at the disco.
5 J'ai **joué** au football. – I played football.
6 Il a **parlé** sur son portable. – He talked on his mobile.
7 On a **visité** le musée. – We visited the museum.
8 Il a **porté** un jean. – He wore jeans.
9 Elle a **rencontré** un beau garçon. – She met a good-looking boy.
10 J'ai **envoyé** des cartes postales. – I sent some postcards.

The perfect tense with *être*

6 *avoir* or *être*? Copy out the sentences, choosing the correct verb in red. Then translate the sentences.

Pupils copy and complete the sentences, choosing the correct verb from the two options given each time. They then translate the sentences into English.

Answers

1 Samedi matin, **je suis** allée en ville avec Julie. – On Saturday morning I went into town with Julie.
2 Elle **a** mangé une glace. – She ate an ice cream.
3 Samedi après-midi, on **a** joué au bowling. – On Saturday afternoon, we went bowling.
4 Samedi soir, tu **es** allée au cinéma? – Did you go to the cinema on Saturday evening?
5 Non, **j'ai** regardé un DVD avec Thomas. – No, I watched a DVD with Thomas.
6 Après, on **a** écouté de la musique. – Afterwards we listened to music.
7 Dimanche matin, **j'ai** joué au foot. – On Sunday morning, I played football.
8 Hier, on **est** allés à la piscine. – Yesterday, we went to the swimming pool.
9 L'année dernière, elle **a** visité Paris. – Last year, she visited Paris.
10 **J'ai** parlé avec mon père. – I spoke to my father.

© Pearson Education Ltd 2013. Copying permitted for purchasing institution only. This material is not copyright free.

(Pupil Book pp. 116–117)

1 À toi

Self-access reading and writing

A Reinforcement

1 Copie et complète le texte. (Reading L2)

Reading. Pupils copy and complete the gap-fill text.

Answers
1 quatorze 2 intelligent 3 marron
4 les cheveux 5 courts

2 Écris un paragraphe en français pour chaque personne. Utilise le texte de l'exercice 1 comme modèle. (Writing L2)

Writing. Pupils write a paragraph for each person, using the exercise 1 text as a model. Draw their attention to the tip box on where to find support.

Example answers
Coucou, je m'appelle **Noah**. J'ai quinze ans. Je suis assez sportif et très intelligent. J'ai les yeux bleus/marron/gris/verts et les cheveux noirs et courts. À mon avis, je ne suis pas timide!
Coucou, je m'appelle **Olivia**. J'ai quatorze ans. Je suis assez belle et très drôle. J'ai les yeux bleus/marron/gris/verts et les cheveux roux et longs. À mon avis, je ne suis pas lunatique!
Coucou, je m'appelle **Quentin**. J'ai quatorze ans. Je suis assez gentil et très sportif. J'ai les yeux bleus/marron/gris/verts et les cheveux blonds et courts. À mon avis, je suis très beau!

3 Fais correspondre les phrases et les images. (Reading L2)

Reading. Pupils match the sentences and pictures.

Answers
1 f 2 e 3 c 4 b 5 a 6 d

4 Écris des textes pour Salim et Fatima. Utilise les images de l'exercice 3. (Writing L3)

Writing. Pupils write texts for Salim and Fatima with the information in the grid, using the letters of the pictures in exercise 3. A sample text is supplied.

Answers
Salim: Tous les jours, je poste des messages à mes copains et une ou deux fois par semaine, je fais des quiz. Quelquefois, je regarde les photos de mes copains.
Fatima: Tous les jours, je commente des photos et j'invite mes copains à sortir. Une ou deux fois par semaine, je poste des messages à mes copains. Quelquefois, je modifie mes préférences.

B Extension

1 Lis le texte. Copie et complète les phrases en anglais. (Reading L4)

Reading. Pupils read the text, then complete the gap-fill sentences in English.

Answers
1 Facebook is the most popular social network in the world with **600 million** members in 2010.
2 With Facebook, you can connect easily with your **friends**, your **family** and your friends' friends.
3 The average user has **130** friends.
4 The average user spends more than **55 minutes** per day on Facebook.
5 The average user clicks the **'like'** button nine times per day.
6 In France, there are more than **15 million** Facebook users.

2 Lis les textes. C'est vrai (V) ou faux (F)? (Reading L4)

Reading. Pupils read the texts, then decide whether each sentence is true (writing V) or false (writing F).

Answers
1 V 2 F 3 V 4 V 5 F 6 F

3 Écris des phrases pour chaque personne. (Writing L4)

Writing. Pupils write sentences for each person, using the picture prompts. A sample is supplied.

Answers
1 *Samedi, j'ai joué au bowling avec Romain. Après, j'ai mangé un hamburger. C'était génial*/bien/romantique/sympa.
2 Le weekend dernier, je suis allé(e) au cinéma avec Léo. J'ai vu un dessin animé. C'était nul/ennuyeux/un désastre.
3 Samedi, je suis allé(e) à une fête avec Aïcha. J'ai dansé. C'était bien/génial/romantique/sympa.
4 Dimanche, je suis allé(e) en ville avec Larisa. J'ai mangé une glace. C'était bien/génial/romantique/sympa.

© Pearson Education Ltd 2013. Copying permitted for purchasing institution only. This material is not copyright free.

(Pupil Book pp. 30–51)

Module 2: Bien dans sa peau

Unit & Learning objectives	Programme of Study references	Key language	Grammar and other language features
1 Touché! (pp. 32–33) Learning the parts of the body Using à + the definite article	**GV2** Grammatical structures (à + definite article) **GV3** Developing vocabulary **LC5** Accurate pronunciation and intonation **LC6** Reading comprehension	la bouche, le bras, l'épaule (f), les oreilles, etc. Où est-ce que tu es touché(e)? le fairplay, etc.	**G** à + definite article – developing speaking skills
2 Le sport et le fitness (pp. 34–35) Talking about sport Using il faut	**GV2** Grammatical structures (il faut) **GV3** Opinions and discussions **LC3** Conversation **LC6** Reading comprehension	Pour être un bon sportif, il faut avoir un bon programme/ bien manger, etc. J'aime/Je n'aime pas jouer dans une équipe. C'est fatigant/ennuyeux. Je pense que/À mon avis … Je (ne) suis (pas) d'accord avec …	**G** il faut + infinitive – developing reading skills – developing listening skills
3 Manger sain (pp. 36–37) Learning about healthy eating Using du, de la and des	**GV2** Grammatical structures (du/de la/des; negatives) **GV3** Developing vocabulary **LC1** Listening and responding **LC6** Reading comprehension	les céréales/les légumes l'eau le pain/le poisson la viande etc. Je (ne) mange (pas) sain. Je mange des … Je ne mange pas de … Je ne mange jamais de …	**G** de + definite article **G** ne … pas, ne … jamais – developing writing skills
4 Je vais changer ma vie! (pp. 38–39) Making plans to get fit Using the near future tense	**GV1** Tenses (near future) **GV3** Developing vocabulary **LC1** Listening and responding **LC6** Reading comprehension	Je vais faire du sport régulièrement. Je vais manger sain. Je vais prendre des cours d'arts martiaux. Je vais aller au collège à pied. Je vais faire trente minutes d'exercice par jour. Je vais aller au collège à vélo.	**G** the near future tense – developing writing skills
5 Es-tu en forme? (pp. 40–41) Describing levels of fitness Using two tenses together	**GV1** Tenses (present and near future) **LC3** Conversation **LC4** Expressing ideas (speaking) **LC5** Speaking coherently and confidently	actif/active Ça ne m'intéresse pas. J'ai un problème. Je joue à des jeux vidéo.	**G** using two tenses together – developing writing skills

© Pearson Education Ltd 2013. Copying permitted for purchasing institution only. This material is not copyright free.

Bien dans sa peau 2

Unit & Learning objectives	Programme of Study references	Key language	Grammar and other language features
Bilan et Révisions (pp. 42–43) Pupils' checklist and practice exercises			
En plus: Les sportifs français (pp. 44–45) Learning about French sportsmen and women	**LC1** Listening and responding **LC3** Conversation **LC6** Reading comprehension	Review of language from the module	– developing reading skills
J'écris (pp. 46–47) Extended writing practice	**GV3** Developing vocabulary **GV4** Accuracy (grammar; spelling; punctuation) **LC4** Expressing ideas (writing) **LC8** Writing creatively	Review of language from the module	– developing writing skills – checking your work
Studio Grammaire (pp. 48–49) Detailed grammar summary and practice exercises			**G** à + the definite article **G** the partitive article **G** il faut **G** negatives **G** the near future tense **G** je vais or je vais faire?
À toi (pp. 118–119) Self-access reading and writing at two levels			

© Pearson Education Ltd 2013. Copying permitted for purchasing institution only. This material is not copyright free.

(Pupil Book pp. 32–33)

2) 1 Touché!

Learning objectives
- Learning the parts of the body
- Using à + the definite article

Programme of Study references
GV2 Grammatical structures (à + definite article)
GV3 Developing vocabulary
LC5 Accurate pronunciation and intonation
LC6 Reading comprehension

FCSE links
Unit 5: Healthy lifestyle (Sports)

Grammar
- à + definite article

Key language
la bouche
le bras
le corps
le dos
l'épaule
les fesses
le front
le genou
la jambe
la main
le nez
l'oeil
les oreilles
le pied
la tête
le visage
les yeux
Où est-ce que tu es touché(e)?
blessé(e)
gagner
éliminé(e)
le membre
le matériel
le fairplay

PLTS
C Creative thinkers

Cross-curricular
English: the definite and indefinite articles
Art: drawing

Resources
Audio files:
19_Module2_Unit1_Ex1.mp3
20_Module2_Unit1_Ex3.mp3
21_Module2_Unit1_Ex7.mp3
Workbooks:
Cahier d'exercices Vert, page 13
ActiveTeach:
p.032 Flashcards
p.032 Grammar
p.032 Grammar practice
p.033 Reading skills
ActiveLearn:
Listening, Reading
Grammar, Vocabulary

Starter 1
Aim
To introduce vocabulary for the parts of the body

Touch your leg and say *la jambe*. Pupils copy you, repeating the word. Repeat with the other parts of the body. Once pupils are familiar with the words, say the words without pointing. The pupils touch the correct part of their body.

Alternative Starter 1:
Use ActiveTeach p.032 Flashcards to introduce the parts of the body.

1 Écoute et écris la bonne lettre. (1–14)
(Listening L2)

Listening. Pupils listen to the list of parts of the body and for each note the letter of the correct label.

Audioscript Track 19

1 *la jambe*   8 *les fesses*
2 *la bouche*   9 *le genou*
3 *l'épaule*   10 *le nez*
4 *le bras*   11 *la tête*
5 *la main*   12 *les yeux*
6 *le front*   13 *les oreilles*
7 *le dos*   14 *le pied*

Answers
1 h   2 l   3 e   4 f   5 b   6 j   7 g   8 c   9 d
10 n   11 a   12 m   13 k   14 i

2 Copie et complète les parties du corps. (Writing L2)

Writing. Pupils copy and complete the gap-fill words for parts of the body.

Answers
1 la main   2 le pied   3 l'épaule   4 le dos
5 la jambe   6 les yeux   7 la bouche
8 les fesses

3 On joue au paintball. Écoute et remplis le tableau. Utilise les lettres de l'exercice 1. (1–4) (Listening L4)

Listening. Pupils copy out the grid. They listen to four conversations between people playing paintball, and complete the grid with the details, using the letters of the exercise 1 pictures.

Audioscript Track 20

1 – Aïe! Je suis touché.
  – Oh, non, Hélio. Où est-ce que tu es touché?
  – Au bras et aussi à la jambe.
2 – AAAOUUTTT! Je suis touchée.

© Pearson Education Ltd 2013. Copying permitted for purchasing institution only. This material is not copyright free.

1 Touché! Bien dans sa peau

- Oh non! Odyssée est touchée! Où est-ce que tu es touchée, Odyssée?
- Au dos et à l'épaule. Oh, et à la main, aussi. Oh là là.
3 - Aooouut, Je suis touché! Je suis touché!
- Où est-ce que tu es touché?
- Au genou et aux fesses.
4 - Aïe!
- Oh non! Où est-ce que tu es touchée, Fatima?
- Ça fait mal! Je suis touchée à la tête, au front!

Answers

		touché(e)
1	Hélio	f, h
2	Odyssée	g, e, b
3	Charles	d, c
4	Fatima	a, j

Studio Grammaire: à + definite article

Use the *Studio Grammaire* box to review à + definite article (*au, à la, à l', aux*). Ask pupils what the definite and indefinite articles are in English. There is more information and further practice on Pupil Book p. 48.

R Pupils write out all the parts of the body in exercise 1 with the correct form of *à* + the definite article.

4 En tandem. Fais quatre dialogues, suivant le modèle. (Speaking L3)

Speaking. In pairs: pupils make up four dialogues, adapting the model shown using the picture prompts supplied. They take it in turn to ask and answer. Draw pupils' attention to the tip box on how to pronounce the question. Some vocabulary is glossed for support.

Starter 2

Aim

To review vocabulary for the parts of the body; To review the different forms of *à* + the definite article

Give pupils three minutes working in pairs to write down as many parts of the body as they can remember. Tell them their target is 14. You can make the activity more challenging by asking them to write each one with the correct form of *à* + the definite article.

Pupils swap answers with another pair to check, awarding 1 point for each correct body part and 2 points if the form of *à* + definite article is also correct. Reward the pair with the highest score.

Alternative Starter 2:

Use ActiveTeach p.032 Grammar practice to practise *à* + definite article.

5 Lis le texte. Choisis la bonne réponse et écris la phrase complète. (Reading L4)

Reading. Pupils read the text. They then complete the sentences by choosing from the two options given each time. Some vocabulary is glossed for support.

Answers

1 Félix est membre de l'association de paintball de la **côte d'Opale**.
2 Il joue **tous les dimanches**.
3 Pour 30 euros, on peut jouer pendant **120 minutes**.
4 Si on est touché(e) à la jambe ou au bras, **on est blessé(e)**.
5 Pour l'association de paintball de la côte d'Opale, le fairplay **est très important**.

R Translate the exercise 5 text orally round the class.

6 Fais correspondre les phrases et les photos. (Reading L3)

Reading. Pupils match the sentences and pictures. Draw their attention to the tip boxes on using *de* to show possession and *c'est/ce sont*. Pupils check their answers in exercise 7.

7 Écoute et vérifie tes réponses. (1–5) (Listening L3)

Listening. Pupils listen to check their answers to exercise 6. Remind them to look at the tip boxes again.

Audioscript Track 21

1 *Ce sont les yeux de Cheryl Cole. – e*
2 *C'est la main de Catherine, Duchesse de Cambridge. – a*
3 *C'est le nez de Daniel Radcliffe. – b*
4 *C'est la bouche de Beyoncé. – d*
5 *C'est le front de Justin Bieber. – c*

Answers

1 e 2 a 3 b 4 d 5 c

8 En tandem. Ce sont les oreilles (etc.) de qui? Discute! (Speaking L3)

© Pearson Education Ltd 2013. Copying permitted for purchasing institution only. This material is not copyright free.

2 Bien dans sa peau 1 Touché!

Speaking. pairs: pupils discuss which celebrity's body part is shown in each picture, adapting the model exchange supplied. They take it in turn to ask and answer. *Je pense que …* is glossed for support.

Answers

a Ce sont les oreilles du Prince Charles.
b C'est le pied de Wayne Rooney.
c C'est la main d'Arsène Wenger.
d C'est le front de Simon Cowell.
e C'est la bouche de Jamie Oliver.

9 Décris ta personne idéale. (Writing L4)

PLTS C

Writing. Pupils describe their ideal person, who should be made up of the body parts of different people. A sample opening is given. Pupils could also draw the person they design.

Plenary

Review the different forms of *à* + the definite article.

Suggest that pupils use different colours to note the different forms of *à* + the definite article, to help them remember them (e.g. blue for masculine, red for feminine, green for *à l'* and purple for plural). If they use the same colours to write out vocabulary, this will also help them remember the gender of words.

Go round the class. Pupil 1 says the French word for a part of the body and points to it at the same time (e.g. *épaule*, pointing to his/her shoulder); Pupil 2 responds (e.g. *à l'épaule*). Continue in this way round the class.

Workbook, page 13

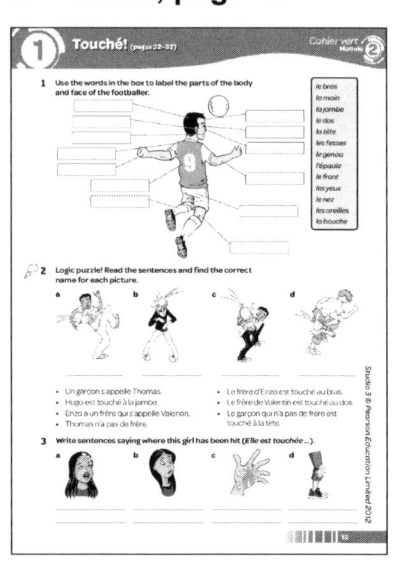

Answers

1 (Parts of body labelled as follows:)
arm = le bras; hand = la main; leg = la jambe; back = le dos; head = la tête; bottom = les fesses; knee = le genou; shoulder = l'épaule; forehead = le front ; eyes = les yeux; nose = le nez; ears = les oreilles; mouth = la bouche

2 a Enzo b Thomas c Valentin d Hugo

3 a Elle est touchée au front.
   b Elle est touchée au nez.
   c Elle est touchée à la main.
   d Elle est touchée au genou.

Worksheet 2.1 Reading unfamiliar texts

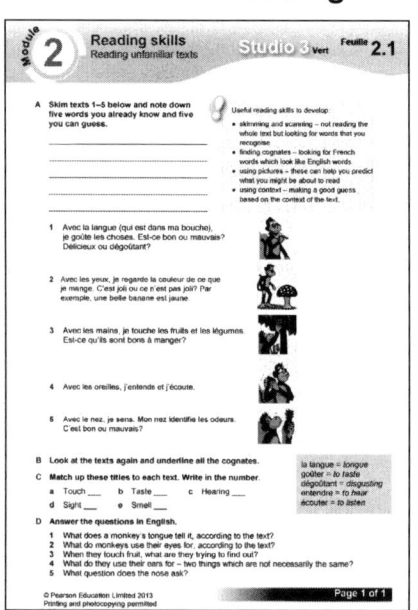

Answers

A (Answers will vary.)

B 1 délicieux
   2 couleur, exemple, banane
   3 touche, fruits
   4 (none)
   5 identifie, odeurs

C a 3 b 1 c 4 d 2 e 5

D 1 If something is good or bad, delicious or disgusting.
   2 To see if the colour of the food is pretty or not.
   3 Whether it is good to eat.
   4 Hearing and listening.
   5 Is the smell good or bad?

© Pearson Education Ltd 2013. Copying permitted for purchasing institution only. This material is not copyright free.

(Pupil Book pp. 34–35)

2 Le sport et le fitness

Learning objectives
- Learning about sport
- Using *il faut*

Programme of Study references
GV2 Grammatical structures (*il faut*)
GV3 Opinions and discussions
LC3 Conversation
LC6 Reading comprehension

FCSE links
Unit 5: Healthy lifestyle (Opinions)

Grammar
- *il faut* + infinitive

Key language
Pour être un bon sportif, …
Il faut …
avoir un bon programme d'entraînement
bien dormir
bien manger
être motivé
aimer la compétition
J'aime …
Je n'aime pas …
jouer dans une équipe
Ça booste le moral.
C'est fatigant.
C'est ennuyeux.
Je pense que …
Je suis d'accord avec …
Je ne suis pas d'accord avec …
À mon avis …

PLTS
I Independent enquirers

Cross-curricular
ICT: internet research
PSHE: healthy lifestyles

Resources
Audio files:
22_Module2_Unit2_Ex1.mp3
23_Module2_Unit2_Ex4.mp3
Workbooks:
Cahier d'exercices Vert, page 14
ActiveTeach:
Starter 1 resource
p.034 Grammar
p.034 Grammar practice
p.035 Video 3
p.035 Video worksheet 3
ActiveLearn:
Listening, Reading

Starter 1
Aim
To review infinitives

Write up the following. Give pupils three minutes working in pairs to write the infinitive form of each verb.

il aime   j'ai   je suis   on mange
elle regarde   je fais

Check answers. (**Answers:** *aimer, avoir, être, manger, regarder, faire*)

1 Écoute et écris la bonne lettre. (1–5)
(Listening L3)

Listening. Pupils listen to five statements on what you need to do to be a successful sportsperson. For each statement they write the letter of the correct picture.

Audioscript Track 22

1 *Pour être un bon sportif, il faut avoir un bon programme d'entraînement.*
2 *Pour être un bon sportif, il faut bien dormir.*
3 *Pour être un bon sportif, il faut aimer la compétition.*
4 *Pour être un bon sportif, il faut bien manger.*
5 *Pour être un bon sportif, il faut être motivé.*

Answers
1 b   2 d   3 a   4 c   5 e

Studio Grammaire: *il faut*

Use the *Studio Grammaire* box to review *il faut* (+ infinitive). There is more information and further practice on Pupil Book p. 48.

R Pupils write out the other *il faut* + infinitive expressions listed in exercise 1, then add two more expressions of their own.

2 Lis les textes. Écris le bon prénom.
(Reading L3)

Reading. Pupils read the five texts, then identify who is being described in each English question. Draw pupils' attention to the tip box on the reading strategy of identifying cognates.

Answers
1 Leïla   2 Damien   3 Fouad   4 Mattéo
5 Candice

3 Tu es d'accord ou pas d'accord avec les jeunes de l'exercice 2? Écris deux phrases pour chaque personne.
(Writing L4)

Writing. Pupils write two sentences for each of the teenagers in exercise 2, saying whether or not they agree with them. A sample is given. Some vocabulary is glossed for support.

© Pearson Education Ltd 2013. Copying permitted for purchasing institution only. This material is not copyright free.

2 Bien dans sa peau 2 Le sport et le fitness

Starter 2

Aim

To review language for giving an opinion about sport

Write up the following. Give pupils three minutes to complete each sentence in two different and appropriate ways.

1 J'aime le sport parce que …
2 Je n'aime pas le sport parce que …

Hear answers. Ask the class to vote by a show of hands on whether they agree with each one.

Alternative Starter 2:

Use ActiveTeach p.034 Grammar practice to practise *il faut*.

4 Écoute et écris la bonne lettre. (1–3) (Listening L4)

Listening. Pupils listen to three people talking about what sport means to them and for each write the letter of the correct picture. Draw pupils' attention to the tip box on the listening skill of prediction. Suggest they add a note to their Skills Notebook on using prediction when getting ready for a listening task.

Audioscript Track 23

1 Moi, j'aime le sport parce que j'aime jouer dans une équipe et j'aime la compétition. À mon avis, pour être un bon sportif, il faut aimer la compétition.
2 Moi, j'aime le sport parce que ça booste le moral. À mon avis, pour être un bon sportif, il faut avoir un bon programme d'entraînement et il faut être motivé.
3 Moi, je n'aime pas le sport parce que c'est ennuyeux et en plus, je n'aime pas la compétition. Je préfère aller sur Facebook.

Answers
1 b 2 a 3 c

5 En tandem. Fais trois dialogues. (Speaking L4)

Speaking. In pairs: pupils make up three dialogues, adapting the model exchange using the symbol prompts.

6 Lis le texte. Mets les phrases en anglais dans l'ordre du texte. (Reading L4)

Reading. Pupils read the text, then put the English sentences into the order the statements are mentioned in the text. Some vocabulary is glossed for support.

Answers
e Renaud Lefèvre is a young tennis player.
a On Saturday mornings, Renaud plays a match.
g In the afternoon, he works with his coach.
f Then he has two hours' training.
c On Sundays, it's the same routine.
h During the week, he exercises daily.
d You have to like competition.
b You have to be motivated.

7 Écris un paragraphe où tu donnes ton opinion sur le sport. (Writing L4)

Writing. Pupils write a paragraph giving their opinion on sport. A framework is supplied.

Pupils research different sports on the internet to compile a list of five sports in French. They should write them out in order from 1 to 5 according to how good they are at keeping you fit, with 1 for the sport that would make you most fit.

Plenary

Ask the class to summarise how *il faut* is used, giving as many examples as possible from the unit.

Ask some pupils to read out their paragraphs from exercise 7. Ask the rest of the class to give constructive feedback.

2 Le sport et le fitness Bien dans sa peau

Workbook, page 14

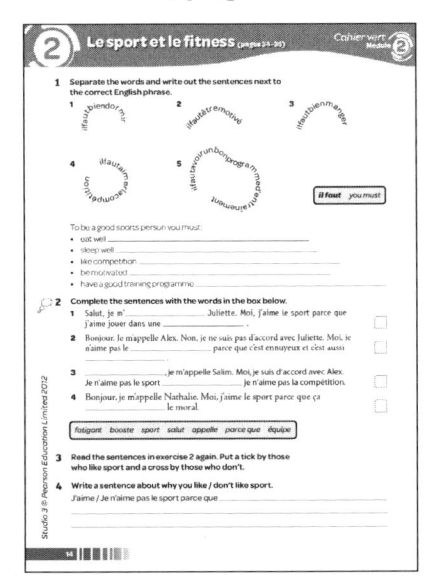

Answers

1
1. il faut bien dormir = sleep well
2. il faut être motivé = be motivated
3. il faut bien manger = eat well
4. il faut aimer la compétition = like competition
5. il faut avoir un bon programme d'entraînement = have a good training programme

2
1. Salut, je m'**appelle** Juliette. Moi, j'aime le sport parce que j'aime jouer dans une **équipe**.
2. Bonjour. Je m'appelle Alex. Moi, je n'aime pas le **sport** parce que c'est ennuyeux et c'est aussi **fatigant**.
3. **Salut**, je m'appelle Salim. Je n'aime pas le sport **parce que** je n'aime pas la compétition.
4. Bonjour, je m'appelle Nathalie. J'aime le sport parce que ça **booste** le moral.

3 1 ✓ 2 ✗ 3 ✗ 4 ✓

4 (Answers will vary.)

Video

Episode 3: La bataille d'eau

The team have a water fight, in which the last person to be hit upon any part of the body is the winner. Video worksheet 3 can be used in conjunction with this episode.

Answers to video worksheet (ActiveTeach)

1 A (Answers will vary.)

2 A *Il fait chaud.*
  B Mehdi.
  C She is horrified and thinks it's a rubbish idea.
  D Alex.
  E Not really – three on one team and two on the other.
  F When you are hit, you are out (you don't play any more).
  G It seems ideal as there are plenty of trees to hide behind.

3 A Eat well (*il faut bien manger*).
  B Fruit and vegetables.
  C Crisps.

4 A Marielle dances every day.
  B To be a good cameraman.

5 A On the leg/knee.
  B She can't play any more.
  C He fails to hit Hugo.
  D Mehdi: forehead (*front*); Alex: stomach (*ventre*).

6 A Who got hit first.
  B The match is void/a draw (*match nul*).
  C Marielle says they will have to play again. The others don't agree and turn their water pistols on Marielle.

© Pearson Education Ltd 2013. Copying permitted for purchasing institution only. This material is not copyright free.

(Pupil Book pp. 36–37)

3 Manger sain

Learning objectives
- Learning about healthy eating
- Using *du, de la* and *des*

Programme of Study references
GV2 Grammatical structures (*du/de la/des*; negatives)
GV3 Developing vocabulary
LC1 Listening and responding
LC6 Reading comprehension

FCSE links
Unit 5: Healthy lifestyle (Food/drink; Healthy/unhealthy eating; Fast food; Eating and drinking)
Unit 6: Food and drink (Food/drink vocabulary; Opinions; Unhealthy/healthy food choices; Food and drink habits)

Grammar
- *de* + definite article
- *ne … pas, ne … jamais*

Key language
les céréales
les chips
l'eau
les fruits
les légumes
les oeufs
le pain
le poisson
les produits laitiers
les sucreries
les boissons gazeuses
la viande
Je mange sain.
Je ne mange pas sain.
Je mange du/de la/de l'/des …
Je ne bois pas de …
Je ne mange pas de …
Je ne mange jamais de …

PLTS
S Self-managers

Cross-curricular
English: the definite and indefinite articles

ICT: word-processing
PSHE: healthy lifestyles

Resources
Audio files:
24_Module2_Unit3_Ex2.mp3
25_Module2_Unit3_Ex4.mp3
Workbooks:
Cahier d'exercices Vert, page 15
ActiveTeach:
Starter 1 resource
Starter 2 resource
p.036 Flashcards
p.036 Grammar
p.036 Grammar practice
p.036 Grammar
p.036 Grammar practice
p.037 Class activity
p.037 Thinking skills
p.037 Grammar skills
ActiveLearn:
Listening, Reading
Grammar, Vocabulary

Starter 1
Aim
To review food and drink vocabulary

Read out the following list. Ask pupils to note the numbers of the items that are food or drinks.

1 *le pain* 2 *la viande* 3 *les yeux*
4 *le poisson* 5 *les magasins* 6 *la fête*
7 *les chips* 8 *les boissons gazeuses*
9 *la bouche* 10 *l'eau*

Check answers, asking pupils to say what the words mean. (**Answers:** 1, 2, 4, 7, 8, 10)

Alternative Starter 1:
Use ActiveTeach p.036 Flashcards to practise food and drink vocabulary.

1 Fais correspondre les photos et les légendes. Utilise la section vocabulaire si nécessaire. (Reading L1)

Reading. Pupils match the pictures and labels. Encourage them to use reading strategies to work out the links, and then to use the vocabulary list on Pupil Book p. 51 if necessary.

Answers
See audioscript for exercise 2: pupils listen to the exercise 2 recording to check their answers.

2 Écoute et vérifie tes réponses. (1–10) (Listening L1)

Listening. Pupils listen and check their answers to exercise 1.

Audioscript Track 24

1 *des fruits – f*
2 *des légumes – g*
3 *de l'eau – d*
4 *des produits laitiers – e*
5 *du pain – a*
6 *de la viande – c*
7 *du poisson – b*
8 *des chips – h*
9 *des sucreries – j*
10 *des boissons gazeuses – i*

Answers
1 f 2 g 3 d 4 e 5 a 6 c 7 b 8 h
9 j 10 i

© Pearson Education Ltd 2013. Copying permitted for purchasing institution only. This material is not copyright free.

3 Manger sain Bien dans sa peau

Studio Grammaire: the partitive article

Use the *Studio Grammaire* box to review *de* + definite article (*du, de l', de la, des*). Ask pupils what the definite and indefinite articles are in English. There is more information and further practice on Pupil Book p. 48.

R Write up the following, omitting the underline. Pupils write out the correct forms, choosing from the two options given each time.

1 du/<u>des</u> chips
2 <u>du</u>/de l' pain
3 <u>de la</u>/des viande
4 de la/<u>des</u> légumes
5 du/<u>des</u> sucreries

3 C'est sain ou pas sain? Fais deux listes. (Writing L2)

Writing. Pupils copy and complete the grid, categorising all the food/drinks in exercise 1 according to whether they are healthy or unhealthy.

Answers

sain	pas sain
des fruits	des boissons
du pain	gazeuses
du poisson	des chips
de la viande	des sucreries
de l'eau	
des produits laitiers	
des légumes	

4 Écoute. Copie et complète le tableau en anglais. (1–4) (Listening L3)

Listening. Pupils copy out the grid. They listen to four conversations in which people discuss whether they eat healthily or unhealthily and complete the grid with the details in English.

Audioscript Track 25

1 – *Tu manges sain ou tu ne manges pas sain, Élisa?*
  – *Je mange sain. Je mange des fruits et des légumes. Je ne mange pas de sucreries et je ne bois jamais de boissons gazeuses.*
2 – *Tu manges sain ou tu ne manges pas sain, Artur?*
  – *Je mange sain. Je mange du pain et des légumes. Je ne mange pas de chips et je ne mange jamais de sucreries.*
3 – *Tu manges sain ou tu ne manges pas sain, Clarisse?*
  – *Je ne mange pas sain. Je mange des chips et des sucreries. Je ne bois pas d'eau et je ne mange jamais de poisson.*
4 – *Tu manges sain ou tu ne manges pas sain, Manu?*
  – *Je mange sain. Je mange des fruits et je bois de l'eau. Je ne bois pas de boissons gazeuses et je ne mange jamais de chips.*

Answers

	eats/drinks	doesn't eat/drink	never eats/drinks
1 Élisa	fruit, vegetables	sweet things	fizzy drinks
2 Artur	bread, vegetables	crisps	sweet things
3 Clarisse	crisps, sweet things	water	fish
4 Manu	fruit, water	fizzy drinks	crisps

Studio Grammaire: negatives

Use the *Studio Grammaire* box to review the negatives *ne … pas* and *ne … jamais*. There is more information and further practice on Pupil Book p. 49.

+ Pupils write four sentences of their own using *ne … pas* and *ne … jamais*.

Starter 2

Aim

To review negatives

Write up the following. Give pupils three minutes to rewrite the sentences following the model.

  Je mange des hamburgers. (ne … pas)
→ *Je ne mange pas de hamburgers.*

1 *Je bois des boissons gazeuses. (ne … jamais)*
2 *Je mange de la viande. (ne … pas)*
3 *Je bois de l'eau. (ne … pas)*
4 *Je mange des sucreries. (ne … jamais)*

Check answers. Ask the class to summarise how negatives are used and what happens to *du/de la/de l'/des* after a negative. (**Answers:** 1 Je ne bois jamais de boissons gazeuses. 2 Je ne mange pas de viande. 3 Je ne bois pas d'eau. 4 Je ne mange jamais de sucreries.)

Alternative Starter 2:

Use ActiveTeach p.036 Grammar practice to practise negatives or p.036 Grammar practice to practise the partitive article.

© Pearson Education Ltd 2013. Copying permitted for purchasing institution only. This material is not copyright free.

2 Bien dans sa peau 3 Manger sain

5 Fais un sondage dans ta classe. Note les réponses. (Speaking L3)

Speaking. Pupils carry out a class survey on healthy eating. The question to use is supplied, along with a framework for responses.

6 Lis les textes. Note les bonnes lettres pour chaque personne. (Reading L4)

Reading. Pupils read the texts, then note what each person eats and drinks and doesn't eat and drink by writing the letters of the correct pictures.

> **Answers**
> **Gabriel:** a, j, h, d, i, c
> **Lucas:** l, b, g, f, k, e, m

7 Tu es un ange ou un diable? Tu manges sain ou tu ne manges pas sain? Écris des phrases. (Writing L4)

Writing. Pupils write a paragraph on whether they are an angel or a devil, i.e. whether they eat healthily or unhealthily. Draw pupils' attention to the tip box on improving their writing by using negatives.

Pupils could do the task on computer, making it easier to produce a second draft.

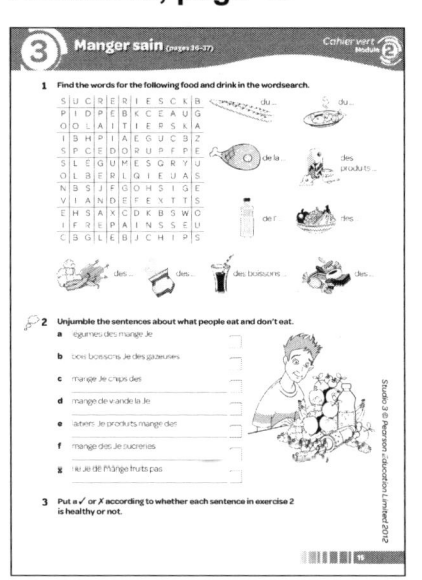

> **Plenary**
>
> **PLTS** S
>
> Review the different forms of *de* + the definite article. Elicit as many examples of foods with the correct form of the partitive article as possible. Suggest pupils use different colours to note the different forms of *de* + the definite article, as they did with *à* + the definite article. Remind them that using colour coding in this way, and linking it to the gender of nouns, really makes remembering the different forms a lot easier.
>
> *Alternative plenary*
>
> Use ActiveTeach p.037 Class activity to practise talking about healthy eating.

Workbook, page 15

Answers

1

S	U	C	R	E	R	I	E	S	C	K	B
P	I	D	P	E	B	K	C	E	A	U	G
O	O	L	A	I	T	I	E	R	S	K	A
I	B	H	P	I	A	E	G	U	C	B	Z
S	P	C	E	D	O	R	U	P	F	P	E
S	L	É	G	U	M	E	S	Q	R	Y	U
O	L	B	E	R	L	Q	I	E	U	A	S
N	B	S	J	F	G	O	H	S	I	G	E
V	I	A	N	D	E	F	E	X	T	T	S
E	H	S	A	X	C	D	K	B	S	W	O
I	F	R	E	P	A	I	N	S	S	E	U
C	B	G	L	E	B	J	C	H	I	P	S

2 a Je mange des légumes.
  b Je bois des boissons gazeuses.
  c Je mange des chips.
  d Je mange de la viande.
  e Je mange des produits laitiers.
  f Je mange des sucreries.
  g Je ne mange pas de fruits.

3 a ✓ b ✗ c ✗ d ✓ (but not too much!)
  e ✓ (but not too many!) f ✗ g ✗

3 Manger sain Bien dans sa peau

Worksheet 2.2 Odd one out!

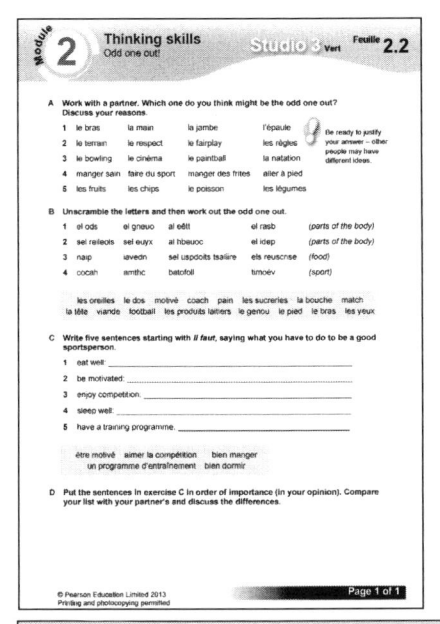

Answers

A (Only the most obvious answers are given. There are other possibilities.)

1 la jambe (in the lower half of the body)
2 le terrain (the others are to do with how the game is conducted)
3 la natation (none of the others are water sports)
4 manger des frites (the others are healthy)
5 les chips (the others are healthy)

B (The odd one out for each group is underlined.)

1 le dos   le genou   <u>la tête</u> *(feminine)*   le bras
2 les oreilles   les yeux   la bouche   <u>le pied</u> *(not on head)*
3 pain   viande   les produits   laitiers   <u>les sucreries</u> *(not savoury)*
4 coach   match   football   motivé (only adjective)

C 1 Il faut bien manger.
2 Il faut être motivé.
3 Il faut aimer la compétition.
4 Il faut bien dormir.
5 Il faut avoir un programme d'entraînement.

D (Answers will vary.)

Worksheet 2.3 Using negatives

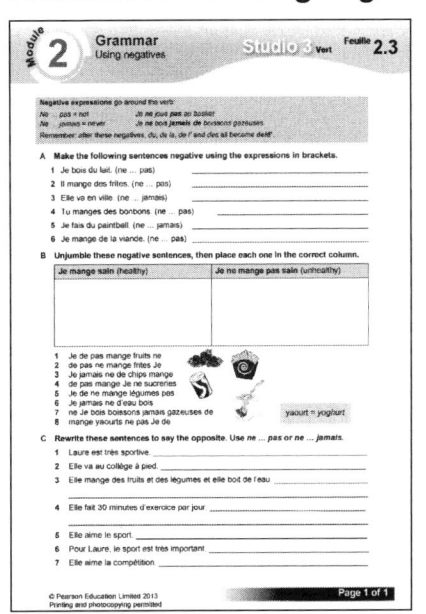

Answers

A 1 Je ne bois pas de lait.
2 Il ne mange pas de frites.
3 Elle ne va jamais en ville.
4 Tu ne manges pas de bonbons.
5 Je ne fais jamais de paintball.
6 Je ne mange pas de viande.

B

Je mange sain (healthy)	Je ne mange pas sain (unhealthy)
Je ne mange pas de frites.	Je ne mange pas de fruits.
Je ne mange jamais de chips.	Je ne mange pas de légumes.
Je ne mange pas de sucreries.	Je ne bois jamais d'eau.
Je ne bois jamais de boissons gazeuses.	Je ne mange pas de yaourts.

C 1 Laure n'est pas très sportive.
2 Elle ne va jamais/pas au collège à pied.
3 Elle ne mange jamais/pas de fruits et de légumes et elle ne boit jamais/pas d'eau.
4 Elle ne fait jamais/pas 30 minutes d'exercice par jour.
5 Elle n'aime pas le sport.
6 Pour Laure, le sport n'est pas très important.
7 Elle n'aime pas la compétition.

© Pearson Education Ltd 2013. Copying permitted for purchasing institution only. This material is not copyright free.

4 Je vais changer ma vie!

(Pupil Book pp. 38–39)

Learning objectives
- Making plans to get fit
- Using the near future tense

Programme of Study references
GV1 Tenses (near future)
GV3 Developing vocabulary
LC1 Listening and responding
LC6 Reading comprehension

FCSE links
Unit 3: Education and future plans (Sequence)
Unit 5: Healthy lifestyle (Healthy living; Healthy/unhealthy eating; Fast food; Exercise; Sports; Health farms; Activities; Eating and drinking)
Unit 6: Food and drink (Unhealthy/healthy food choices; Food and drink choices)

Grammar
- the near future tense

Key language
Je vais faire du sport régulièrement.
Je vais manger sain.
Je vais prendre des cours d'arts martiaux.
Je vais aller au collège à pied.
Je vais faire trente minutes d'exercice par jour.
Je vais aller au collège à vélo.

PLTS
T Team workers

Cross-curricular
ICT: using a DTP package
PSHE: healthy lifestyles

Resources
Audio files:
26_Module2_Unit4_Ex1.mp3
27_Module2_Unit4_Ex4.mp3
Workbooks:
Cahier d'exercices Vert, pages 16 & 17
ActiveTeach:
Starter 1 resource
p.039 Video 4
p.039 Video worksheet 4
p.039 Class activity
p.039 Grammar skills
p.039 Thinking skills
ActiveLearn:
Listening, Reading Grammar

Starter 1
Aim
To work out meaning using context

Write up the following. Explain that they are all resolutions for the future. Give pupils three minutes working in pairs to translate the sentences into English.

1 *Je vais faire du sport régulièrement.*
2 *Je vais manger sain.*
3 *Je vais prendre des cours d'arts martiaux.*
4 *Je vais aller au collège à pied.*
5 *Je vais faire trente minutes d'exercice par jour.*
6 *Je vais aller au collège à vélo.*

Check answers, asking pupils how they worked them out. (**Answers:** 1 I'm going to do sport regularly. 2 I'm going to eat healthily. 3 I'm going to take martial arts classes. 4 I'm going to go to school on foot/walk to school. 5 I'm going to do 30 minutes of exercise a day. 6 I'm going to go to school by bike/cycle to school.)

1 Écoute et écris la bonne lettre. (1–6)
(Listening L3)

Listening. Pupils listen to six conversations in which people say what they are going to do to keep in shape. For each they write the letter of the correct picture.

Audioscript Track 26

1 – *Qu'est-ce que tu vas faire pour être en forme?*
   – *Je vais prendre des cours d'arts martiaux.*
2 – *Qu'est-ce que tu vas faire pour être en forme?*
   – *Je vais faire trente minutes d'exercice par jour.*
3 – *Qu'est-ce que tu vas faire pour être en forme?*
   – *Je vais aller au collège à pied.*
4 – *Qu'est-ce que tu vas faire pour être en forme?*
   – *Je vais aller au collège à vélo.*
5 – *Qu'est-ce que tu vas faire pour être en forme?*
   – *Je vais manger sain.*
6 – *Qu'est-ce que tu vas faire pour être en forme?*
   – *Euh … Je vais faire du sport régulièrement.*

Answers
1 c   2 e   3 d   4 f   5 b   6 a

Studio Grammaire: the near future tense
Use the *Studio Grammaire* box to cover the near future tense. There is more information and further practice on Pupil Book p. 49.

R Pupils identify all the infinitives used in the sentences in exercise 1.

© Pearson Education Ltd 2013. Copying permitted for purchasing institution only. This material is not copyright free.

4 Je vais changer ma vie! Bien dans sa peau 2

2 Lis les textes. Note les bonnes lettres pour chaque personne. (Reading L3)

Reading. Pupils read the texts, then identify which pictures relate to Pol and which to Laëtitia, noting the correct letters. Draw pupils' attention to the tip box pointing out the effectiveness of including sequencers and connectives to make their writing more interesting. Say that this would be a useful strategy to note in their Skills Notebook.

Answers
Pol: d, a, f, h, i, j
Laëtitia: k, b, c, g, e

Starter 2

Aim

To review the near future tense

Give pupils three minutes working in pairs to identify, write down and translate into English all the near future tense forms in the texts in exercise 2 (Pupil Book p. 38). Check answers.

Alternative Starter 2:

Use ActiveTeach p.039 Class activity to practise the language for being healthy and the near future tense.

3 En tandem. Joue! Jette le dé et fais des phrases. (Speaking L3)

PLTS T

Speaking. In pairs: pupils take it in turn to throw the dice. The first pupil asks the question; the second throws the dice and answers, using the appropriate picture prompts. The question and answer opening are supplied.

Pupils write a list of resolutions in French, detailing changes they are going to make to live more healthily. Ask them to design this on computer, encouraging them to be creative. Revisit the lists at the end of the module and ask pupils to say (honestly) if they have managed to make the changes.

4 Écoute. Qu'est-ce qu'ils vont faire pour être en forme? Copie et complète le tableau en anglais. (1–3) (Listening L4)

Listening. Pupils copy out the grid. They listen to three conversations in which people talk about what they are going to do to keep in shape, then complete the grid with the details in English.

Audioscript Track 27

1 – Qu'est-ce que tu vas faire pour être en forme, Nico?
 – Alors, d'abord, je vais faire du sport régulièrement. Ensuite, je ne vais pas boire de boissons gazeuses et je vais aussi aller au collège à vélo! Ça va être intéressant.
2 – Et toi, Coline, qu'est-ce que tu vas faire pour être en forme?
 – D'abord, je vais aller au collège à pied. Ensuite, je ne vais pas manger de sucreries et je vais aussi prendre des cours d'arts martiaux. Ça va être fatigant!
3 – Qu'est-ce que tu vas faire pour être en forme, Axelle?
 – Euh, voyons ... D'abord, je vais manger sain. Je ne vais pas manger de frites et je ne vais pas manger de hamburgers. Ensuite, je vais faire trente minutes d'exercice par jour. Voilà!

Answers

	resolutions
1 Nico	do sport regularly, not drink fizzy drinks, go to school by bike
2 Coline	walk to school, not eat sweet things, take martial arts classes
3 Axelle	eat healthily, not eat chips, not eat burgers, do 30 minutes' exercise a day

5 Lis l'histoire. C'est vrai (V) ou faux (F)? (Reading L5)

Reading. Pupils read the story, then decide whether each sentence is true (writing V) or false (writing F). *l'échec* is glossed for support.

Answers
1 V 2 V 3 F 4 F 5 V

Draw pupils' attention to *Stratégie 2* on Pupil Book p. 51 on 'false friends'. They work out the correct meaning of the words listed. Ask them if they know any other *faux amis*.

Translate the story round the class, with each pupil translating one sentence.

6 Copie et complète les règles pour un camp anti-fitness. (Writing L3)

Writing. Pupils copy and complete the rules for an anti-fitness camp, using the picture prompts.

© Pearson Education Ltd 2013. Copying permitted for purchasing institution only. This material is not copyright free.

2 Bien dans sa peau 4 Je vais changer ma vie!

Answers

1 *Au camp anti-fitness, on va manger des* **sucreries**.
2 Au camp anti-fitness, on va manger des **frites**.
3 Au camp anti-fitness, on va manger des **chips**.
4 Au camp anti-fitness, on va boire des **boissons gazeuses**.
5 Au camp anti-fitness, on ne va pas manger de **fruits**.
6 Au camp anti-fitness, on ne va pas boire d'**eau**.

Plenary

Review the near future tense by prompting in English to elicit different forms, e.g. *je vais prendre, je vais manger*, etc.

Ask pupils to make up more rules for the anti-fitness camp, using on in the near future tense. Take a class vote by a show of hands (1) on whether they agree with each rule and (2) on the best rule.

Workbook, pages 16 and 17

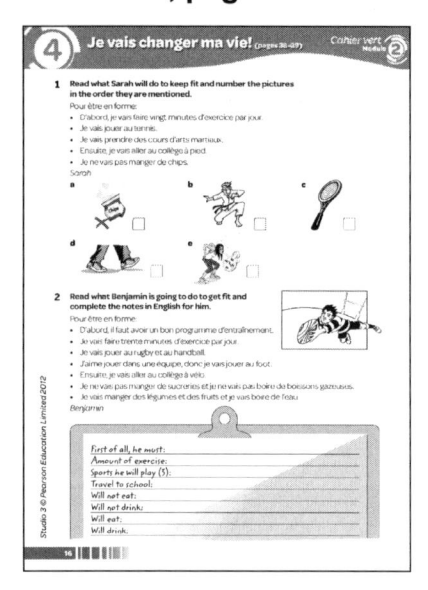

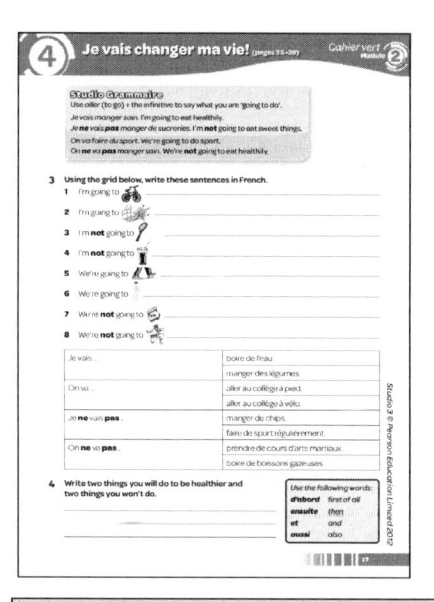

Answers

1 1 e   2 c   3 b   4 d   5 a

2 First of all he must have a good training programme.
   Amount of exercise: 30mn per day
   Sports he will play (3): rugby, handball and football
   Travel to school: by bike
   Will not eat: sweet things
   Will not drink: fizzy drinks
   Will eat: fruit and veg
   Will drink: water

3 1 Je vais aller au collège à vélo.
   2 Je vais manger des légumes.
   3 Je ne vais pas faire de sport régulièrement.
   4 Je ne vais pas boire de boissons gazeuses.
   5 On va aller au collège à pied.
   6 On va boire de l'eau.
   7 On ne va pas manger de chips.
   8 On ne va pas prendre de cours d'arts martiaux.

4 (Answers will vary.)

© Pearson Education Ltd 2013. Copying permitted for purchasing institution only. This material is not copyright free.

4 Je vais changer ma vie! Bien dans sa peau 2

Worksheet 2.4 The near future

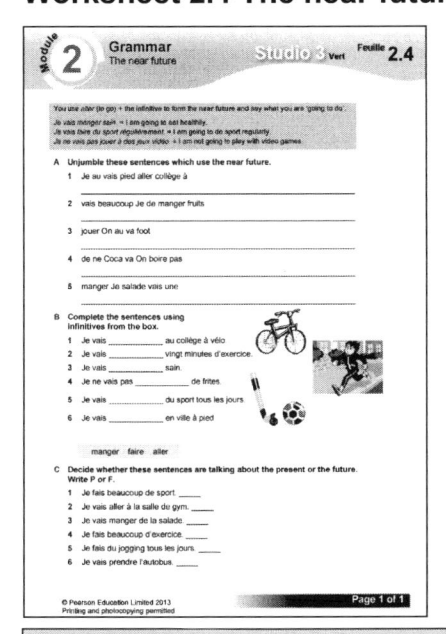

Answers

A 1 Je vais aller au collège à pied.
2 Je vais manger beaucoup de fruits.
3 On va jouer au foot.
4 On ne va pas boire de coca.
5 Je vais manger une salade.

B 1 aller 2 faire 3 manger 4 manger 5 faire 6 aller

C 1 P 2 F 3 F 4 P 5 P 6 F

Worksheet 2.5 Making connections

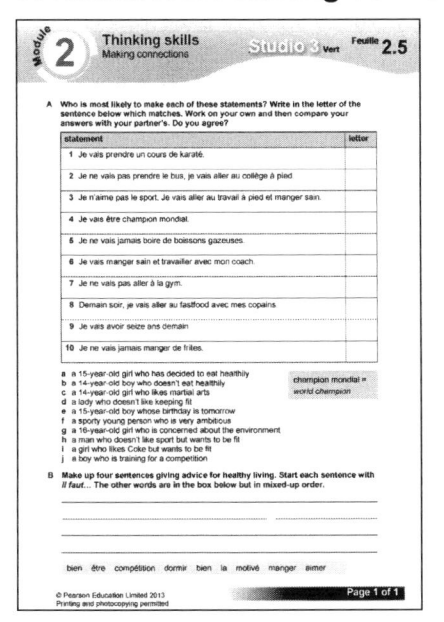

Answers

A 1 c 2 g 3 h 4 f 5 i 6 j 7 d 8 b 9 e 10 a

B (Answers will vary.)

Video

Episode 4: La danse

Marielle teaches the reluctant team to dance, in preparation for the Studio party. Video worksheet 4 can be used in conjunction with this episode.

Answers to video worksheet (ActiveTeach)

1 A It is likely that the boys will not be keen, while the girls will be.

2 A A *Studio* party in two weeks.
  B They are not keen at all.
  C It means 'dancing isn't for boys'.
  D Do sport with him.
  E He says he'll film rather than dance.
  F No, Samira insists that he join in.

3 A Shoulder, arm, head, back, hand, leg.
  B Take their jackets off (and line up in front of Marielle).
  C Because he doesn't eat well.
  D Chips and hamburgers.
  E Judo or martial arts.
  F He's dancing (badly) because he's enjoying it and he wants to get fit.
  G They laugh and tell him to stop.

© Pearson Education Ltd 2013. Copying permitted for purchasing institution only. This material is not copyright free.

(Pupil Book pp. 40–41)

5 Es-tu en forme?

Learning objectives
- Describing levels of fitness
- Using two tenses together

Programme of Study references
GV1 Tenses (present and near future)
LC3 Conversation
LC4 Expressing ideas (speaking)
LC5 Speaking coherently and confidently

FCSE links
Unit 5: Healthy lifestyle (Exercise, Activities)

Grammar
- using two tenses together

Key language
En général …
je ne fais pas beaucoup d'activité physique
je ne mange pas très sain
je vais au collège en bus
à midi, je mange un hamburger
je joue à des jeux vidéo
… mais à l'avenir …
je vais manger/aller/jouer, etc.
actif/active
Ça ne m'intéresse pas.
J'ai un problème.

PLTS
E Effective participator

Cross-curricular
PSHE: healthy lifestyles

Resources
Audio files:
28_Module2_Unit5_Ex1.mp3
29_Module2_Unit5_Ex3.mp3
Workbooks:
Cahier d'exercices Vert, pages 18 & 19
ActiveTeach:
Starter 1 resource
p.041 Grammar skills
ActiveLearn:
Listening, Reading
Grammar

Starter 1
Aim
To review the present and near future tenses
Write up the following. Give pupils three minutes working in pairs to copy and complete the grid.

present tense	English	near future tense	English
je fais			
	I eat	je vais manger	
			I'm going to go
		je vais boire	
je joue			

Check answers.
(**Answers:**
– *je fais*, I make/do, *je vais faire*, **I'm going to make/do**
– *je mange*, I eat, *je vais manger*, **I'm going to eat**
– *je vais*, I go, *je vais aller*, I'm going to go
– *je bois*, I drink, *je vais boire*, **I'm going to drink**
– *je joue*, I play, *je vais jouer*, **I'm going to play**)

1 Écoute et lis. Qui parle? Écris le bon prénom. (1–5) (Listening L5)

Listening. Pupils listen to five people talking about their current unhealthy habits and what they are going to do to improve their lifestyle in the future,
and read the text at the same time. They identify who's speaking each time by writing the correct name.

Audioscript Track 28

1 *En général, je vais au collège en bus, mais à l'avenir, je vais aller au collège à pied.*
2 *En général, je ne mange pas très sain, mais à l'avenir, je vais manger des fruits et des légumes.*
3 *En général, je joue à des jeux vidéo, mais à l'avenir, je vais jouer au foot deux fois par semaine.*
4 *En général, je ne fais pas beaucoup d'activité physique, mais à l'avenir, je vais faire trente minutes d'exercice par jour.*
5 *En général, à midi, je mange un hamburger, mais à l'avenir, à midi, je vais manger une salade.*

Answers
1 Djamel 2 Élise 3 Marco 4 Barnabé 5 Leïla

2 Lis les textes de l'exercice 1 et écris le bon prénom. (Reading L5)

Reading. Pupils read the texts in exercise 1, then identify which person is being described in each of the English questions.

Answers
1 Élise 2 Marco 3 Barnabé 4 Djamel 5 Leïla
6 Barnabé 7 Marco 8 Djamel

© Pearson Education Ltd 2013. Copying permitted for purchasing institution only. This material is not copyright free.

5 Es-tu en forme? Bien dans sa peau 2

3 Écoute les interviews. Copie et complète le tableau en anglais. (1–4) (Listening L5)

Listening. Pupils copy out the grid. They listen to four people talking about whether they are in shape or not and what their plans are for the future, then complete the grid with the details in English.

Audioscript Track 29

1 – Tu es en forme, Loïc?
   – En général, je ne suis pas très actif. Je ne fais pas beaucoup d'activité physique, mais à l'avenir, je vais aller au collège à pied.
2 – Tu es en forme, Estelle?
   – Eh bien … Je ne mange pas très sain et je ne suis pas très active. Mais à l'avenir, je vais manger des fruits et des légumes et je vais aller au collège à vélo.
3 – Tu es en forme, Patrice?
   – Euh … non, pas trop. Je ne fais pas d'exercice, je préfère jouer à des jeux vidéo. Mais à l'avenir, je vais jouer au foot deux fois par semaine.
4 – Tu es en forme, Sahda?
   – Oui, je suis active et en général, je mange sain, mais je bois des boissons gazeuses et j'adore les bonbons. À l'avenir, je ne vais pas manger de sucreries.

Answers

	in general	in the future
1 Loïc	not very active, doesn't do much exercise	is going to walk to school
2 Estelle	doesn't eat very healthily, not very active	is going to eat fruit and vegetables and go to school by bike
3 Patrice	doesn't do exercise, prefers playing video games	is going to play football twice a week
4 Sahda	active, eats healthily but drinks fizzy drinks and loves sweets	is not going to eat sweet things

4 En tandem. Fais trois dialogues. Change les mots soulignés. (Speaking L5)

Speaking. In pairs: pupils make up three dialogues, changing the underlined details in the model dialogue and using the picture prompts supplied. They take it in turn to ask and answer.

Studio Grammaire: present tense and near future tense

Use the *Studio Grammaire* box to review the present and near future tenses. There is more information and further practice on Pupil Book p. 49.

Starter 2

Aim

To practise using two tenses together

Write up the following. Give pupils three minutes to write a short text which uses the present and near future tenses together. They should include at least two details in each section.

En général, …

Mais à l'avenir, …

Pupils swap with a partner and check each other's texts. Hear some examples.

5 Lis l'article. C'est vrai (V) ou faux (F)? (Reading L5)

Reading. Pupils read the magazine article and decide whether each sentence is true (writing V) or false (writing F).

Answers

1 F 2 V 3 F 4 F 5 V 6 F

Pupils work in pairs. They make up more true/false sentences based on the exercise 5 texts, to test each other.

6 Imagine que tu es Noëlle. Prépare un exposé. (Speaking L3)

PLTS E

Speaking. Pupils imagine that they are Noëlle and prepare and give a presentation using the prompts supplied.

7 Écris ton exposé. (Writing L5)

PLTS E

Writing. Pupils write out their presentation in full. Draw their attention to the tip box on using two tenses in their writing if they want to aim for a higher level, and the importance of checking verb forms. Point out that this would be a useful tip to note in their Skills Notebook.

© Pearson Education Ltd 2013. Copying permitted for purchasing institution only. This material is not copyright free.

2 Bien dans sa peau 5 Es-tu en forme?

Plenary

Write up *En général ...* and *Mais à l'avenir, ...* Ask pupils to make a statement which could follow on from one of these. (They shouldn't include *En général ...* or *Mais à l'avenir, ...* at the start of their sentence.) The class identify whether the present tense or near future tense is used each time.

Remind pupils of the importance of using more than one tense if they want to aim for a higher level.

Workbook, pages 18 and 19

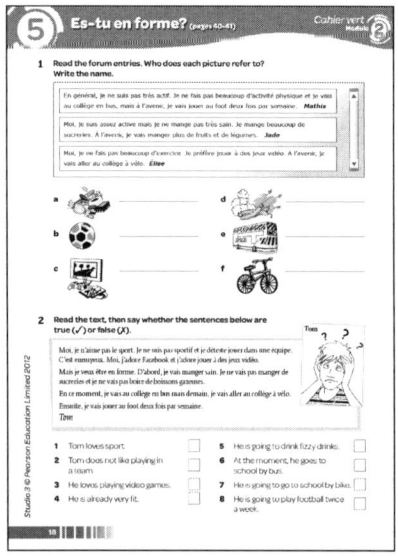

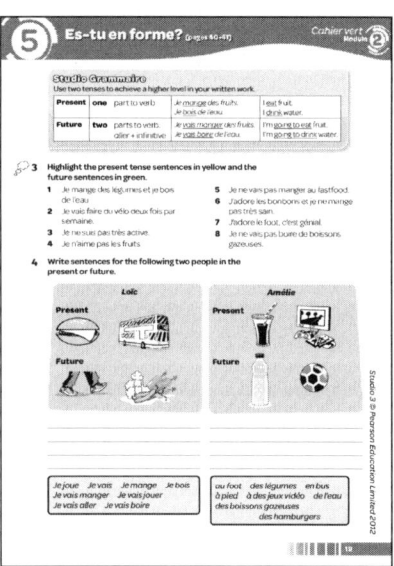

Answers

1 a Jade b Mathis c Élise d Jade e Mathis f Élise

2 1 ✗ 2 ✓ 3 ✓ 4 ✗ 5 ✗ 6 ✓ 7 ✓ 8 ✓

3 Present tense sentences: 1, 3, 4, 6, 7
Future tense sentences: 2, 5, 8

4 (Example answers:)
Loïc: En général, je ne mange pas très sain. Je mange des hamburgers. Je vais au collège en bus. À l'avenir, je vais manger des légumes et je vais aller au college à pied.
Amélie: Moi, je ne fais pas beaucoup d'exercice. Je joue à des jeux vidéo et je bois des boissons gazeuses. À l'avenir, je vais boire de l'eau et je vais jouer au foot.

Worksheet 2.6 Using three tenses together

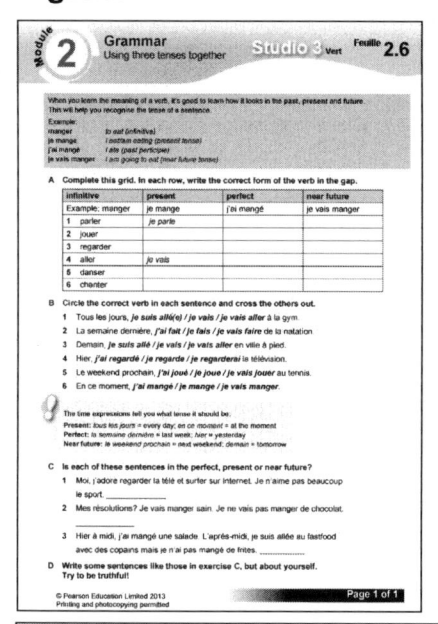

Answers

A

infinitive	present	perfect	near future
1 parler	je parle	j'ai parlé	je vais parler
2 jouer	je joue	j'ai joué	je vais jouer
3 regarder	je regarde	j'ai regardé	je vais regarder
4 aller	je vais	je suis allé(e)	je vais aller
5 danser	je danse	j'ai dansé	je vais danser
6 chanter	je chante	j'ai chanté	je vais chanter

B 1 je vais 2 j'ai fait 3 je vais aller 4 j'ai regardé 5 je vais jouer 6 je mange

C 1 present 2 near future 3 perfect

D (Answers will vary.)

© Pearson Education Ltd 2013. Copying permitted for purchasing institution only. This material is not copyright free.

(Pupil Book pp. 42–43)

Bilan et Révisions (2)

Bilan
Pupils use this checklist to review language covered in the module, working on it in pairs in class or on their own at home. Encourage them to follow up any areas of weakness they identify. There are Target Setting Sheets included in the Assessment Pack, and an opportunity for pupils to record their own levels and targets on the *J'avance* page in the Workbook, p. 24. You can also use the *Bilan* checklist as an end-of-module plenary option.

Révisions
These revision exercises can be used for assessment purposes or for pupils to practise before tackling the assessment tasks in the Assessment Pack.

Resources
Audio files:
30_Module2_Rev_Ex1.mp3
Workbooks:
Cahier d'exercices Vert, pages 20 & 21

1 Écoute et écris les bonnes lettres. (1–4) (Listening L3)

Listening. Pupils listen to four conversations about paintballing and for each note the letters of the two correct pictures.

Audioscript Track 30

1 – Aïe, je suis touché, je suis touché!
  – Mince, où est-ce que tu es touché?
  – Au bras et à la jambe.
2 – Aïe!
  – Ça va? T'as un problème?
  – Je suis touchée!
  – Oh non, où est-ce que tu es touchée?
  – Aux fesses et au front.
3 – Aïe, je suis touchée, je suis touchée.
  – Mince, où est-ce que tu es touchée?
  – Au genou et à l'oreille.
4 – Ça va? T'as un problème? Qu'est-ce qui s'est passé?
  – Je suis touché!
  – Oh non, où est-ce que tu es touché?
  – À l'épaule et au dos.

Answers
1 a, c **2** h, e **3** f, g **4** d, b

2 En tandem. Réponds aux questions. (Speaking L5)

Speaking. In pairs: pupils make up a dialogue about their own attitude to sport and approach to healthy eating. A framework is supplied.

3 Lis le texte. Copie et complète les phrases en anglais. (Reading L5)

Reading. Pupils read the text, then complete the gap-fill sentences in English.

Answers
1 Every day, Jade does **one hour of training** before school.
2 At the weekend, she has lessons from **8 o'clock** to **10 o'clock**.
3 Once a month, there are **competitions**.
4 You have to be **disciplined** and you have to like **competition**.
5 One day, Jade is going to **go to the Olympic Games**.

4 Écris correctement les résolutions pour être en forme. (Writing L4)

Writing. Pupils write out each jumbled sentence in the correct order.

Answers
1 Je vais aller au collège à pied.
2 Je vais faire trente minutes d'exercice par jour.
3 Je vais aller au collège à vélo.
4 Je vais faire du sport régulièrement.
5 Je vais manger sain.
6 Je vais prendre des cours d'arts martiaux.

© Pearson Education Ltd 2013. Copying permitted for purchasing institution only. This material is not copyright free.

2 Bien dans sa peau Bilan et Révisions

Workbook, pages 20 and 21

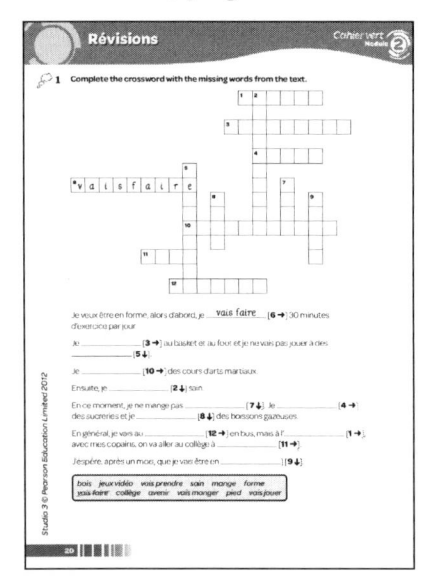

Answers

1. 1 avenir 2 vais manger 3 vais jouer
   4 mange 5 jeux vidéo 6 vais faire 7 sain
   8 bois 9 forme 10 vais prendre 11 pied
   12 collège

2. Ann'Onyme3: ✓ Clacla34: ✗ la miss6: ✓

3. 1 Clacla34 2 la miss6 3 Ann'Onyme3
   4 Ann'Onyme3 5 Clacla34
   6 la miss6 and Ann'Onyme3 7 la miss6
   8 Clacla34

4. (Answers will vary.)

En plus: Les sportifs français

(2)

(Pupil Book pp. 44–45)

Learning objective
- Learning about French sportsmen and women

Programme of Study references
LC1 Listening and responding
LC3 Conversation
LC6 Reading comprehension

FCSE links
Unit 5: Healthy lifestyle (Exercise; Activities)

Key language
Review of language from the module

PLTS
R Reflective learners

Resources
Audio files:
31_Module2_EnPlus_Ex2.mp3
ActiveTeach:
p.045 Assignment 2
p.045 Assignment 2: prep

Starter

Aim

To practise reading for gist; To introduce the topic

Give pupils one minute to skim-read the text in exercise 1.

Ask what the text was about and how they worked it out (looking at pictures, reading headings and questions, scanning for key words, looking for special features – here question/answer structure, etc.). Remind them that reading for gist in this way is a useful technique: it gives an overview of the topic, which makes the next stage of working out the detail in context much easier.

Ask the class to name all the famous French sportspeople they can think of.

1 Lis l'interview avec Mathilde Bergeron. Copie et complète la fiche en anglais. (Reading L5)

Reading. Pupils read the interview with the pentathlete Mathilde Bergeron. They then copy and complete the profile in English. Some vocabulary is glossed for support.

Answers
Sports: pentathlon: running, fencing, shooting, riding, swimming
Training programme: 9.30 to 12.30 then 15.45 to 19.00: running, swimming, fencing every day; four sessions of weights, two sessions of shooting and two horse-riding sessions per week
Favourite sport: fencing
Ambition: to qualify for the Olympic Games

2 Écoute et choisis la bonne réponse. (Listening L4)

Listening. Pupils listen to the feature on Gwladys Épangue, a French taekwondo competitor, then complete the sentences by choosing the correct option from the two given each time (a or b).

Audioscript Track 31

Gwladys Épangue est une taekwondoïste française, championne du monde et d'Europe. Elle est née le 15 août 1983 à Clichy-La-Garenne. Quand Gwladys est très jeune, elle est très sportive. Elle s'intéresse à l'athlétisme, au tennis de table et au badminton. Un jour, elle a commencé le taekwondo!

Elle s'entraîne tous les jours. Son programme commence à 8 heures et se termine à 7 heures du soir. Son objectif, pour cette année, ce sont les Jeux olympiques.

Answers
1 b **2** a **3** b **4** a **5** a **6** a

3 En tandem. Prépare une interview avec Djamel Monfils (un triathlète imaginaire). Utilise les renseignements suivants et invente d'autres idées si tu veux. (Speaking L5)

PLTS R

Speaking. In pairs: pupils prepare an interview with the fictional triathlete Djamel Monfils, using the details supplied. They can supplement these with ideas of their own, if they want to. A framework is supplied.

© Pearson Education Ltd 2013. Copying permitted for purchasing institution only. This material is not copyright free.

2   Bien dans sa peau En plus: Les sportifs français

Pairs perform their interview in front of another pair. One pair gives feedback on the other's performance and suggests two improvements. Ask pupils what they will do to improve their performance next time they do an extended speaking task.

4 Lis les textes. Dans quel texte trouves-tu les informations? Écris la bonne lettre. (Reading L5)

Reading. Pupils read the four sections of the article about judo. They then identify which section (from A–D) contains the information given in each English description (from 1–4). Draw pupils' attention to the tip box on reading strategies to use. *le palmarès* is glossed for support.

> **Answers**
> 1 C   2 B   3 A   4 D

Pupils identify in the text the information specified in the English descriptions 1–4.
(**Answers: 1** one   **2** 115 kilos   **3** (more than) half a million/500,000   **4** ten years old)

5 Relis les textes. C'est vrai (V) ou faux (F)? (Reading L5)

Reading. Pupils read the texts in exercise 4 again, then decide whether each sentence is true (writing V) or false (writing F).

> **Answers**
> 1 F   2 V   3 F   4 V   5 F

> **Plenary**
> Ask the class to tell you about the French sportspeople featured in this section, with each pupil giving one fact.

Worksheet 2.7 Le sport et le fitness. Assignment 2: speaking

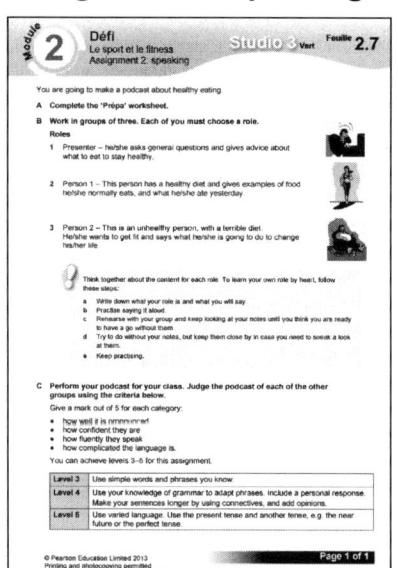

Worksheet 2.8 Le sport et le fitness: Prépa

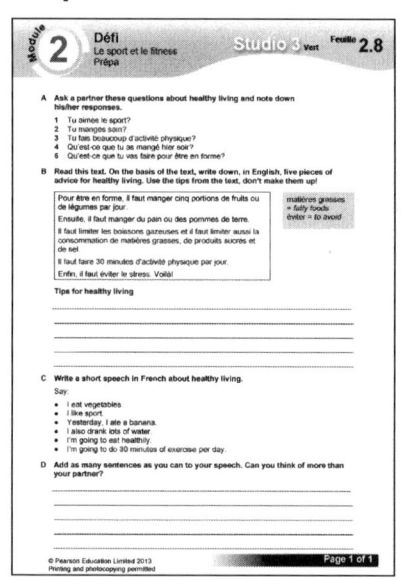

> **Answers**
>
> **A** (Answers will vary.)
>
> **B** Eat five portions of fruit and vegetables a day.
> Eat bread or potatoes.
> Limit fizzy drinks, fatty foods, sugar products and salt.
> Do 30 minutes of physical activity a day.
> Avoid stress.
>
> **C** Je mange des légumes.
> J'aime bien le sport.
> Hier, j'ai mangé une banane.
> J'ai aussi bu beaucoup d'eau.
> Je vais manger sain.
> Je vais faire 30 minutes d'exercice par jour.
>
> **D** (Answers will vary.)

© Pearson Education Ltd 2013. Copying permitted for purchasing institution only. This material is not copyright free.

(Pupil Book pp. 46–47)

② J'écris

The challenge
- Writing a 100-word blog entry on your decision to adopt a healthier lifestyle

Overview
Explain how this section works.
- Pupils read the context and what they need to do to complete the challenge.
- They then read the list of suggested details to include. Explain that they should use this both to help structure their content and as a checklist as part of their final preparations.
- Explain that the exercises which follow in this section are structured to help them prepare for the extended writing task.
- Before starting, pupils read the POSM feature: this will help them to improve their performance. Encourage them to use this approach routinely in writing tasks.

Programme of Study references
GV3 Developing vocabulary
GV4 Accuracy (grammar; spelling; punctuation)
LC4 Expressing ideas (writing)
LC8 Writing creatively

---

1 Unjumble these sentences in the present tense. Choose three to use in your answer.

Pupils unscramble the jumbled words to make sentences in the present tense. They then choose three of the sentences to use in their blog entry. Draw pupils' attention to the tip box on using time phrases and connectives to make links between their sentences.

> **Answers**
> 1 Je regarde la télé.
> 2 Je joue à des jeux vidéo.
> 3 Je regarde des DVD.
> 4 Je vais sur Facebook.
> 5 Je surfe sur Internet.

2 Make a list of five unhealthy things that you eat and drink at the moment. You can use the prompts given below.

Pupils use the picture prompts to write five sentences, each on a different unhealthy thing that they currently eat or drink.

> **Answers**
> 1 Je mange des chips.
> 2 Je mange des frites.
> 3 mange des sucreries/bonbons.
> 4 Je mange des hamburgers.
> 5 bois des boissons gazeuses.

3 Put these words in order so that they mean 'But I am going to change my life!'.

Pupils unscramble the words to make the French version of the sentence 'But I am going to change my life!'

> **Answers**
> Mais je vais changer ma vie!

4 Find four healthy things that you are going to eat and drink in this apple. Add four more of your own.

Pupils identify in the word snake four healthy items of food or drink that they can use to complete the sentence opening supplied (À l'avenir, je vais manger …). Draw pupils' attention to the tip box on sequencers.

> **Answers**
> des fruits, du poisson, des légumes, des produits laitiers

5 Decode these sentences in the near future tense. Choose three you could use in your blog entry.

Pupils work out what the half-visible sentences say, writing them out correctly. They then choose three to use in their blog entry. Remind pupils to use the sequencers in the tip box to improve their writing.

> **Answers**
> 1 Je vais aller au collège à vélo.
> 2 Je vais faire trente minutes d'exercice par jour.
> 3 Je vais jouer au foot deux fois par semaine.
> 4 Je vais prendre des cours d'arts martiaux.
> 5 Je ne vais pas manger de frites et je ne vais pas manger de hamburgers.

© Pearson Education Ltd 2013. Copying permitted for purchasing institution only. This material is not copyright free.

2 Bien dans sa peau J'écris

6 Copy the table and put these sentences into the right column.

Pupils copy out and complete the table by writing the sentences in the correct column.

Answers

present	future
2, 4	1, 3, 5, 6

7 Put the sentences in exercise 6 into a logical order. Start with 2. Look back at the 'Your challenge!' box on page 46 to help you decide on the order.

Pupils put the sentences in exercise 6 in a logical order, using sentence 2 as the starting point. They should use the 'Your challenge!' box on p. 46 to help them work out the order.

Answers

2 En général, je ne fais pas beaucoup d'exercice.

4 Je surfe sur Internet et je regarde la télé.

6 Mais à l'avenir, je vais changer ma vie!

3 Pour être en forme, d'abord, je vais manger sain. Je vais manger des fruits et des légumes et ensuite, je vais boire de l'eau.

1 Je ne vais pas manger de hamburgers, je ne vais pas manger de sucreries et je ne vais jamais boire de boissons gazeuses.

5 Je vais aussi faire trente minutes d'exercice par jour, alors je vais aller au collège à vélo et je vais prendre des cours d'arts martiaux.

8 Plan and write your blog entry.

Pupils plan and write their blog entry. Draw their attention to the tip box on how to check their work. They might also find it useful to look again at the tips on Pupil Book p. 128.

(Pupil Book pp. 48–49)

Studio Grammaire (2)

The *Studio Grammaire* section provides a more detailed summary of the key grammar covered in the module, along with further exercises to practise these points. The activities on ActiveTeach pages 48 and 49 are repeated from elsewhere in the module.

Grammar topics
- à + definite article
- the partitive article
- *il faut*
- negatives
- the near future tense
- *je vais* or *je vais faire*?

à + definite article

1 Copy the text and decide whether you need to use *au, à la, à l'* or *aux*.

Pupils copy and complete the gap-fill text, using the correct form of à + the definite article (*au, à la, à l'* or *aux*).

Answers
1 à la 2 au 3 à l' 4 à la 5 à la 6 aux 7 au 8 au

The partitive article

2 Copy the table and write each food or drink in the correct column.

Pupils copy and complete the table by writing the food and drink items in the correct column, depending on whether each word is masculine or feminine, begins with a vowel, or is plural.

Answers

masculine	feminine	beginning with a vowel	plural
du pain du poisson du poulet	de la viande de la pizza de la glace	de l'eau	des chips des sucreries des oeufs des céréales des fruits

Il faut

3 Choose the correct verb form in each sentence. Clue – it's the infinitive! Then match the English to the French.

Pupils complete the sentences by identifying the correct verb form from the two options given each time. They then match the completed French sentences with their English translations.

Answers
1 Il faut **aimer** la compétition.
c You must like competition.
2 Il faut **être** motivé.
d You must be motivated.
3 Il faut **faire** de l'exercice.
b You have to do exercise.
4 Il ne faut pas **manger** trop de sucreries.
a You must not eat too many sweets.
5 Il ne faut pas **boire** trop de boissons gazeuses.
e You must not drink too many fizzy drinks.

Negatives

4 Make these sentences negative using the construction in brackets.

Pupils make the sentences negative, using the negative constructions supplied.

Answers
1 Je **n'**aime **pas** le fastfood.
2 Elle **ne** va **pas** faire 30 minutes d'exercice par jour.
3 Je **ne** mange **jamais** malsain.
4 Je **ne** vais **jamais** à la salle de gym.
5 Il **ne** va **jamais** au collège à pied.
6 Je **ne** vais **pas** au fastfood.
7 Je **ne** mange **pas** sain.
8 Elle **ne** va **pas** à la piscine à vélo.

The near future tense

5 Fill in the gaps with the correct infinitive.

Pupils complete the sentences with the correct infinitive.

Answers
1 manger 2 aller 3 faire 4 jouer 5 boire 6 être

© Pearson Education Ltd 2013. Copying permitted for purchasing institution only. This material is not copyright free.

2 Bien dans sa peau **Studio Grammaire**

Je fais or *je vais faire*?
6 Choose the correct verb each time.

Pupils complete the sentences by choosing the correct verb form from the two options given each time.

> **Answers**
> 1 En général, **je vais** au collège en bus, mais à l'avenir, **je vais aller** au collège à pied.
> 2 En général, **je joue** à des jeux vidéo, mais à l'avenir, **je vais jouer** au foot deux fois par semaine.
> 3 En général, **je fais** trente minutes d'exercice par jour, mais à l'avenir, **je vais faire** deux heures d'exercice par jour.
> 4 En général, **je ne mange pas** sain, mais à l'avenir, **je vais manger** des fruits et des légumes.

À toi 2

Self-access reading and writing

A Reinforcement

1 C'est quelle partie du corps?
(Reading L2)

Reading. Pupils match each word to the correct label.

Answers

1 la bouche (n)   2 le bras (d)   3 le dos (e)
4 l'épaule (b)   5 les oreilles (l)   6 les fesses (c)
7 les yeux (m)   8 le front (j)   9 le nez (k)
10 le genou (f)   11 la jambe (g)   12 la main (h)
13 la tête (a)   14 le pied (i)

2 Écris correctement les phrases.
(Writing L3)

Writing. Pupils write out each jumbled sentence correctly.

Answers

1 Au camp fitness, on va manger des fruits.
2 Au camp fitness, on va boire de l'eau.
3 Au camp fitness, on va manger des légumes.
4 Au camp fitness, on va faire du sport régulièrement.
5 Au camp fitness, on ne va pas manger de sucreries.
6 Au camp fitness, on ne va pas manger de frites.

3 Regarde le tableau. Écris un paragraphe pour Flavie et Romain.
(Writing L4)

Writing. Pupils write a paragraph each for Flavie and Romain, using the information in the table.

Answers

Je m'appelle Flavie. Je mange des bananes *et des* légumes *et j'adore les* fraises, *mais je ne mange pas de* sucreries et *je ne bois pas de* boissons gazeuses.

Je m'appelle Romain. Je mange des légumes et des fraises et j'adore les hamburgers, mais je ne mange pas de chips et je ne bois pas de boissons gazeuses.

B Extension

1 Lis le texte. C'est vrai (V) ou faux (F)?
(Reading L4)

Reading. Pupils read the text, then decide whether each sentence is true (writing V) or false (writing F).

Answers

1 V   2 F   3 F   4 V   5 V   6 F

2 Lis le texte. Complète les phrases en anglais. (Reading L4)

Reading. Pupils read the text, then complete the gap-fill sentences in English. Draw their attention to the tip box on using the questions to help them identify the details they need to work out in the text.

Answers

1 Brandon says that paintball is his life and his **passion**.
2 He likes to play, to travel and to **win**.
3 The best piece of advice he can give new players is **practice, practice, practice**.
4 In the future, he wants to fill his passport with **visas**.
5 He wants to travel and to win the World Cup for **the third time**.

3 Écris un paragraphe pour chaque personne. (Writing L5)

Writing. Pupils write a paragraph for each person, using the picture prompts supplied. A sample text is given, with the structures to change underlined.

Answers

Je m'appelle **Sierra**. En général, je vais au collège en bus, mais je vais changer ma vie. Alors à l'avenir, d'abord, je vais aller au collège à pied et je ne vais pas manger de sucreries. Ensuite, je ne vais pas manger de frites.

Je m'appelle **Gilles**. En général, je ne fais pas beaucoup d'activité physique, mais je vais changer ma vie.
Alors à l'avenir, d'abord, je vais jouer au foot deux fois par semaine et je vais prendre des cours d'arts martiaux.
Ensuite, je vais manger des légumes et je vais boire de l'eau.

© Pearson Education Ltd 2013. Copying permitted for purchasing institution only. This material is not copyright free.

Module 3: À l'horizon

(Pupil Book pp. 52–73)

Unit & Learning objectives	Programme of Study references	Key language	Grammar and other language features
1 Mon avenir (pp. 54–55) Discussing your future Using the near future tense	**GV1** Tenses (near future) **LC1** Listening and responding **LC4** Expressing ideas (writing) **LC6** Reading comprehension	*Dans deux/quatre ans, … Un jour, … Je vais … aller au lycée avoir un emploi bien payé faire un apprentissage faire des études à la fac quitter le collège travailler voyager*	**G** the near future tense – developing speaking skills
2 Le monde est un village (pp. 56–57) Learning languages Using *on peut*	**GV2** Grammatical structures (*on peut*) **GV3** Opinions and discussions **LC6** Reading comprehension **LC8** Writing creatively	*Avec les langues, on peut … comprendre les gens travailler dans un autre pays, etc.* *À mon avis, parler une autre langue, c'est … un avantage/important/ un plus parce que …*	**G** modal verbs – *on peut* + infinitive – developing speaking skills
3 Du matin au soir (pp. 58–59) Talking about your job More practice with common irregular verbs	**GV1** Tenses (present: irregular verbs) **LC3** Conversation **LC6** Reading comprehension **LC8** Translation into French	*d'abord/ensuite/l'après-midi, etc.* *créatif/intéressant/ motivant, etc.* *l'emploi/le travail, etc.*	**G** *je fais, je prends, je vais* **G** *ne … pas* – developing writing skills
4 Mon boulot (pp. 60–61) Describing what your job involves Asking questions	**GV2** Grammatical structures (questions) **GV3** Developing vocabulary **LC6** Translation into English **LC4** Expressing ideas (writing)	*Qu'est-ce que tu fais comme travail? Quelles sont tes responsabilités? acheter/contacter/ inventer/organiser/ répondre au téléphone, etc.*	**G** asking questions – developing writing skills
5 Mes ambitions (pp. 62–63) Talking about your ambitions Using masculine and feminine nouns	**GV2** Grammatical structures (gender) **GV3** Opinions and discussions **LC1** Listening and responding **LC3** Conversation	*Qu'est-ce que tu voudrais faire plus tard? Je voudrais être … acteur/actrice contrôleur aérien designer de chaussures directeur/directrice de magasin etc.*	**G** masculine and feminine nouns for jobs – developing speaking skills

© Pearson Education Ltd 2013. Copying permitted for purchasing institution only. This material is not copyright free.

À l'horizon 3

Unit & Learning objectives	Programme of Study references	Key language	Grammar and other language features
Bilan et Révisions (pp. 64–65) Pupils' checklist and practice exercises			
En plus: Un portrait professionnel (pp. 66–67) Investigating unusual jobs	**GV3** Developing vocabulary **LC1** Listening and responding **LC6** Reading comprehension	Review of language from the module	– developing writing skills – developing listening skills
Je parle (pp. 68–69) Extended speaking practice	**LC4** Expressing ideas (speaking) **LC5** Speaking coherently and confidently	Review of language from the module	– developing speaking skills – checking your work
Studio Grammaire (pp. 70–71) Detailed grammar summary and practice exercises			**G** the near future tense **G** some common irregular verbs **G** asking questions **G** *je fais* or *je voudrais faire?*
À toi (pp. 120–121) Self-access reading and writing at two levels			

(Pupil Book pp. 54–55)

1 Mon avenir

Learning objectives
- Discussing your future
- Using the near future tense

Programme of Study references
GV1 Tenses (near future)
LC1 Listening and responding
LC4 Expressing ideas (writing)
LC6 Reading comprehension

FCSE links
Unit 2: Education and future plans (Future plans: after school, jobs and careers, future study)

Grammar
- the near future tense

Key language
Dans deux/quatre ans, …
Un jour, …
Je vais …
aller au lycée
avoir un emploi bien payé
faire un apprentissage
faire des études à la fac
quitter le collège
travailler
voyager

PLTS
I Independent enquirers

Cross-curricular
PSHE: exploring options and choices in career contexts

Resources
Audio files:
32_Module3_Unit1_Ex1.mp3
33_Module3_Unit1_Ex3.mp3
Workbooks:
Cahier d'exercices Vert, page 25
ActiveTeach:
Starter 1 resource
Starter 2 resource
p.054 Flashcards
p.054 Grammar
p.054 Grammar practice
p.055 Thinking skills
ActiveLearn:
Listening, Reading
Grammar, Vocabulary

Starter 1

Aim

To review the near future tense; To use reading strategies

Write up the following, omitting the underline. Give pupils three minutes to circle the correct verb forms to complete the sentences.

1 *Je vais quitte / quitter le collège.*
2 *Je vais faire / fais un apprentissage.*
3 *Je vais aller / va à la fac.*
4 *Je vais ai / avoir un emploi bien payé.*

Check answers, asking pupils to translate the sentences into English. Ask them to summarise how the near future tense is formed and how they worked out the meaning of new words. Remind them as necessary of the various reading strategies (identifying cognates, using context, using educated guesses, etc.).
(**Answers:** as underlined above. **Translations:** 1 I'm going to leave school. 2 I'm going to do an apprenticeship. 3 I'm going to go to university. 4 I'm going to have a well-paid job.)

Alternative Starter 1:
Use ActiveTeach p.054 Flashcards to introduce language for future plans.

1 Écoute et lis. Qui parle? Écris le bon prénom. (1–6) (Listening L5)

Listening. Pupils listen to six young people talking about their future plans, and read the text at the same time. They identify who's speaking each time by writing the correct name.

Audioscript Track 32

1 – *Qu'est-ce que tu vas faire plus tard?*
  – *Dans deux ans, je vais aller au lycée.*
2 – *Qu'est-ce que tu vas faire plus tard?*
  – *Dans quatre ans, je vais travailler.*
3 – *Qu'est-ce que tu vas faire plus tard?*
  – *Dans deux ans, je vais quitter le collège.*
4 – *Qu'est-ce que tu vas faire plus tard?*
  – *Dans quatre ans, je vais faire des études à la fac.*
5 – *Qu'est-ce que tu vas faire plus tard?*
  – *Dans deux ans, je vais faire un apprentissage.*
6 – *Qu'est-ce que tu vas faire plus tard?*
  – *Dans deux ans, je vais avoir un emploi bien payé.*

Answers
1 Latifa 2 Chloë 3 Matthieu 4 Amélie
5 Salif 6 Vincent

2 Lis les textes. Écris le bon prénom. (Reading L5)

Reading. Pupils read the texts, then identify who is being described in each of the English questions. Draw pupils' attention to the tip box on the false friend *travailler*.

Answers
1 Hassan 2 Seb 3 Yasmine 4 Éloïse 5 Seb
6 Hassan

© Pearson Education Ltd 2013. Copying permitted for purchasing institution only. This material is not copyright free.

1 Mon avenir À l'horizon   **3**

Studio Grammaire: the near future tense
Use the *Studio Grammaire* box to review the near future tense (singular). There is more information and further practice on Pupil Book p. 70.

Starter 2
Aim
To review the near future tense; To review language for future plans
Write up the following, jumbling the order of each sentence (e.g. **1** *voyager va elle*). Give pupils three minutes to write out the sentences correctly. If necessary, include capital letters and full stops on/after the appropriate words for support.
1 *elle va voyager*
2 *il va travailler*
3 *elle va aller au lycée*
4 *je vais faire un apprentissage*
5 *il va avoir un emploi bien payé*
Check answers. Ask pupils to summarise how the near future tense is formed.
Alternative Starter 2:
Use ActiveTeach p.054 Grammar practice to practise the near future tense.

3 Écoute et choisis les bons mots pour compléter chaque phrase. (Listening L4)

Listening. Pupils listen to Margaux and Omar talking about what they are going to do in the future, then complete the sentences by choosing the correct option from the two given each time (**a** or **b**). Draw pupils' attention to the tip box on the speaking skill of using 'filler' words to buy time. Suggest they add this advice to their Skills Notebook.

Audioscript Track 33

– *Qu'est-ce que tu vas faire plus tard, Margaux?*
– *Alors, dans deux ans, je vais aller au lycée et puis … euh … dans quatre ans, euh … ça dépend … je ne sais pas … je vais travailler, je crois.*
– *Et toi, Omar, qu'est-ce que tu vas faire plus tard?*
– *Voyons, euh … Dans deux ans, je vais faire un apprentissage chez Renault et puis dans quatre ans, je vais avoir un emploi bien payé.*

Answers
1 a **2** a **3** a **4** b

4 En tandem. Fais trois dialogues. (Speaking L4)

Speaking. In pairs: pupils adapt the model given to make up three dialogues, using the picture prompts supplied. They take it in turn to ask and answer.

5 Copie et complète le texte. (Reading L5)

Reading. Pupils copy and complete the gap-fill text, using the words supplied. Some vocabulary is glossed for support.

Answers
1 quitter **2** aller **3** faire **4** avoir **5** habiter

6 Fais un sondage dans ta classe. Pose la question suivante à cinq personnes. (Speaking L4)

PLTS I

Speaking. Pupils carry out a class survey, asking five people *Qu'est-ce que tu vas faire à l'avenir?* Remind them that they can use the fillers in the tip box to buy time and sound more French.

7 Imagine que tu es Pedro ou Lou-Anne. Écris un paragraphe pour décrire ton avenir. (Writing L5)

Writing. Pupils imagine they are Pedro or Lou-Anne and use the English prompts to write a paragraph describing what they're going to do in the future. A framework is supplied.

➕ Pupils could rewrite their paragraph using the 3rd person (*Il/Elle va aller,* etc.).

Plenary
Review the topic and the near future tense by making up sentences about future plans round the class. Each pupil adds a word. When a sentence is complete, start a new one.

© Pearson Education Ltd 2013. Copying permitted for purchasing institution only. This material is not copyright free.

3 À l'horizon 1 Mon avenir

Workbook, page 25

Answers

1 1 T 2 M 3 M 4 T 5 M 6 T 7 T 8 M

2 Dans deux ans, je vais aller au lycée.

Dans quatre ans, je vais faire des études à la fac.

Dans sept ans, je vais voyager.

Dans dix ans, je vais avoir un emploi bien payé.

3 (Answers will vary.)

Worksheet 3.1 Cracking the code

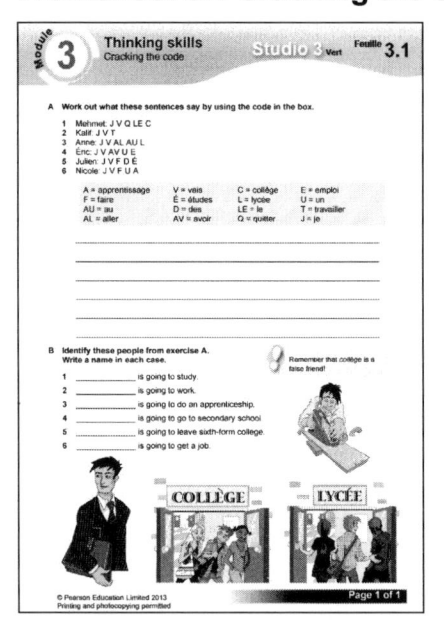

Answers

A 1 Je vais quitter le collège.

2 Je vais travailler.

3 Je vais aller au lycée.

4 Je vais avoir un emploi.

5 Je vais faire des études.

6 Je vais faire un apprentissage.

B 1 Julien 2 Kalif 3 Nicole 4 Anne

5 Mehmet 6 Éric

© Pearson Education Ltd 2013. Copying permitted for purchasing institution only. This material is not copyright free.

2 Le monde est un village

(Pupil Book pp. 56–57)

Learning objectives
- Learning languages
- Using *on peut*

Programme of Study references
GV2 Grammatical structures (*on peut*)
GV3 Opinions and discussions
LC6 Reading comprehension
LC8 Writing creatively

Grammar
- modal verbs – *on peut* + infinitive

Key language
Avec les langues, on peut …
comprendre les gens
habiter à l'étranger
travailler dans un autre pays
communiquer avec les jeunes de son âge
voyager
regarder la télévision
écouter de la musique dans une autre langue
À mon avis, parler une autre langue, c'est …
un avantage
important
un plus
parce que …
moniteur de ski

PLTS
E Effective participators

Cross-curricular
ICT: internet research
PSHE: assessing interests in relation to options in learning and work

Resources
Audio files:
34_Module3_Unit2_Ex1.mp3
35_Module3_Unit2_Ex4.mp3
Workbooks:
Cahier d'exercices Vert, page 26
ActiveTeach:
p.057 Video 5
p.057 Video worksheet 5
ActiveLearn:
Listening, Reading

Starter 1

PLTS E

Aim
To introduce the topic

Have a short class discussion in English on the usefulness of learning foreign languages. How important are they? What can you do with them? Elicit examples of jobs using foreign languages. Ask what the title of the unit means.

1 Écoute et écris la bonne lettre. (1–6) (Listening L4)

Listening. Pupils listen to six sentences on what you can do with foreign languages, and for each sentence write the letter of the correct picture.

Audioscript Track 34

1 *Avec les langues, on peut habiter à l'étranger.*
2 *Avec les langues, on peut comprendre les gens.*
3 *Avec les langues, on peut voyager.*
4 *Avec les langues, on peut communiquer avec les jeunes de son âge.*
5 *Avec les langues, on peut travailler dans un autre pays.*
6 *Avec les langues, on peut regarder la télévision ou écouter de la musique dans une autre langue.*

Answers
1 c   2 e   3 a   4 d   5 b   6 f

2 Trouve les expressions en français dans l'exercice 1. (Reading L4)

Reading. Pupils find in exercise 1 the French expressions for the English phrases listed.

Answers
1 habiter à l'étranger
2 travailler dans un autre pays
3 comprendre les gens
4 regarder la télévision ou écouter de la musique dans une autre langue
5 communiquer avec des jeunes de son âge
6 voyager

Studio Grammaire: modal verbs – *on peut* + infinitive

Use the *Studio Grammaire* box to review *on peut* + infinitive.

R Pupils write out all the *on peut* + infinitive expressions from exercise 1, then add two more of their own.

3 Lis les opinions et écris le bon prénom. (Reading L4)

Reading. Pupils read the three opinions, then identify the person being described in each English question. Draw pupils' attention to the tip box on improving speaking and writing by including opinions and reasons, as the people here have done. Some vocabulary is glossed for support.

© Pearson Education Ltd 2013. Copying permitted for purchasing institution only. This material is not copyright free.

3 À l'horizon 2 Le monde est un village

Answers

1 David 2 Amira 3 Géraldine 4 Géraldine
5 David 6 Amira

Starter 2

Aim

To review *on peut* + infinitive

Write up *On peut* ... Give pupils three minutes working in pairs to come up with four sentences using this opening, each giving a different reason for learning languages.

Hear answers. (See the key language listed in exercise 1 on Pupil Book p. 56.)

4 Écoute. Complète les phrases en anglais. (1–6) (Listening L4)

Listening. Pupils listen to three people saying why they think speaking foreign languages is important, then complete the gap-fill sentences in English.

Audioscript Track 35

– Je m'appelle Nadège. À mon avis, parler une autre langue, c'est un avantage, parce qu'avec les langues, on peut communiquer avec les jeunes de son âge et aussi regarder la télévision ou écouter de la musique dans une autre langue.

– Je m'appelle Rachid. À mon avis, parler une autre langue, c'est important, parce qu'avec les langues, on peut travailler dans un autre pays et comprendre les gens.

– Salut, je m'appelle Loïc. À mon avis, parler une autre langue, c'est un plus, parce qu'avec les langues, on peut voyager et même habiter à l'étranger.

Answers

1 Nadège thinks that speaking a language is **an advantage.**
2 She believes that, with languages, you can **communicate with young people your own age** and **watch TV** or **listen to music in another language.**
3 Rachid thinks that learning languages is **important.**
4 He thinks that, with languages, you can **work in another country** and **understand people.**
5 Loïc thinks that learning languages is **a bonus.**
6 He thinks that, with languages, you can **travel** and even **live abroad.**

5 En tandem. Jette le dé pour faire des phrases. (Speaking L4)

Speaking. In pairs: pupils take it in turn to start a sentence and to throw the dice. They use the number on the dice to make up a sentence according to the appropriate photo prompt. A sample exchange is given.

6 Lis le texte. Corrige les erreurs dans les phrases. (Reading L5)

Reading. Pupils read the text. Ask whether Declan enjoys his job. Pupils then correct the errors in the sentences summarising the text.

Answers

1 Declan Mullen est **irlandais**.
2 Declan travaille en **France**.
3 Declan est moniteur de **ski**.
4 Declan est **(très) patient**.
5 Declan parle **français** tous les jours.
6 Declan **aime** communiquer en français.

Translate the text round the class, with each pupil translating one sentence.

7 Fais un poster pour encourager l'apprentissage des langues. Utilise les mots à droite. (Writing L4)

Writing. Pupils design a poster to encourage people to learn languages, using the words supplied. Remind them to include opinions and reasons.

Pupils do research on the internet to identify three jobs requiring a knowledge of foreign languages.

Plenary

Put the class in teams. Give them three minutes to write as many reasons as possible for learning languages, using *On peut* ... They then swap answers with another team to check, awarding 2 points for a completely correct answer and 1 point for an answer with an error in any part apart from the *On peut* + infinitive structure. The team with the most points wins.

© Pearson Education Ltd 2013. Copying permitted for purchasing institution only. This material is not copyright free.

2 Le monde est un village À l'horizon 3

Workbook, page 26

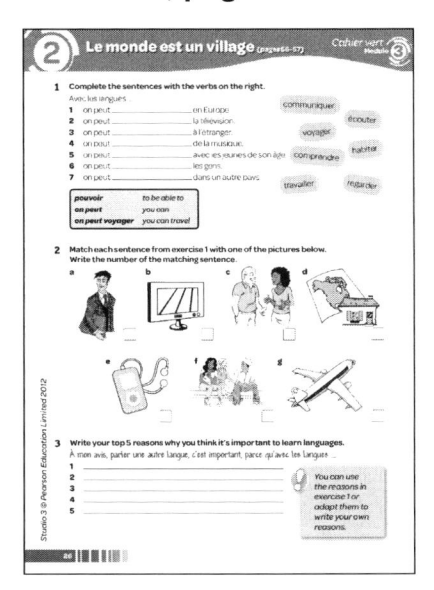

Answers

1 (NB Some sentences have several possible answers.)
   1 voyager/travailler/habiter
   2 regarder
   3 voyager/travailler/habiter
   4 écouter
   5 communiquer/habiter
   6 comprendre
   7 voyager/travailler/habiter

2 a 1, 3, or 7 b 2 c 6 d 3 or 7 e 4
  f 5 or 6 g 1, 3 or 7

3 (Answers will vary.)

Video

Episode 5: Les langues au travail

The team do a survey on the use of foreign languages in various professions, to help Hugo with his homework on the importance of languages at work. Video worksheet 5 can be used in conjunction with this episode.

Answers to video worksheet (ActiveTeach)

1 Suggestions of what might be discussed:
  – Languages enable you to talk and correspond with people from other countries. They provide the opportunity to work abroad and understand foreign documents.
  – Examples: teaching; anything export- or import-related; any job that involves foreign travel, translating and interpreting.
  – Any European language, plus Mandarin, Japanese and Indonesian.

2 A Hugo
  B Marielle
  C Mehdi
  D Alex
  E Samira

3 A Examples: communicating with customers; ordering stock from abroad.
  B A perfume/make-up shop/pharmacy.
  C What do you do for a living?
  D A diploma/qualification in commerce/business.
  E Communicating with foreign customers.

4 A They are going to the local tourist office.
  B Samira.
  C Organising tours; updating the website (*j'organise aussi des tours et je mets l'information sur notre site Internet*).
  D A school exchange group from Spain (*il y avait un groupe de jeunes Espagnols qui sont venus pour un échange scolaire*).
  E Flemish, spoken in Belgium.

5 A He's still not sure.
  B French.
  C Her company has branches in 50 countries.
  D Chinese, Thai, Indonesian. China, Thailand, Indonesia.
  E For work.

6 A Yes.
  B He says it's essential to speak another language because we are in Europe. (*Comme nous habitons en Europe, c'est essentiel d'avoir une autre langue.*)
  C 'The language of love'. The others groan.

© Pearson Education Ltd 2013. Copying permitted for purchasing institution only. This material is not copyright free.

(Pupil Book pp. 58–59)

3 Du matin au soir

Learning objectives
- Talking about your job
- More practice with common irregular verbs

Programme of Study references
GV1 Tenses (present: irregular verbs)
LC3 Conversation
LC6 Reading comprehension
LC8 Translation into French

FCSE links
Unit 2: Education and future plans (Future plans: advantages and disadvantages of jobs)

Grammar
- je fais, je prends, je vais
- ne ... pas

Key language
d'abord
ensuite
l'après-midi
le lendemain
le matin
puis
tous les jours
très tôt
créatif
intéressant
motivant
stimulant
varié
le boulot
l'emploi
le travail
le job
je prends
je vais
je fais
journaliste
pâtissier/pâtissière
serveur/serveuse

PLTS
S Self-managers

Cross-curricular
ICT: word-processing

Resources
Audio files:
36_Module3_Unit3_Ex4.mp3
37_Module3_Unit3_Ex5.mp3
Workbooks:
Cahier d'exercices Vert, page 27
ActiveTeach:
Starter 1 resource
p.058 Grammar
p.059 Class activity
ActiveLearn:
Listening, Reading
Vocabulary

Starter 1
Aim
To review time expressions

Write up the following, jumbling the order of the second column. Give pupils three minutes to match the French and English versions.

le soir	in the evening
ensuite	next
l'après-midi	in the afternoon
puis	then
le matin	in the morning
d'abord	first

Check answers.

1 Lis le texte et complète les phrases en anglais. (Reading L4)

Reading. Pupils read the text, then complete the gap-fill sentences in English. Some vocabulary is glossed for support.

PLTS S

Remind pupils that as well as writing down and learning the key vocabulary in each unit, it will also help them to note new words in texts that they can use in their own speaking and writing. Ask them to identify in the exercise 1 text three words or phrases that they think will be useful. Give them time to write these down. Encourage them to learn and use them.

Answers
1 Salim creates reports for **TV**.
2 In the morning, his boss gives him **a subject**.
3 He does some research, then goes off with his **video camera** and his **microphone**.
4 In town, he interviews and **films** people.
5 In the afternoon, he puts **the pictures** together.
6 Then he writes **the/his text**.

Studio Grammaire: *je fais, je prends, je vais*

Use the *Studio Grammaire* box to review *je vais*, *je prends* and *je vais*. There is more information and further practice on Pupil Book p. 70.

2 Copie et complète les expressions. Trouve les expressions dans le texte de l'exercice 1. (Reading L4)

© Pearson Education Ltd 2013. Copying permitted for purchasing institution only. This material is not copyright free.

3 Du matin au soir À l'horizon

Reading. Pupils copy and complete the time expressions with the missing letters, finding the expressions in exercise 1 if they need to. Draw pupils' attention to the tip box on improving their writing by using sequencers.

Answers
1 le matin 2 d'abord 3 ensuite 4 l'après-midi
5 puis

3 Mets le texte dans le bon ordre.
(Reading L4)

Reading. Pupils read the sentences and reorder them in the correct sequence.

Answers
See audioscript for exercise 4: pupils listen to the exercise 4 recording to check their answers.

4 Écoute et vérifie tes réponses.
(Listening L4)

Listening. Pupils listen and check their answers to exercise 3.

Audioscript Track 36

Salut! Je m'appelle Hamid et je suis serveur dans un restaurant.
Le matin, je vais au travail.
D'abord, je fais la mise en place des tables.
Puis les clients arrivent. Je prends les commandes et j'apporte les plats.
L'après-midi, je range les tables et je fais la vaisselle.
Ensuite, je fais la mise en place des tables pour le service du soir.

Answers
c, e, a, d, b, f

Ask questions about Hamid's daily routine, e.g. *Qu'est-ce que Hamid fait le matin?*, etc., for pupils to answer orally.

Starter 2
Aim

To review *je fais, je prends, je vais*

Write up the following. Give pupils three minutes working in pairs to complete the three sentences.

1 Je fais …
2 Je prends …
3 Je vais …

Hear answers. Ask pupils to give the infinitive forms of these three verbs.

Alternative Starter 2:
Use ActiveTeach p.059 Class activity to practise infinitives related to jobs and work.

5 Écoute et écris la bonne lettre. (1–5)
(Listening L4)

Listening. Pupils listen to five people saying whether or not they like their job and why. For each they identify the correct picture.

Audioscript Track 37

1 – Tu aimes ton job?
   – Oui, j'aime mon job parce que c'est varié.
2 – Tu aimes ton job?
   – Oui, j'aime mon job parce que c'est motivant.
3 – Tu aimes ton job?
   – Oui, j'aime mon job parce que c'est créatif.
4 – Tu aimes ton job?
   – Oui, j'aime mon job parce que c'est intéressant.
5 – Tu aimes ton job?
   – Oui, j'aime mon job parce que c'est stimulant.

Answers
1 b 2 d 3 a 4 e 5 c

6 Traduis les phrases en français. (Writing L4)

Writing. Pupils translate the sentences into French.

Answers
1 Je n'aime pas mon job parce que ce n'est pas motivant.
2 Je n'aime pas mon job parce que ce n'est pas stimulant.
3 Je n'aime pas mon job parce que ce n'est pas créatif.
4 Je n'aime pas mon job parce que ce n'est pas varié.
5 Je n'aime pas mon job parce que ce n'est pas intéressant.

Studio Grammaire: *ne … pas*
Use the *Studio Grammaire* box to review *ne … pas.* There is more information and further practice on Pupil Book p. 49

7 En tandem. Fais cinq conversations.
(Speaking L4)

Speaking. In pairs: pupils adapt the model to make up five conversations, using the picture prompts supplied. They take it in turn to ask and answer.

3 · À l'horizon 3 Du matin au soir

Remind them to think carefully about how to use *ne ... pas*, and to include sequencers to improve their speaking.

8 Lis le texte. C'est vrai (V) ou faux (F)? (Reading L4)

Reading. Pupils read the text, then decide whether each sentence is true (writing V) or false (writing F). Some vocabulary is glossed for support.

Answers
1 F   2 V   3 F   4 V   5 F

Pupils work in pairs. They pretend they do the same job as Salim (exercise 1), Hamid (exercise 3) or Arthur (exercise 8). They say what they do and whether they like it or not, giving reasons. They don't need to agree with the people in the exercises.

9 Choisis un job. Écris un paragraphe. (Writing L4)

Writing. Pupils choose a job and write a paragraph about what they do. If they don't know the word for the job, they look it up in a dictionary. Remind them to include sequencers, opinions and reasons. A framework is supplied.

Pupils could do the task on computer, making it easier for them to produce a second draft.

Plenary
Ask some pupils to read out the description of their job from exercise 9, omitting the name of the job. The rest of the class try to work out what the job is.

Answers
1 1 puis   2 l'après-midi   3 très tôt   4 ensuite
   5 le matin   6 d'abord   7 quelquefois

2 1 She is a presenter on the **television**.
   2 First of all, she does **research**.
   3 Then, she **telephones** people and sometimes she **does interviews**.
   4 In the afternoon, she **writes** scripts.
   5 Next, at **four o'clock**, she does the programme.
   6 She **likes** her job because it's **creative** and **varied**.

3 (Example answer:)
Je m'appelle Juliette et je suis serveuse dans un café.
Le matin, j'arrive au café à huit heures.
D'abord, je range les tables et puis je fais la vaisselle.
Quelquefois, je prends les commandes et ensuite j'apporte les plats.
L'après-midi, je fais la mise en place des tables.
J'aime mon job parce que c'est intéressant et varié.

Workbook, page 27

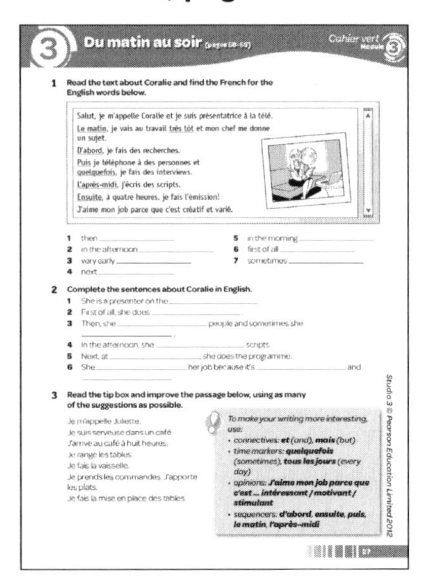

© Pearson Education Ltd 2013. Copying permitted for purchasing institution only. This material is not copyright free.

(Pupil Book pp. 60–61)

4 Mon boulot

Learning objectives
- Describing what your job involves
- Asking questions

Programme of Study references
GV2 Grammatical structures (questions)
GV3 Developing vocabulary
LC6 Translation into English
LC4 Expressing ideas (writing)

Grammar
- asking questions

Key language
Qu'est-ce que tu fais comme travail?
Quelles sont tes responsabilités?
Tu travailles seul(e) ou avec d'autres personnes?
Est-ce que tu aimes ton boulot?
acheter
contacter
créer
inventer
organiser
répondre au téléphone
travailler en équipe
trouver
chauffeur de camion
contrôleur aérien
designer de chaussures
game designer
secrétaire médicale
trader

PLTS
R Reflective learners

Cross-curricular
PSHE: exploring options and choices in career contexts

Resources
Audio files:
38_Module3_Unit4_Ex1.mp3
39_Module3_Unit4_Ex3.mp3
Workbooks:
Cahier d'exercices Vert, pages 28 & 29
ActiveTeach:
Starter 1 resource
Starter 2 resource
p.060 Grammar
p.060 Grammar practice
p.061 Grammar skills
p.061 Learning skills
ActiveLearn:
Listening, Reading Grammar

Starter 1

Aim
To review language for jobs; To use reading strategies

Write up the following. Give pupils two minutes to number them according to their order of preference (with 1 their favourite). Pupils then discuss in pairs why they would like to do the job they marked 1 and wouldn't like to do the job they marked 8.

acteur/actrice
designer de chaussures
footballeur
game designer
trader
journaliste
moniteur de ski
serveur/serveuse

1 Écoute et lis. (Listening L4)

Listening. Pupils listen to Vincent, a game designer, talking about his job, and read the text at the same time. Some vocabulary is glossed for support.

Audioscript Track 38

- Qu'est-ce que tu fais comme travail, Vincent?
- Je suis game designer à Paris.
- Quelles sont tes responsabilités?
- Moi, je crée des jeux vidéo. J'invente les règles, les personnages et l'univers où les personnages habitent.
- Tu travailles seul ou avec d'autres personnes?
- Quelquefois, je travaille seul, mais quelquefois, je travaille en équipe avec les programmeurs ou les animateurs.
- Est-ce que tu aimes ton boulot?
- Ah oui, j'adore ça! C'est motivant et créatif. À mon avis, j'ai l'emploi idéal.

Studio Grammaire: asking questions

Use the *Studio Grammaire* box to review how to form questions. There is more information and further practice on Pupil Book p. 71.

3 À l'horizon 4 Mon boulot

2 Copie et remplis la fiche pour Vincent. (Reading L4)

Reading. Pupils copy and complete the profile for Vincent.

> **Answers**
> **Name:** Vincent
> **Job:** game designer
> **Responsibilities/Tasks:** creates video games, invents the rules, the characters and the universe/world in which they live
> **Works alone/with others:** sometimes alone, sometimes with others/in a team
> **Opinion of job:** loves it – it's motivating and creative, he has the ideal job

3 Écoute et choisis le bon mot pour compléter chaque phrase. (Listening L4)

Listening. Pupils listen to Christine, a clothes buyer, talking about her job, and complete the sentences by choosing the correct option from the two given each time (**a** or **b**). Some vocabulary is glossed for support.

> **Audioscript Track 39**
> – Qu'est-ce que tu fais comme travail, Christine?
> – Je suis acheteuse habillement.
> – Quelles sont tes responsabilités?
> – J'achète des vêtements. Je dois trouver les meilleurs vêtements à la mode à un prix raisonnable.
> – Tu travailles seule ou avec d'autres personnes?
> – Normalement, je travaille seule.
> – Est-ce que tu aimes ton boulot?
> – J'aime beaucoup mon job parce que c'est très créatif.

> **Answers**
> 1 a 2 a 3 b 4 a

4 Écris correctement les questions. (Writing L3)

Writing. Pupils write out each jumbled question correctly.

> **Answers**
> 1 Qu'est-ce que tu fais comme travail?
> 2 Quelles sont tes responsabilités?
> 3 Tu travailles seul(e) ou avec d'autres personnes?
> 4 Est-ce que tu aimes ton boulot?

Pupils choose a job. They write a sentence saying they don't like it, giving a reason.

Starter 2

Aim

To review language for talking about your job

Write up the following. Give pupils three minutes to work out which question in exercise 5 each sentence answers.

1 *Je crée des jeux vidéo.*
2 *Je travaille en équipe.*
3 *J'aime beaucoup mon job parce que c'est très créatif.*
4 *Je suis chauffeur de taxi.*

Check answers. (**Answers: 1** *Quelles sont tes responsabilités?* **2** *Tu travailles seul(e) ou avec d'autres personnes?* **3** *Est-ce que tu aimes ton boulot?* **4** *Qu'est-ce que tu fais comme travail?*)

Alternative Starter 2:

Use ActiveTeach p.060 Grammar practice to practise forming questions.

5 En tandem. Fais deux interviews. Une personne pose les questions, l'autre répond. (Speaking L4)

Speaking. In pairs: pupils make up two interviews, taking it in turn to ask the questions listed and to answer as Coralie or Joseph, using the prompts supplied.

6 Lis le texte. Copie et complète les phrases en anglais. (Reading L4)

Reading. Pupils read the text, then copy and complete the gap-fill sentences in English.

> **Answers**
> 1 Éva works as a **shoe designer**.
> 2 She chooses the materials and **the colours**.
> 3 Normally, she works **alone**, but she **works in a team** too.
> 4 She likes her job because **it's creative, motivating and (also) very varied**.

7 Écris une interview avec Éric ou Marie-Aude. Utilise les questions de l'exercice 5. (Writing L4)

PLTS R

Writing. Pupils write an interview with Éric or Marie-Aude, using the questions in exercise 5 and the details supplied. Draw pupils' attention to the tip box on improving their writing skills.

When they have finished, ask pupils to check their work using the tip box as a checklist and to identify two areas in which they can improve. Also draw their attention to *Stratégie 3* on Pupil Book p. 73. Suggest they add this checklist to their Skills Notebook.

© Pearson Education Ltd 2013. Copying permitted for purchasing institution only. This material is not copyright free.

4 Mon boulot À l'horizon

Plenary
Tell the class to imagine that they are game designers. Ask the following questions, eliciting appropriate responses:
- *Qu'est-ce que tu fais comme travail?*
- *Quelles sont tes responsabilités?*
- *Tu travailles seul(e) ou avec d'autres personnes?*
- *Est-ce que tu aimes ton boulot?*

Ask for suggestions for a different job. This time pupils ask the questions, eliciting appropriate responses from different pupils.

Workbook, pages 28 and 29

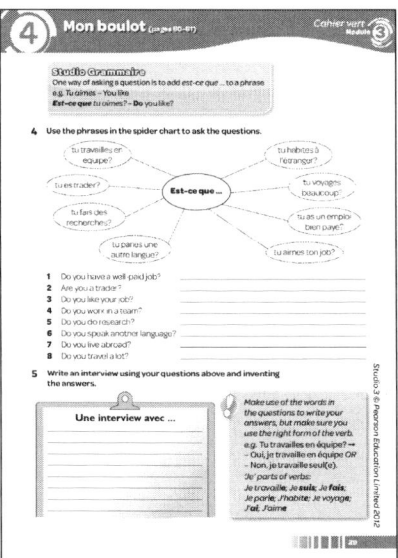

Answers
1 1 b 2 d 3 a 4 c
2
– Qu'est-ce que tu fais comme travail?
– Quelles sont tes responsabilités?
– Tu travailles seul ou avec d'autres personnes?
– Est-ce que tu aimes ton boulot?

3 1 The young man is called **Robert**.
2 He is **29** years old.
3 He is a buyer of **shoes**.
4 He has to **buy** the best shoes.
5 He has to find the best shoes at the **most reasonable** price.
6 He works **alone**.
7 He **likes** his job.
8 He finds his job **varied/stimulating**.

4 1 Est-ce que tu as un emploi bien payé?
2 Est-ce que tu es trader?
3 Est-ce que tu aimes ton job?
4 Est-ce que tu travailles en équipe?
5 Est-ce que tu fais des recherches?
6 Est-ce que tu parles une autre langue?
7 Est-ce que tu habites à l'étranger?
8 Est-ce que tu voyages beaucoup?

5 (Answers will vary.)

Worksheet 3.2 Irregular verbs and asking questions

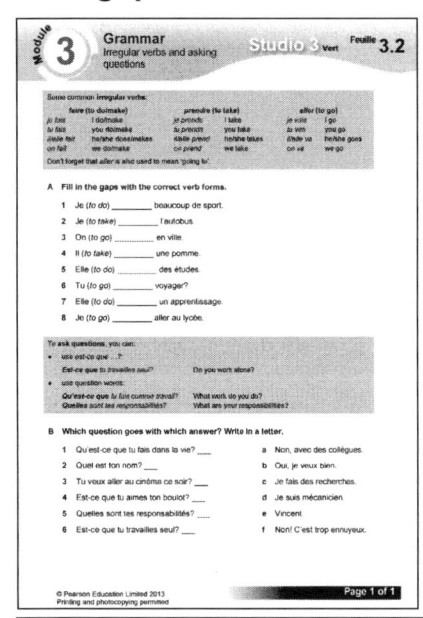

Answers
A 1 fais 2 prends 3 va 4 prend 5 fait
6 vas 7 fait 8 vais

B 1 d 2 e 3 b 4 f 5 c 6 a

3 À l'horizon 4 Mon boulot

Worksheet 3.3 Looking up nouns in a dictionary

Answers

A

masculine	feminine	English
chanteur	chanteuse	singer
acteur	actrice	actor/actress
directeur	directrice	manager
pilote	pilote	pilot
pâtissier	pâtissière	confectioner
vétérinaire	vétérinaire	vet
professeur	professeur	teacher
ingénieur	ingénieure	engineer

B

English	masculine	feminine
1 baker	boulanger	boulangère
2 waiter	serveur	serveuse
3 hairdresser	coiffeur	coiffeuse
4 nurse	infirmier	infirmière
5 farmer	fermier	fermière
6 architect	architecte	architecte

C (Answers will vary.)

(Pupil Book pp. 62–63)

3 | 5 Mes ambitions

Learning objectives
- Talking about your ambitions
- Using masculine and feminine nouns

Programme of Study references
GV2 Grammatical structures (gender)
GV3 Opinions and discussions
LC1 Listening and responding
LC3 Conversation

FCSE links
Unit 2: Education and future plans (Future plans: jobs and careers)

Grammar
- masculine and feminine nouns for jobs

Key language
Qu'est-ce que tu voudrais faire plus tard?
Je voudrais être …
acteur/actrice
chanteur/chanteuse
chauffeur de taxi/camion
contrôleur aérien
designer de chaussures
directeur/directrice de magasin
footballeur
guide touristique
ingénieur/ingénieure
journaliste
pilote
professeur
réceptionniste
serveur/serveuse
secrétaire
vétérinaire
webdesigner
Ce serait …
cool/ennuyeux
génial/intéressant
fatigant/nul
stimulant
Ça ne m'intéresse pas.
Non, merci!
Jamais de la vie!

PLTS
T Team workers

Cross-curricular
PSHE: exploring options and choices in career contexts

Resources
Audio files:
40_Module3_Unit5_Ex1.mp3
41_Module3_Unit5_Ex3.mp3
42_Module3_Unit5_Ex5.mp3
Workbooks:
Cahier d'exercices Vert, pages 30 & 31
ActiveTeach:
Starter 1 resource
p.062 Flashcards
p.063 Video 6
p.063 Video worksheet 6
p.063 Class activity
p.063 Grammar skills
p.063 Learning skills
p.063 Thinking skills
p.063 Reading skills
ActiveLearn:
Listening, Reading
Vocabulary

Starter 1
Aim

To introduce more language for jobs

Write up the following. Say that they are all jobs and give pupils three minutes working in pairs to translate them into English. If necessary, supply the English versions in jumbled order for support.

directeur/directrice de magasin
webdesigner
vétérinaire
chanteur/chanteuse
acteur/actrice
ingénieur/ingénieure
guide touristique
pilote
footballeur

Alternative Starter 1:
Use ActiveTeach p.062 Flashcards to introduce language for jobs.

1 Écoute et écris la bonne lettre. (1–8)
(Listening L4)

Listening. Pupils listen to eight people saying what job they would like to do in the future. For each speaker they write the letter of the correct picture.

Audioscript Track 40

1 – *Qu'est-ce que tu voudrais faire plus tard?*
  – *Je voudrais être pilote.*
2 – *Qu'est-ce que tu voudrais faire plus tard?*
  – *Je voudrais être vétérinaire.*
3 – *Qu'est-ce que tu voudrais faire plus tard?*
  – *Je voudrais être webdesigner.*
4 – *Qu'est-ce que tu voudrais faire plus tard?*
  – *Je voudrais être directeur de magasin.*
5 – *Qu'est-ce que tu voudrais faire plus tard?*
  – *Je voudrais être guide touristique.*
6 – *Qu'est-ce que tu voudrais faire plus tard?*
  – *Je voudrais être actrice.*
7 – *Qu'est-ce que tu voudrais faire plus tard?*
  – *e voudrais être chanteur.*
8 – *Qu'est-ce que tu voudrais faire plus tard?*
  – *Je voudrais être ingénieur.*

© Pearson Education Ltd 2013. Copying permitted for purchasing institution only. This material is not copyright free.

3 À l'horizon 5 Mes ambitions

Answers
1 h 2 c 3 b 4 a 5 g 6 e 7 d 8 f

Studio Grammaire: masculine and feminine nouns for jobs
Use the *Studio Grammaire* box to review masculine and feminine nouns for jobs.

2 Pose la question à dix personnes dans la classe. Note les réponses. (Speaking L4)

Speaking. Pupils ask ten people in the class *Qu'est-ce que tu voudrais faire plus tard?* and write down their answers. A framework is supplied.

3 Écoute. Copie et complète le tableau en anglais. (1–4) (Listening L4)

Listening. Pupils copy out the table. They listen to four conversations about future jobs, then complete the table with the details in English.

Audioscript Track 41

1 – Tu voudrais être chanteuse plus tard?
   – Non, ça ne m'intéresse pas, je voudrais être pilote.
2 – Tu voudrais être ingénieur plus tard?
   – amais de la vie! Je voudrais être directeur de magasin.
3 – Tu voudrais être acteur plus tard?
   – Non, c'est ennuyeux. Je voudrais être webdesigner.
4 – Tu voudrais être guide touristique plus tard?
   – Non merci, ça ne m'intéresse pas. Je voudrais être vétérinaire.

Answers

	job suggested	job preferred
1	singer	pilot
2	engineer	store manager
3	actor	web designer
4	tourist guide	vet

R Pupils use their answers to exercise 3 to write out a sentence for each speaker, saying what they would like to do using *Je voudrais …*

4 En tandem. Fais quatre dialogues. (Speaking L4)

Speaking. In pairs: pupils adapt the model to make up four conversations about what they would like to do in the future, using the picture prompts. Draw pupils' attention to the tip box on improving their speaking skills by including reactions and opinions.

Starter 2

PLTS T

Aim
To review job vocabulary

Give pupils three minutes working in pairs to write down as many different jobs in French as they can. Encourage them to include masculine and feminine forms. They then swap lists with another pair, and check each other's work. Reward the pair with the longest list – each correct feminine form counts as a separate job.

Alternative Starter 2:
Use ActiveTeach p.063 Class activity to practise language from the module.

5 Écoute et écris les bonnes lettres. (1–4) (Listening L4)

Listening. Pupils listen to four conversations in which people talk about what they would like to be in the future and why. For each, they write down the letter of the job mentioned (from **a–d**) and the letter of the opinion (from **e–h**). *Ce serait…* is glossed for support.

Audioscript Track 42

1 – Qu'est-ce que tu voudrais faire plus tard, dans la vie?
   – Je voudrais être trader. À mon avis, ce serait cool.
2 – Qu'est-ce que tu voudrais faire plus tard, dans la vie?
   – Je voudrais être réceptionniste. À mon avis, ce serait intéressant.
3 – Qu'est-ce que tu voudrais faire plus tard, dans la vie?
   – Je voudrais être chauffeur de taxi. À mon avis, ce serait génial.
4 – Qu'est-ce que tu voudrais faire plus tard, dans la vie?
   – Je voudrais être game designer. À mon avis, ce serait stimulant.

Answers
1 b, g 2 d, f 3 c, e 4 a, h

6 En tandem. Commente les jobs contre la montre. (Speaking L4)

Speaking. In pairs: pupils take it in turn to comment on the jobs listed, using the emoticon prompts and range of opinions supplied. They can either time themselves to see how long it takes them to cover all the jobs, or you can set a time limit and see how many jobs each pair can cover. A sample comment is given.

© Pearson Education Ltd 2013. Copying permitted for purchasing institution only. This material is not copyright free.

5 Mes ambitions À l'horizon

7 Lis les textes. Copie et complète le tableau en anglais. (Reading L5)

Reading. Pupils read the texts, then copy and complete the table with the details in English.

Answers			
name	likes	would like to be …	thinks it would be …
Inès	multimedia, surfing the net	web designer	cool
Albane	travelling, speaking languages	tourist guide	interesting
Dimitri	animal	vet	motivating
Yann	children	teacher	stimulating
Clarisse	films and theatre	actress	great

8 Écris un paragraphe sur un job que tu voudrais faire à l'avenir. (Writing L5)

Writing. Pupils write a paragraph on the job they would like to do in the future, also including details of a job that doesn't appeal. A framework is supplied.

Plenary

Tell the class you are going to play a game. You will throw a ball to a pupil and ask him/her a question. He/She replies, then chooses another pupil to throw the ball to, asking the same question as he/she throws it. The question is *Qu'est-ce que tu voudrais faire plus tard?* Pupils reply using *Je voudrais …* and include a reason.

Workbook, pages 30 and 31

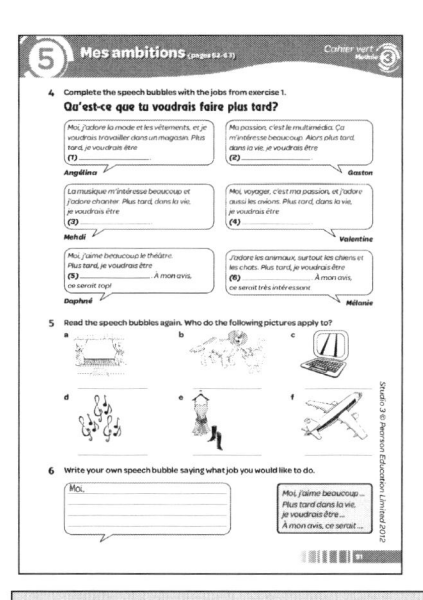

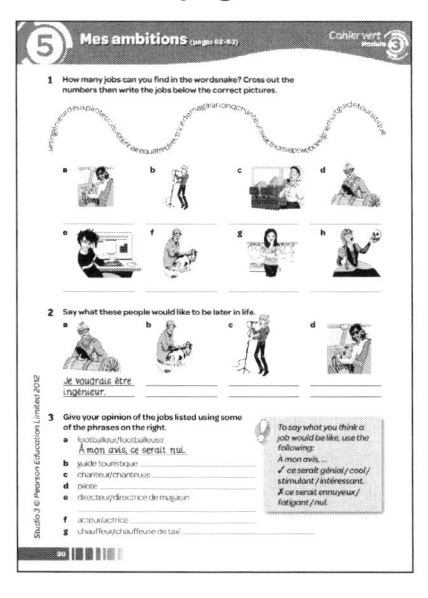

Answers

1 a pilote   b chanteur   c guide touristique
   d ingénieur   e webdesigner   f vétérinaire
   g directrice de magasin   h actrice

2 a Je voudrais être ingénieur.
   b Je voudrais être vétérinaire.
   c Je voudrais être chanteur.
   d Je voudrais être pilote.

3 (Answers will vary.)

4 1 directrice de magasin   2 webdesigner
   3 chanteur   4 pilote   5 actrice   6 vétérinaire

5 a Daphné   b Mélanie   c Gaston   d Mehdi
   e Angélina   f Valentine

6 (Answers will vary.)

Worksheet 3.4 The near future and *je voudrais*

© Pearson Education Ltd 2013. Copying permitted for purchasing institution only. This material is not copyright free.

3 À l'horizon 5 Mes ambitions

Answers

A
1. Elle va faire des études.
2. On va regarder la télé.
3. Tu vas travailler dans un café.
4. Je vais faire du ski.
5. Il va aller au bowling.
6. Je vais poster des messages sur Facebook.

B
1. Je voudrais parler français.
2. Je voudrais prendre le petit déjeuner.
3. Je voudrais regarder la télévision.
4. Je voudrais travailler dans un restaurant.
5. Je voudrais faire un apprentissage.
6. Je voudrais aller au collège à pied.

Worksheet 3.5 Using different tenses

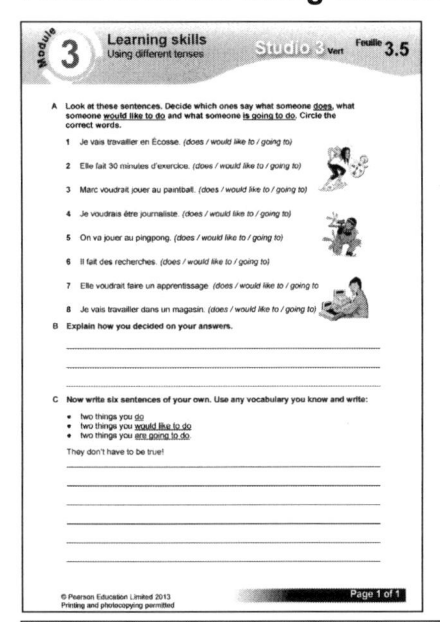

Answers

A
1. going to 2. does 3. would like to
4. would like to 5. going to 6. does
7. would like to 8. going to

B (Answers will vary.)

C (Answers will vary.)

Worksheet 3.6 Making logical connections

Answers

A 1. pilote 2. webdesigner 3. professeur
4. footballeur 5. journaliste 6. vétérinaire
7. pâtissier 8. réceptionniste

B (Answers will vary.)

C 1 e 2 c 3 a 4 b 5 f 6 d

Video
Episode 6: Le judo

Alex films Mehdi's day of work experience as a judo instructor, and they learn more about the qualities needed for the job. Video worksheet 6 can be used in conjunction with this episode.

Answers to video worksheet (ActiveTeach)

1. – It definitely has to be Mehdi, as he is the sporty one and has talked about judo in previous videos.
   – (Answers will vary.)
2. **A** He's a bit nervous (*nerveux*).
   B Alex also says Mehdi is *rapide* (quick).
3. **A** For ten years.
   B He wants to become a judo teacher.
   C Politeness, respect, honour.
   D Afternoon (*après-midi*).
   E Hop.
   F Fifteen (*quinze pompes*).
4. **A** The different levels of skill.
   B Yellow.
   C He has a brown belt, meaning he is nearly an expert.
5. **A** Yes, he thinks he has done well.
   B Mehdi has been polite and inventive but too serious.
   C To become a sports journalist.
   D He takes on Mehdi and ends up on the floor.

5 Mes ambitions À l'horizon 3

Worksheet 3.7 Reading a poem – 'The best jobs'

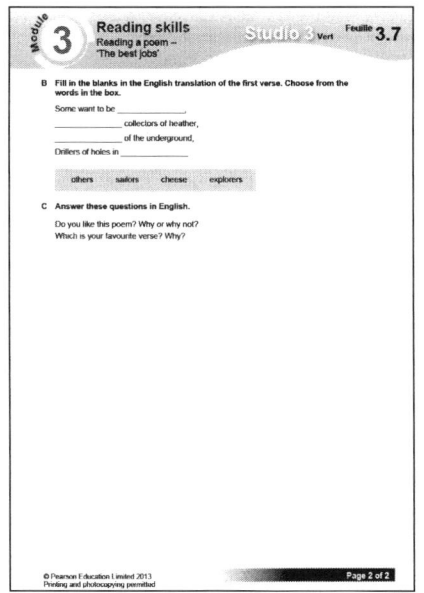

Answers

A
3 unusual jobs: (3 from:) ramasseurs de bruyère, explorateurs de souterrains, perceurs de trous dans le gruyère, goûteurs de tartes à la crème
3 things to eat: (3 from:) gruyère, tartes, crème, chocolat, babas
2 animals: (2 from:) faon, singes, éléphant, giraffe

B
Some want to be <u>sailors</u>,
<u>Others</u> collectors of heather,
<u>Explorers</u> of the underground,
Drillers of holes in <u>cheese</u>.

C
Answers will vary.

© Pearson Education Ltd 2013. Copying permitted for purchasing institution only. This material is not copyright free.

(Pupil Book pp. 64–65)

3 Bilan et Révisions

Bilan

Pupils use this checklist to review language covered in the module, working on it in pairs in class or on their own at home. Encourage them to follow up any areas of weakness they identify. There are Target Setting Sheets included in the Assessment Pack, and an opportunity for pupils to record their own levels and targets on the *J'avance* page in the Workbook, p. 36. You can also use the *Bilan* checklist as an end-of-module plenary option.

Révisions

These revision exercises can be used for assessment purposes or for pupils to practise before tackling the assessment tasks in the Assessment Pack.

Resources

Audio files:
43_Module3_Rev_Ex1.mp3

Workbooks:
Cahier d'exercices Vert, pages 32 & 33

1 Écoute. C'est vrai (V) ou faux (F)? (Listening L4)

Listening. Pupils listen to Monique talking about her job, then decide whether each English sentence is true (writing V) or false (writing F).

Audioscript Track 43

Salut! Je m'appelle Monique et je suis directrice de magasin.
Le matin, je vais au travail et j'ouvre le magasin.
D'abord, je parle avec mes collègues.
Puis je fais le tour du magasin.
L'après-midi, j'ai des meetings.
Ensuite, je parle avec des clients.
J'aime beaucoup mon job, c'est top.

Answers
1 F 2 V 3 F 4 V 5 F

2 En tandem. Prépare des réponses aux questions. (Speaking L5)

Speaking. In pairs: pupils make up a conversation about the future, taking it in turn to ask the questions listed and to answer using the picture prompts.

3 Fais correspondre les questions et les réponses. (Reading L4)

Reading. Pupils match the questions and answers.

Answers
1 d 2 a 3 b 4 c

4 Tu es Jamel. Décris tes projets d'avenir en français. (Writing L5)

Writing. Pupils pretend that they are Jamel and write a paragraph describing their future projects, using the English prompts supplied. A framework is also given.

Workbook, pages 32 and 33

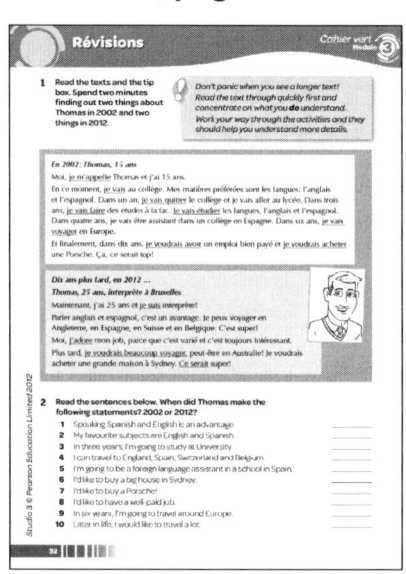

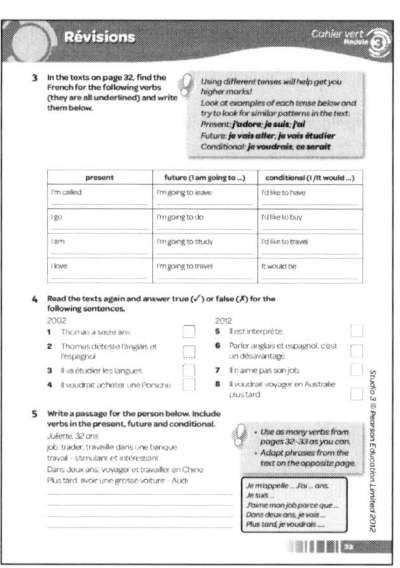

© Pearson Education Ltd 2013. Copying permitted for purchasing institution only. This material is not copyright free.

Bilan et Révisions À l'horizon **3**

Answers

1 (Answers will vary.)

2 **1** 2012 **2** 2002 **3** 2002 **4** 2012 **5** 2002 **6** 2012 **7** 2002 **8** 2002 **9** 2002 **10** 2012

3

present	future (I am going to …)	conditional (I /It would …)
I'm called Je m'appelle	I'm going to leave Je vais quitter	I'd like to have Je voudrais avoir
I go Je vais	I'm going to do Je vais faire	I'd like to buy Je voudrais acheter
I am Je suis	I'm going to study Je vais étudier	I'd like to travel Je voudrais voyager
I love J'adore	I'm going to travel Je vais voyager	It would be Ce serait

4 **1** ✗ **2** ✗ **3** ✓ **4** ✓ **5** ✓ **6** ✗ **7** ✗ **8** ✓

5 (Example answer:)

Je m'appelle Juliette et j'ai 32 ans. Je suis trader et je travaille dans une banque.

Moi, j'adore mon job, parce que c'est stimulant et c'est toujours intéressant. Je rencontre de nouvelles personnes tous les jours.

Dans deux ans, je voudrais beaucoup voyager, peut-être en Chine!

Plus tard, je voudrais acheter une Audi. Ce serait super!

En plus: Un portrait professionnel

(Pupil Book pp. 66–67)

Learning objective
Investigating unusual jobs

Programme of Study references
GV3 Developing vocabulary
LC1 Listening and responding
LC6 Reading comprehension

Key language
Review of language from the module

PLTS
C Creative thinkers

Cross-curricular
PSHE: exploring options and choices in career contexts

Resources
Audio files:
44_Module3_EnPlus_Ex1.mp3
45_Module3_EnPlus_Ex5.mp3
ActiveTeach:
p.067 Assignment 3
p.067 Assignment 3: prep

Starter

Aim

To practise locating information

Give pupils one minute to look at the text in exercise 1. Their aim is to find out what it takes to be a good team mascot.

Hear answers. Remind pupils that when they are looking for a specific piece of information, they should identify key words – not just the ones relating to the information, but also those which clearly don't. Here, the whole section starting *Voici une journée typique*, with a list of sentences starting with time expressions, can be disregarded.

1 Écoute et lis. (Listening L5)

Listening. Pupils listen to Pierre talking about his job as a team mascot at sports events, and read the text at the same time. Some vocabulary is glossed for support.

Audioscript Track 44

Pour être une mascotte, il faut être imaginatif et créatif, acrobatique et athlétique et surtout, avoir le sens de l'humour! Il faut aussi être un bon danseur.

On doit aussi être en forme. C'est très important parce que quelquefois, il fait très chaud à l'intérieur du costume!

Je m'entraîne tous les jours. J'ai une routine précise.

Voici une journée typique:
Je me lève.
Je prends mon petit déjeuner.
Je fais de l'exercice.
L'après-midi, je ne travaille pas.
Le soir, je me prépare.
J'arrive deux heures avant le spectacle et je me change.
Pendant le spectacle, je bois beaucoup d'eau. C'est essentiel.

J'aime beaucoup mon job parce que c'est varié et amusant. Je fais des sketches et des cascades et j'adore ça. Être devant beaucoup de personnes, c'est aussi très motivant.

Un jour, je vais aller aux Jeux olympiques où je voudrais être mascotte pour l'équipe canadienne. C'est mon rêve!

2 Relis le texte et réponds aux questions en anglais. (Reading L5)

PLTS C

Reading. Pupils read the text again and answer the questions in English. Draw their attention to the tip box on reading strategies.

Answers
1 You have to be imaginative, creative, acrobatic and athletic, have a sense of humour and be a good dancer.
2 Because sometimes it's very hot inside the costume.
3 He exercises/does exercise.
4 He doesn't work.
5 He drinks a lot of water.
6 It's varied and fun.
7 It's very motivating./He does sketches and stunts, which he loves.
8 To be the mascot for the Canadian Olympic team.

3 Trouve les expressions en français dans le texte. (Reading L5)

Reading. Pupils read the text in exercise 1 again and find the French versions of the English expressions listed.

Answers
1 On doit aussi être en forme.
2 Voici une journée typique.
3 Je fais de l'exercice.
4 Je fais des sketches et des cascades et j'adore ça.
5 Un jour, je vais aller aux Jeux olympiques.

© Pearson Education Ltd 2013. Copying permitted for purchasing institution only. This material is not copyright free.

En plus: Un portrait professionnel À l'horizon 3

4 Lis le texte en français et complète le texte en anglais. (Reading L4)

Reading. Pupils read the French text, then complete the gap-fill passage in English.

> **Answers**
>
> 1 school 2 artists 3 start 4 the opportunity
> 5 dance 6 horse riding 7 animals
> 8 (registration) fee

5 Écoute Mélody. Choisis les bons mots pour compléter chaque phrase. (Listening L5)

Listening. Pupils listen to Mélody, then complete each sentence by choosing the correct word/phrase from the two options given each time (**a** or **b**). Draw pupils' attention to the tip box on identifying synonyms as a means of improving their listening skills.

> **Audioscript Track 45**
>
> *Je joue dans le spectacle Les Vikings au Puy du Fou. J'habite dans le village que les Vikings attaquent. Il faut être acrobatique et athlétique parce que je cours beaucoup. On doit être en forme, quoi! Je m'entraîne tous les jours pour mon rôle.*
> *Voici une journée type:*
> *Je me lève.*
> *Je prends mon petit déjeuner et puis je fais de l'exercice.*
> *L'après-midi, je me change pour le spectacle.*
> *Le soir, on fait le spectacle une deuxième fois.*
> *J'aime beaucoup mon job parce que c'est amusant. Un jour, je vais jouer le rôle de Marguerite dans le spectacle Le Secret de la Lance. C'est mon rêve!*

> **Answers**
>
> 1 a 2 a 3 a 4 a 5 b

6 Copie et complète le texte. (Writing L4)

Writing. Pupils copy and complete the gap-fill text, using the words supplied.

> **Answers**
>
> 1 journée 2 petit déjeuner 3 du footing
> 4 l'après-midi 5 être 6 parce que 7 rôle
> 8 génial

> **Plenary**
>
> Read out sentences in random order from the profiles of Pierre, Mélody and Mathias, e.g. *Elle veut jouer dans le spectacle Le Secret de la Lance.* Pupils compete to be the first to say who is speaking.

Worksheet 3.8 Mon CV

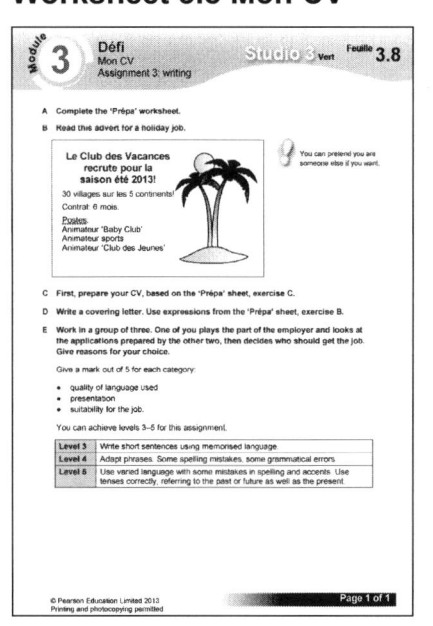

Worksheet 3.9 Mon CV: Prépa

> **Answers**
>
> **A** 1 J'ai vu votre annonce 2 site Internet
>   3 poser ma candidature pour le poste
>   4 animateur 5 J'ai beaucoup d'expérience
>   6 diplôme 7 Veuillez trouver ci-joint mon CV
>
> **B** (Answers will vary.)
>
> **C Prénom:** Mathilde
>   **Nom de famille:** Leclerc
>   **Date de naissance:** le 3 juillet 1992
>   **Lieu de naissance:** Paris
>   **Formation:** diplôme d'animateur
>   **Informatique:** maîtrise de Word, Excel, PowerPoint
>   **Langues:** français, anglais
>   **Intérêts:** musique, cinema
>   **Sport(s):** danse, tennis

(Pupil Book pp. 68–69)

③ Je parle

The challenge
- Giving a two-minute podcast about your job and your ambitions for the future

Overview
Explain how this section works.
- Pupils read the context and what they need to do to complete the challenge.
- They then read the English questions supplied. Explain that they should use these both to help structure their content and as a checklist as part of their final preparations.
- Explain that the exercises which follow in this section are structured to help them prepare for their presentation.
- Before starting, pupils read the POSM feature: this will help them to improve their performance. Encourage them to use this approach routinely in speaking tasks.

Programme of Study references
LC4 Expressing ideas (speaking)
LC5 Speaking coherently and confidently

Resources
Audio files:
46_Module3_Jeparle_Ex3.mp3

---

1 These are the questions you will be asked. Find the English equivalents of these questions in the 'Your challenge!' box.

Pupils find in the 'Your challenge!' box the English versions of the questions listed in French.

Answers
1 Qu'est-ce que tu vas faire plus tard? What are you going to do later on? 2 Tu travailles seul(e) ou en équipe? Do you work alone or in a team? 3 Quelle est ta journée typique? What is your typical day like? 4 Tu aimes ton job? Do you like your job? 5 Qu'est-ce que tu fais comme travail? What kind of work do you do?

2 Find ten jobs in this word snake. Think of the job you are going to say you do.

Pupils write out the ten jobs contained in the word snake. They then decide on the job they are going to talk about in their podcast. It does not have to be one of those in the word snake.

Answers
secrétaire médicale contrôleur aérien designer de chaussures pâtissier journaliste vétérinaire ingénieur guide touristique pilote acteur

3 Listen to the sentences. Which person (a, b or c) would say each sentence? (1–9)

Pupils listen to the sentences and identify each speaker's job, writing the letter of the correct picture.

Audioscript Track 46
1 Je fais des reportages. 2 Je prends les commandes et j'apporte les plats. 3 Je fais des recherches. 4 Je fais la mise en place des tables. 5 Je contacte des clients. 6 Je prends ma caméra. 7 Je réponds au téléphone. 8 Je range les tables et je fais la vaisselle. 9 J'organise les rendez-vous.

Answers
1 a 2 c 3 a 4 c 5 b 6 a 7 b 8 c 9 b

4 Unjumble these sequencers. Choose three to use in your podcast.

Pupils unjumble the sequencers, writing them out correctly. They choose three to use in their podcast.

Answers
le matin (in the morning) d'abord (first) l'après-midi (in the afternoon) puis (then) ensuite (next)

© Pearson Education Ltd 2013. Copying permitted for purchasing institution only. This material is not copyright free.

Je parle À l'horizon 3

5 Make a list of six things you do in a typical day in your job.

Pupils write six short sentences describing what they do in a typical day in their job. Draw their attention to the tip box on using what they know, rather than trying to invent details that require complicated language.

6 Note down five more adjectives you could use to describe a great job.

Pupils think up five adjectives (in addition to *super*, *génial* and *intéressant*) that they could use to say how good their job is.

7 Match up the English to the French.

Pupils match the French and English sentences.

Answers
1 d 2 b 3 e 4 c 5 a

8 Read the interview and choose the correct verbs.

Pupils read and complete the interview by choosing the correct word from the two options given each time.

Answers
1 fais 2 vais 3 travaille 4 contacte 5 travaille 6 varié 7 vais 8 J'adore

9 Write out in full what you are going to say for the job challenge. Check that what you have written is accurate and makes sense.

Pupils write out the complete text of their podcast, using the language they have developed in the course of the challenge. They then check their texts, making sure that they are accurate and logical.

10 Now memorise your podcast and rehearse it!

Pupils memorise and practise their podcast. Draw their attention to the tip box on presentation skills. They might also find it useful to look again at the tips on Pupil Book p. 128.

Pupils can then record or deliver their podcasts. They should ask their audience to give constructive feedback. Pupils can then use this to identify areas for improvement in the next extended speaking task they do.

Studio Grammaire

(Pupil Book pp. 70–71)

The *Studio Grammaire* section provides a more detailed summary of the key grammar covered in the module, along with further exercises to practise these points. The interactive activities on ActiveTeach pages 70 and 71 are repeated from elsewhere in the module.

Grammar topics
- the near future tense
- some common irregular verbs
- asking questions
- *je fais* or *je voudrais faire*?

The near future tense

1 Use the table to help you translate these sentences into French.

Pupils translate the English sentences into French, using the verb table supplied for support.

Answers
1 Je vais avoir un emploi bien payé.
2 Elle va travailler.
3 Tu vas faire un apprentissage.
4 On va voyager.
5 Il va aller au lycée.
6 Je vais faire des études à la fac.

2 Decode these sentences in the near future tense. Then translate the sentences into English.

Pupils work out what the sentences featuring the near future tense say, writing them out correctly. They then translate the sentences into English.

Answers
1 Un jour, je vais voyager.
  One day I am going to travel.
2 Un jour, je vais habiter à l'étranger.
  One day I am going to live abroad.
3 Un jour, je vais travailler dans un autre pays.
  One day I am going to work in another country.
4 Un jour, je vais avoir des enfants.
  One day I am going to have children.
5 Un jour, je vais gagner beaucoup d'argent.
  One day I am going to earn lots of money.

Some common irregular verbs

3 Write the verbs in brackets in the correct form.

Pupils write out the sentences, replacing the infinitive prompts with the correct verb forms.

Answers
1 Je **vais** au collège.
2 Tu **prends** des cours d'arts martiaux?
3 Il **fait** du ski.
4 Elle **fait** des recherches.
5 On **va** en ville.
6 Tu **fais** beaucoup de sport.

4 Copy the text and fill in the gaps.

Pupils copy and complete the gap-fill text, using the words supplied. *le téléphérique* is glossed for support.

Answers
1 fais   2 vais   3 prends   4 prend   5 fait

Asking questions

5 Unjumble the questions so that they make sense.

Pupils unjumble the questions and write them out correctly.

Answers
1 Est-ce que tu fais du sport?
2 Est-ce que tu manges sain?
3 Est-ce que tu vas au collège à pied?
4 Est-ce que tu prends des cours d'arts martiaux?
5 Est-ce que tu habites à l'étranger?

6 Rewrite the questions so that they all begin with *Est-ce que* …?

Pupils rewrite the questions using *est-ce que*.

Answers
1 Est-ce que tu aimes ton job?
2 Est-ce que tu travailles seule?
3 Est-ce que tu travailles en équipe?
4 Est-ce que tu as un ordinateur dans ta chambre?
5 Est-ce que tu fais des quiz sur Facebook?

© Pearson Education Ltd 2013. Copying permitted for purchasing institution only. This material is not copyright free.

Studio Grammaire À l'horizon 3

je fais or *je voudrais faire?*

7 Match up the sentences and the pictures. Translate the sentences into English.

Pupils match the sentences and pictures, then translate the sentences into English.

> **Answers**
> 1 c I am a teacher, but I would like to be an actress.
> 2 a I am doing research, but I would like to be making cakes.
> 3 b I work alone, but I would like to work in a team.

8 Fill in the gaps using the verbs on the right. Choose the present tense or *je voudrais* + infinitive.

Pupils complete the gap-fill sentences, using the verb forms supplied.

> **Answers**
> 1 **Je vais** au collège, mais **je voudrais aller** en ville.
> 2 **Je parle** français, mais **je voudrais parler** espagnol.
> 3 **J'organise** les rendez-vous, mais **je voudrais organiser** des concerts.
> 4 **Je travaille** en France, mais **je voudrais travailler** dans un autre pays.
> 5 **Je fais** un apprentissage chez Peugeot, mais je **voudrais faire** un apprentissage chez Mercedes.

© Pearson Education Ltd 2013. Copying permitted for purchasing institution only. This material is not copyright free.

(Pupil Book pp. 120–121)

3 À toi

Self-access reading and writing

A Reinforcement

1 Décode les jobs et copie les phrases. Puis trouve la bonne photo pour chaque phrase. (Writing L2)

Writing. Pupils decode the job words using the key and write out the sentences correctly. They then match each sentence to the correct picture.

Answers
1 Je voudrais être pilote. (f)
2 Je voudrais être webdesigner. (b)
3 Je voudrais être vétérinaire. (c)
4 Je voudrais être ingénieur. (d)
5 Je voudrais être guide touristique. (e)
6 Je voudrais être directeur de magasin. (a)

2 Copie et complète les phrases. (Reading L3)

Reading. Pupils match the sentence halves, writing out the complete sentences.

Answers
1 Avec les langues, on peut voyager.
2 On peut travailler dans un autre pays.
3 On peut habiter à l'étranger.
4 On peut communiquer avec les jeunes de son âge.
5 On peut comprendre les gens.
6 On peut regarder la télévision dans une autre langue.

3 Lis les phrases. C'est logique ou pas logique? Écris L ou PL. (Reading L3)

Reading. Pupils read the sentences and decide whether each is logical (writing L) or illogical (writing PL).

Answers
1 L   2 PL   3 L   4 PL   5 PL   6 L

4 Corrige les phrases de l'exercice 3 qui ne sont pas logiques. Utilise tes propres idées. (Writing L3)

Writing. Pupils write correct versions of the illogical sentences in exercise 3, using their own ideas. Draw their attention to the tip box giving ideas on this.

Example answers
2 J'aime mon job parce que c'est intéressant./Je n'aime pas mon job parce que c'est ennuyeux./Je n'aime pas mon job parce que ce n'est pas intéressant.
4 J'aime mon job parce que c'est varié./Je n'aime pas mon job parce que ce n'est pas varié.
5 Je n'aime pas mon job parce que ce n'est pas motivant./J'aime mon job parce que c'est motivant.

B Extension

1 Lis les textes et complète le tableau. (Reading L5)

Reading. Pupils read the texts, then copy and complete the table with the details in English, writing the letters of the correct pictures.

Answers

	when?	what?	then what?
Anaïs	in 2 years	a	e
Frédéric	in 1 year	a	c
Nadia	in 1 year	b	(in 3 years) d

2 Lis les textes et réponds aux questions. Écris le bon prénom. (Reading L4)

Reading. Pupils read the texts and answer the questions by identifying the person described in each one. *le même boulot que* is glossed for support.

Answers
1 Jade   2 Astrid   3 Abdoul   4 Astrid   5 Jade
6 Abdoul

3 Regarde le tableau. Écris des phrases pour Vincent, Nadia … et toi! (Writing L4)

Writing. Pupils use the information in the table to write sentences about Vincent and Nadia. They then write about themselves in a similar way. Draw their attention to the tip box on adding an opinion to their writing using *À mon avis, ce serait …*

Example answers

*Je m'appelle **Vincent**. Je voudrais être vétérinaire parce que j'adore les animaux. Je ne voudrais pas être webdesigner parce que je n'aime pas les ordinateurs. À mon avis, ce serait ennuyeux.*

Je m'appelle **Nadia**. Je voudrais être directrice de magasin parce que j'adore la mode. À mon avis, ce serait génial. Je ne voudrais pas être professeur parce que je n'aime pas les enfants.

© Pearson Education Ltd 2013. Copying permitted for purchasing institution only. This material is not copyright free.

Module 4: Spécial vacances

(Pupil Book pp. 74–95)

Unit & Learning objectives	Programme of Study references	Key language	Grammar and other language features
1 Question de vacances (pp. 76–77) Discussing holidays Asking questions using question words	**GV2** Grammatical structures (question words) **GV3** Developing vocabulary **LC3** Conversation (dealing with the unexpected) **LC4** Expressing ideas (writing)	*Je passe mes vacances …* *au bord de la mer/en colo,* etc. *Je vais en vacances avec ma famille/avec mes copains,* etc. *Je reste une semaine/quinze jours,* etc. *Je fais …* *du canoë-kayak/du VTT/de la voile,* etc.	**G** asking questions using question words – developing writing skills
2 J'adore les sensations fortes! (pp. 78–79) Imagining adventure holidays Using *je voudrais* + infinitive	**GV2** Grammatical structures (*je voudrais* + infinitive) **GV3** Opinions and discussions **LC3** Conversation **LC5** Accurate pronunciation and intonation	*Un jour, je voudrais …* *aller au pôle Nord* *descendre l'Amazone en canoë* *faire de la plongée sous-marine* etc. *Ouais! Cool!* *Quelle horreur!* *Ce n'est pas mon truc.* etc.	**G** *je voudrais* + infinitive – developing speaking skills
3 C'est indispensable! (pp. 80–81) Talking about what you take with you on holiday Using reflexive verbs	**GV2** Grammatical structures (reflexive verbs) **GV3** Developing vocabulary **LC1** Listening and responding **LC5** Accurate pronunciation and intonation	*un chargeur (pour mon mp3)* *un portable* *des palmes* *des tongs* etc. *Je me baigne.* *Je me coiffe.* *Je m'ennuie.* etc.	**G** reflexive verbs – developing speaking skills – developing writing skills
4 Quel désastre! (pp. 82–83) Describing holiday disasters Using perfect tense verbs	**GV1** Tenses (perfect) **LC1** Listening and responding **LC3** Conversation **LC6** Reading comprehension	*J'ai oublié mon passeport.* *J'ai perdu mon portemonnaie.* *On a raté l'avion.* etc. *Aïe!/Mince!/Oh là là!* etc.	**G** the perfect tense – developing speaking skills

© Pearson Education Ltd 2013. Copying permitted for purchasing institution only. This material is not copyright free.

4 Spécial vacances

Unit & Learning objectives	Programme of Study references	Key language	Grammar and other language features
5 À la base de loisirs (pp. 84–85) Visiting a tourist attraction More practice with the perfect tense	**GV1** Tenses (perfect) **GV2** Grammatical structures (possessive adjectives) **LC5** Speaking coherently and confidently **LC8** Writing creatively	J'ai … Il/Elle a … fait du tir à l'arc fait du trampoline fait de l'escalade Je suis … Il/Elle est … allé(e) à la pêche	**G** the perfect tense **G** possessive adjectives – developing reading skills
Bilan et Révisions (pp. 86–87) Pupils' checklist and practice exercises			
En plus: Des vacances au collège! (pp. 88–89) Debating the idea of 'open school' in the holidays	**LC1** Listening and responding **LC6** Reading comprehension **LC6** Translation into English **LC8** Writing creatively	Review of language from the module	– developing reading skills – developing writing skills
J'écris (pp. 90–91) Extended writing practice	**GV3** Developing vocabulary **GV4** Accuracy (grammar; spelling; punctuation) **LC4** Expressing ideas (writing) **LC8** Writing creatively	Review of language from the module	– developing writing skills – checking your work
Studio Grammaire (pp. 92–93) Detailed grammar summary and practice exercises			**G** asking questions using question words **G** *je voudrais* + infinitive **G** the perfect tense **G** using the perfect tense to say what other people did
À toi (pp. 122–123) Self-access reading and writing at two levels			

© Pearson Education Ltd 2013. Copying permitted for purchasing institution only. This material is not copyright free.

(Pupil Book pp. 76–77)

4) 1 Question de vacances

Learning objectives
- Discussing holidays
- Asking questions using question words

Programme of Study references
GV2 Grammatical structures (question words)
GV3 Developing vocabulary
LC3 Conversation (dealing with the unexpected)
LC4 Expressing ideas (writing)

FCSE links
Unit 3: Holidays and travel (Holidays; Activities; Accommodation; Destination)
Unit 7: Local area and environment (Locations)

Grammar
- asking questions using question word

Key language
Où passes-tu tes vacances?
Je passe mes vacances …
au bord de la mer
à la campagne
à la montagne
en colo
Avec qui vas-tu en vacances?
Je vais en vacances …
avec ma famille
avec mes parents
avec mes copains
Combien de temps restes-tu en vacances?
Je reste …
une semaine
quinze jours
dix jours
Que fais-tu quand tu vas en vacances?
Je fais …
du canoë-kayak
du ski
du snowboard
du VTT
de la voile
de la planche à voile
de l'équitation

PLTS
R Reflective learners

Resources
Audio files:
47_Module4_Unit1_Ex1.mp3
48_Module4_Unit1_Ex5.mp3
Workbooks:
Cahier d'exercices Vert, page 37
ActiveTeach:
Starter 2 resource
p.076 Flashcards
p.076 Grammar
p.076 Grammar practice
p.076 Class activity
p.077 Grammar skills
p.077 Listening skills
ActiveLearn:
Listening, Reading
Grammar, Vocabulary

Starter 1
Aim
To review question words; To use reading strategies

Write up the following. Give pupils three minutes to read the questions in exercise 2 and use them to work out the meaning of the question words.

Où? Qui? Combien? Que?

Check answers, asking pupils how they worked them out. (**Answers:** Where? Who? How much? What?)

Alternative Starter 1:
Use ActiveTeach p.076 Grammar practice to practise forming questions.

1 Écoute et note les bonnes lettres pour chaque personne. (1–4) (Listening L3)

Listening. Pupils listen to four conversations about holidays. For each person they note the letters of the four correct pictures, to give details of where they usually go, who they go with, how long they stay and what they do.

Audioscript Track 47

1 – Pardon. Où passes-tu tes vacances?
 – Normalement, je passe mes vacances à la montagne.
 – Avec qui vas-tu en vacances?
 – Je vais en vacances avec ma famille.
 – Combien de temps restes-tu en vacances?
 – Je reste une semaine.
 – Que fais-tu quand tu vas en vacances?
 – Je fais du ski.
2 – Salut! Où passes-tu tes vacances?
 – Euh … Je passe mes vacances au bord de la mer.
 – Avec qui vas-tu en vacances?
 – Je vais en vacances avec mes parents.
 – Combien de temps restes-tu en vacances?
 – Normalement, je reste dix jours.
 – Que fais-tu quand tu vas en vacances?
 – Je fais de la voile. J'adore ça!
3 – Bonjour. Où passes-tu tes vacances?
 – Normalement, je passe mes vacances à la campagne.
 – Avec qui vas-tu en vacances?
 – Je vais en vacances avec ma famille.
 – Combien de temps restes-tu en vacances?
 – Ben … Je reste quinze jours.
 – Que fais-tu quand tu vas en vacances?
 – Je fais du VTT! C'est génial, le VTT!

© Pearson Education Ltd 2013. Copying permitted for purchasing institution only. This material is not copyright free.

4 Spécial vacances 1 Question de vacances

4 – *Pardon. Où passes-tu tes vacances?*
– *Je passe mes vacances en colo.*
– *Avec qui vas-tu en vacances?*
– *Je vais en colo avec mes copains.*
– *Combien de temps restes-tu en vacances?*
– *Normalement, je reste une semaine.*
– *Que fais-tu quand tu vas en vacances?*
– *Alors, moi, je fais du canoë-kayak.*

Answers
1 c, e, h, l
2 a, f, j, n
3 b, e, i, m
4 , g, h, k

2 Trouve la bonne réponse à chaque question. (Reading L2)

Reading. Pupils match the questions and answers.

Answers
1 b 2 d 3 a 4 c

R Pupils work in pairs to practise the dialogue they have just made by matching the questions and answers in exercise 2. They take it in turn to ask and answer.

Studio Grammaire: asking questions using question words

Use the *Studio Grammaire* box to review forming questions using question words. There is more information and further practice on Pupil Book p. 92.

3 En tandem. Fais une conversation. Choisis les images A ou B. (Speaking L4)

Speaking. In pairs: pupils make up a conversation, taking it in turn to ask and answer. Each chooses a set of prompts, A or B. Remind pupils that the letters 'gne' (e.g. *montagne, compagne*) are pronounced a bit like 'n' quickly followed by 'yuh'.

Starter 2

Aim

To review talking about holidays

Write up the following. Give pupils three minutes working in pairs to write an answer to each question.

1 *Où passes-tu tes vacances?*
2 *Avec qui vas-tu en vacances?*
3 *Combien de temps restes-tu en vacances?*
4 *Que fais-tu quand tu vas en vacances?*

Hear answers.

Alternative Starter 2:

Use ActiveTeach p.076 Flashcards to review holiday language or p.076 Class activity to practise answering questions on holidays.

4 Lis les textes, puis regarde les images. C'est Blaise (B) ou Laëtitia (L)? (Reading L4)

Reading. Pupils read the texts. They then identify whether each picture relates to Blaise (writing B) or Laëtitia (writing L).

Answers
1 L 2 L 3 B 4 B 5 L 6 B 7 L 8 L

5 Écoute l'interview avec une célébrité. Copie et complète le tableau en anglais. (Listening L4)

Listening. Pupils copy out the grid. They listen to an interview with a celebrity, then complete the grid with the details in English. *ma petite amie* is glossed for support.

Audioscript Track 48

– *Bonjour, j'ai avec moi le chanteur Daniel Dugrand. Daniel, où vas-tu normalement en vacances?*
– *Ça dépend. En juillet, je vais au bord de la mer.*
– *Au bord de la mer?*
– *Oui. J'ai une villa en Espagne. J'adore le soleil! Et en février, je vais à la montagne. Je vais à la montagne en Suisse.*
– *Avec qui vas-tu en vacances?*
– *Alors … Je vais en vacances avec ma petite amie.*
– *Avec ta petite amie? Elle s'appelle comment?*
– *Elle s'appelle Laura.*
– *Et combien de temps restes-tu en vacances?*
– *Normalement, je reste trois semaines au bord de la mer.*
– *Trois semaines! Et combien de temps à la montagne?*
– *Je reste quinze jours à la montagne.*

© Pearson Education Ltd 2013. Copying permitted for purchasing institution only. This material is not copyright free.

1 Question de vacances Spécial vacances 4

– *Et finalement, Daniel. Que fais-tu quand tu vas en vacances? Quelles activités aimes-tu?*
– *Quand je vais au bord de la mer, je fais du jet-ski. J'adore faire du jet-ski! J'ai aussi un bateau, donc je fais de la voile.*
– *Et quand tu vas à la montagne, tu fais du ski?*
– *Non, je n'aime pas faire de ski. Je préfère faire du snowboard.*

Answers

where?	1 seaside
	2 mountains (in Switzerland)
who with?	his girlfriend, Laura
for how long?	1 three weeks (seaside)
	2 two weeks (mountains)
activities	1 jet-skiing, sailing (seaside)
	2 snowboarding (mountains)
any other details?	Goes to seaside in July. Has villa in Spain. Loves the sun. Goes to Switzerland in February. Loves jet-skiing. Has a boat. Doesn't like skiing.

6 Imagine que tu es une célébrité. Décris tes vacances. (Writing L4)

Writing. Pupils imagine that they are a celebrity and write a paragraph describing their usual holiday. A list of features to include is supplied in the form of a framework. Draw pupils' attention to the tip box on improving their writing by including impressive extra details. Suggest they add this advice to their Skills Notebook and keep a list of the types of details they could include.

7 En tandem. Interviewe ton/ta camarade. Il/Elle joue le rôle de la célébrité de l'exercice 6. (Speaking L4)

PLTS R

Speaking. In pairs: pupils take it in turn to interview each other in the role of the celebrity they wrote about in exercise 6. A sample opening is supplied. *J'ai avec moi* is glossed for support.

If possible, record the interviews on a CD or DVD and play them back, either to the relevant pairs or to the whole class. Encourage pupils to identify two areas in which they think they could improve.

Plenary

Ask the class to recall the four questions used in the unit.

Then tell them you are going to play a game. You will throw a ball to a pupil and ask him/her one of the questions. He/She replies (using real holiday details or making them up), then chooses another pupil to throw the ball to, asking a different question as he/she throws it.

Workbook, page 37

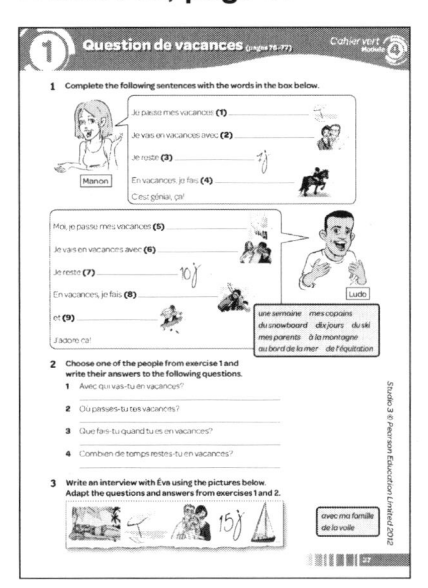

Answers

1 1 au bord de la mer   2 mes parents
   3 une semaine   4 de l'équitation
   5 à la montagne   6 mes copains   7 dix jours
   8 du ski   9 du snowboard
2 (One of each answer, depending on the person they have chosen:)
   1 Manon: Je vais en vacances avec **mes parents**.
   Ludo: Je vais en vacances **avec mes copains**.
   2 Manon: Je passe mes vacances **au bord de la mer**.
   Ludo: Moi, je passe mes vacances **à la montagne**.
   3 Manon: En vacances, je fais **de l'équitation**.
   Ludo: En vacances, je fais **du ski** et **du snowboard**.
   4 Manon: Je reste **une semaine**.
   Ludo: Je reste **dix jours**.
3 (Example answers:)
   Je vais en vacances avec ma famille.
   Je passe mes vacances au bord de la mer/je me fais bronzer sur la plage.
   En vacances, je fais de la voile.
   Je reste quinze jours/deux semaines.

© Pearson Education Ltd 2013. Copying permitted for purchasing institution only. This material is not copyright free.

4 Spécial vacances 1 Question de vacances

Worksheet 4.1 Asking questions using question words

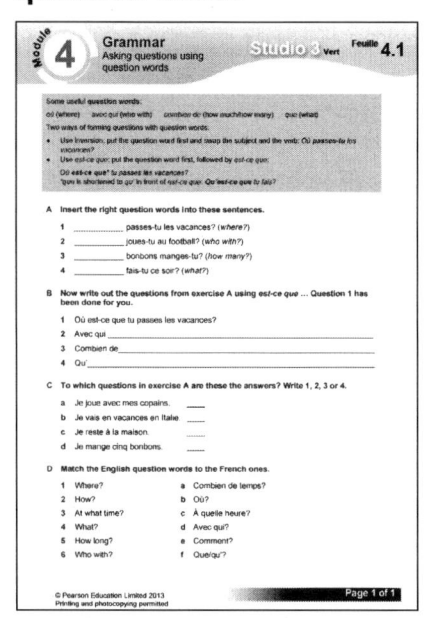

Answers

A
a 1
b 3
c 5
d 2
e 4

B
1 Her family: her mum, her step dad, her brother and her sister
2 By the sea in France
3 In February
4 All sorts of activities: mountain biking, horse riding and sailing
5 Snowboarding
6 One week

Answers

A 1 Où 2 Avec qui 3 Combien de 4 Que

B 1 Où est-ce que tu passes les vacances?
  2 Avec qui est-ce que tu joues au football?
  3 Combien de bonbons est-ce que tu manges?
  4 Qu'est-ce que tu fais ce soir?

C a 2 b 1 c 4 d 3

D 1 b 2 e 3 c 4 f 5 a 6 d

Worksheet 4.2 Listening for gist and detail

2 J'adore les sensations fortes!

(Pupil Book pp. 78–79)

Learning objectives
- Imagining adventure holidays
- Using *je voudrais* + infinitive

Programme of Study references
GV2 Grammatical structures (*je voudrais* + infinitive)
GV3 Opinions and discussions
LC3 Conversation
LC5 Accurate pronunciation and intonation

FCSE links
Unit 3: Holidays and travel (Types of holiday; Camping; Activities)

Grammar
- *je voudrais* + infinitive

Key language
Un jour, je voudrais …
aller au pôle Nord
descendre l'Amazone en canoë
faire de la plongée sous-marine
faire des sports extrêmes
faire un safari en Afrique
habiter sur une île déserte
Ouais! Cool!
Bonne idée!
Pourquoi pas?
Quelle horreur!
Tu rigoles!
Ce n'est pas mon truc.

PLTS
I Independent enquirers

Resources
Audio files:
49_Module4_Unit2_Ex2.mp3
50_Module4_Unit2_Ex4.mp3
51_Module4_Unit2_Ex5.mp3
Workbooks:
Cahier d'exercices Vert, page 38
ActiveTeach:
p.078 Flashcards
p.078 Grammar
p.078 Grammar practice
ActiveLearn:
Listening, Reading
Vocabulary

Starter 1
Aim
To introduce the topic

Ask the class what they think the title of the unit means. Have a short class discussion in English on the topic of thrill-seeking, eliciting pupils' ideas for dream activities along the lines of those in exercise 1.

Alternative Starter 1:
Use ActiveTeach p.078 Flashcards to introduce vocabulary for adventure holidays.

1 Trouve la bonne photo pour chaque phrase. (Reading L2)

Reading. Pupils match the phrases to the pictures. *un jour* is glossed for support.

Answers
See audioscript for exercise 2: pupils listen to the exercise 2 recording to check their answers.

2 Écoute et vérifie. (1–6) (Listening L2)

Listening. Pupils listen and check their answers to exercise 1.

Audioscript Track 49

1 Un jour, je voudrais aller au pôle Nord. – E
2 Un jour, je voudrais descendre l'Amazone en canoë. – F
3 Un jour, je voudrais faire un safari en Afrique. – D
4 Un jour, je voudrais faire de la plongée sous-marine. – B
5 Un jour, je voudrais faire des sports extrêmes. – A
6 Un jour, je voudrais habiter sur une île déserte. – C

Answers
1 E 2 F 3 D 4 B 5 A 6 C

Studio Grammaire: *je voudrais* + infinitive

Use the *Studio Grammaire* box to review *je voudrais* + infinitive. There is more information and further practice on Pupil Book p. 92.

Pupils translate the following sentences into French.

1 I'd like to go to the swimming pool.
2 I'd like to play football.

3 En tandem. Jeu de mime. (Speaking L3)

Speaking. In pairs: pupils play a mime game, taking it in turn to mime something they would like to do in the future and to guess. A sample exchange is given. Draw pupils' attention to the tip box on pronunciation.

© Pearson Education Ltd 2013. Copying permitted for purchasing institution only. This material is not copyright free.

4 Spécial vacances 2 J'adore les sensations fortes!

4 Écoute. Note l'activité (utilise les lettres de l'exercice 1) et note si la réaction est positive ☺ ou négative ☹. (1–6) (Listening L3)

Listening. Read together through the language boxes on positive and negative responses. Pupils then listen to six conversations in which people talk about what they would like to do in the future. For each they note whether the reaction to the question asked is positive (drawing a smiley face) or negative (drawing a sad face).

Audioscript Track 50

1 – Est-ce que tu voudrais faire un safari en Afrique?
– Oui, pourquoi pas? J'adore les animaux!
2 – Est-ce que tu voudrais aller au pôle Nord?
– Ah non! Quelle horreur! Je n'aime pas le froid!
3 – Est-ce que tu voudrais faire des sports extrêmes?
– Oua-a-a-is! Cool!
4 – Est-ce que tu voudrais descendre l'Amazone en canoë?
– Bonne idée! J'aime faire du canoë!
5 – Est-ce que tu voudrais faire de la plongée sous-marine?
– Ben ... Ce n'est pas mon truc.
6 – Est-ce que tu voudrais habiter sur une île déserte?
– Tu rigoles! Moi, j'aime aller au centre commercial!

Answers

1 D ☺ 2 E ☹ 3 A ☺ 4 F ☺
5 B ☹ 6 C ☹

Starter 2

Aim
To review *je voudrais*; To review language for the topic

Write up the following. Give pupils three minutes to choose three things they would like to do and write three sentences, using *Je voudrais ...*

Je voudrais ...
faire de la plongée sous-marine
descendre l'Amazone en canoë
habiter sur une île déserte
faire un safari en Afrique
aller au pôle Nord
faire des sports extrêmes

Hear answers, asking pupils to translate their sentences into English. Ask the class to summarise how *je voudrais* is used.

Alternative Starter 2:
Use ActiveTeach p.078 Grammar practice to practise *je voudrais*.

5 Écoute et lis le quiz. Utilise le Mini-dictionnaire, si nécessaire. Note tes réponses. (Listening L4)

Listening. Pupils listen to a quiz, reading the text at the same time. They should try to use reading strategies as a first resort to work out any words they don't know; they can then look up words in the *Mini-dictionnaire* at the back of the Pupil Book. They should then write down their own answers to the quiz. *les sensations fortes* is glossed for support.

Audioscript Track 51

– Aimes-tu les sensations fortes? Réponds aux questions! Un. Voudrais-tu faire du camping toute seule dans une forêt?
– A Pourquoi pas?
– B Tu rigoles!
– Deux. Voudrais-tu nager avec des requins?
– A Oua-a-a-is! Cool!
– B Quelle horreur!
– Trois. Voudrais-tu passer des vacances dans un château hanté?
– A Bonne idée!
– B Tu rigoles!
– Quatre. Voudrais-tu faire de la randonnée dans une jungle?
– A Pourquoi pas?
– B Ce n'est pas mon truc.
– Cinq. Voudrais-tu manger des insectes?
– A Miam-miam! J'adore ça!
– B Beurk! Quelle horreur!

6 En tandem. Fais le quiz avec ton/ta camarade. (Speaking L4)

Speaking. In pairs: pupils do the quiz orally with a friend. They take it in turn to ask the questions. As well as asking and answering, they should respond to what their partner has said. A sample exchange is given.

7 Fais un sondage. Pose les questions du tableau à trois personnes et écris les prénoms dans la bonne case. (Speaking L4)

PLTS

Speaking. Pupils carry out a survey, asking three people the questions in the grid and writing their names in the correct box. A sample exchange is given.

Pupils could make up their own questions to use instead of the ones given.

© Pearson Education Ltd 2013. Copying permitted for purchasing institution only. This material is not copyright free.

2 J'adore les sensations fortes! Spécial vacances 4

8 Écris les résultats de ton sondage.
(Writing L4)

Writing. Pupils write up the results of their survey, following the model given.

> **Plenary**
>
> Ask the class to summarise how *je voudrais* is used.
>
> Pupils then take it in turn to say something that they dream of doing, either using the examples in the unit or coming up with their own ideas. For each suggestion, ask another pupil *Tu es d'accord?* to elicit his/her response to the idea.

Workbook, page 38

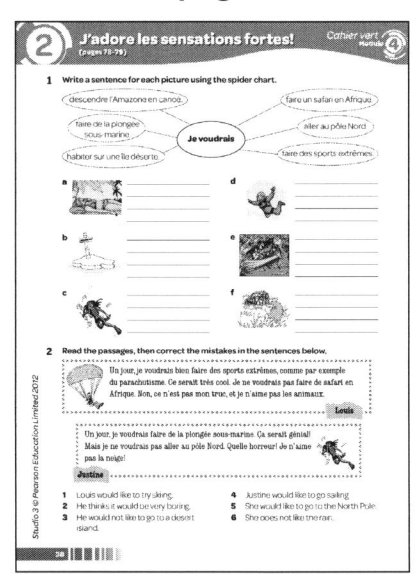

> **Answers**
>
> 1 a Je voudrais habiter sur une île déserte.
>
>   b Je voudrais aller au pôle Nord.
>
>   c Je voudrais faire de la plongée sous-marine.
>
>   d Je voudrais faire des sports extrêmes.
>
>   e Je voudrais descendre l'Amazone en canoë.
>
>   f Je voudrais faire un safari en Afrique.
>
> 2 1 Louis would like to **try parachuting**.
>
>   2 He thinks it would be **very cool**.
>
>   3 He would not like to go **on a safari**.
>
>   4 Justine would like to go **scuba diving**.
>
>   5 She **would not like** to go to the North Pole.
>
>   6 She does not like **the snow**.

4 · 3 C'est indispensable!

(Pupil Book pp. 80–81)

Learning objectives
- Talking about what you take with you on holiday
- Using reflexive verbs

Programme of Study references
GV2 Grammatical structures (reflexive verbs)
GV3 Developing vocabulary
LC1 Listening and responding
LC5 Accurate pronunciation and intonation

FCSE links
Unit 3: Holidays and travel (Activities)

Grammar
- reflexive verbs

Key language
Qu'est-ce que tu prends quand tu vas en vacances?
Je prends …
un chargeur (pour mon mp3/ ma PlayStation Portable)
un portable
un tuba
une bombe anti-insectes
du gel coiffant
de la crème solaire
des lunettes de plongée
des palmes
des tongs
Je me baigne.
Je me coiffe.
Je me douche.
Je me fais bronzer.
Je me fais piquer.
Je m'ennuie.

PLTS
T Team workers

Resources
Audio files:
52_Module4_Unit3_Ex1.mp3
53_Module4_Unit3_Ex6.mp3
Workbooks:
Cahier d'exercices Vert, page 39
ActiveTeach:
Starter 1 resource
p.080 Flashcards (a)
p.081 Flashcards (b)
p.081 Video 7
p.081 Video worksheet 7
p.081 Grammar
p.081 Grammar practice
p.081 Learning skills
p.081 Thinking skills
Plenary resource
ActiveLearn:
Listening, Reading
Grammar, Vocabulary

Starter 1
Aim
To use reading strategies

Write up the following, jumbling the order of the second column. Give pupils three minutes to match the French and English words.

un chargeur (pour mon mp3)	a charger (for my mp3)
un portable	a mobile phone
un tuba	a snorkel
une bombe anti-insectes	an insect-repellent spray
du gel coiffant	hair gel
de la crème solaire	sun cream
des lunettes de plongée	swimming goggles
des palmes	flippers
des tongs	flip-flops

Check answers. Ask pupils how they worked out the meanings, eliciting techniques such as cognates, grammar, using what they know, process of elimination, etc.

Alternative Starter 1:
Use ActiveTeach p.080 Flashcards (a) to introduce holiday items.

1 Écoute. Qui parle? Écris le bon prénom. (1–3) (Listening L3)

Listening. Pupils listen to three conversations in which people say what they take when they go on holiday. For each they identify the person answering, using the pictures. *Qu'est-ce que tu prends quand tu vas en vacances?* is glossed for support.

Audioscript Track 52

1 – Qu'est-ce que tu prends quand tu vas en vacances?
 – Je prends … du gel coiffant, … des lunettes de plongée … et des palmes.
2 – Qu'est-ce que tu prends quand tu vas en vacances?
 – e prends … un chargeur pour mon mp3, … des tongs … et de la crème solaire.
3 – Qu'est-ce que tu prends quand tu vas en vacances?
 – Je prends … un tuba, … un portable … et une bombe anti-insectes.

Answers
1 Lucas **2** Laurent **3** Léo

© Pearson Education Ltd 2013. Copying permitted for purchasing institution only. This material is not copyright free.

3 C'est indispensable! Spécial vacances 4

2 En tandem. Jeu de mémoire.
(Speaking L3)

Speaking. In pairs: pupils play a memory game. They each choose one of the people in exercise 1, then take it in turn to ask and answer on what they take on holiday, using the exercise 1 details. Draw pupils' attention to the tip box on the pronunciation of the question.

3 Copie les phrases. Écris correctement les mots en rouge. (Writing L2)

Writing. Pupils copy out the sentences, unjumbling the jumbled words (shown in red within the exercise).

Answers
1 Je prends du **gel coiffant** et de la **crème solaire**.
2 Je prends des **tongs** et un **portable**.
3 Je prends un **tuba** et des **palmes**.
4 Je prends des **lunettes de plongée**.
5 Je prends un **chargeur** pour mon mp3.
6 prends une **bombe anti-insectes**.

Starter 2

PLTS T

Aim

To review language for items you take on holiday

Give pupils three minutes working in pairs to write a list of items they take on holiday. Tell them that they will get 1 point for each item already mentioned in the unit and 2 points for any appropriate item not mentioned.

Ask pairs to swap and check another pair's list. Read out the list of items on Pupil Book p. 80 (exercise 1). Then ask pupils to read out any other items. Confirm whether each is acceptable or not. Find out which pair has the highest score.

Alternative Starter 2:

Use ActiveTeach p.081 Flashcards (b) to introduce reflexive verbs and/or p.081 Grammar practice to practise reflexive verbs.

4 Lis les textes et mets les images dans l'ordre des textes. (Reading L4)

Reading. Pupils read the texts and put the pictures in the order they are mentioned. Some vocabulary is glossed for support.

Answers
b, f, a, d, e, c

5 Relis les textes. Copie et complète les phrases en anglais. (Reading L4)

Reading. Pupils read the texts in exercise 4 again, then copy and complete the gap-fill sentences in English.

Answers
1 When Noah goes on holiday, he **sunbathes** on the beach, so he takes **sun cream**.
2 Sometimes he gets **bored** on holiday, so he takes magazines and **a charger (for his mp3)**.
3 Every day, Julie **swims** in the sea, so she takes her **swimming goggles**.
4 Afterwards, she **showers** and does her hair, so she takes plenty of **hair gel**.
5 Baptiste loves scuba diving, so he takes a **snorkel** and **flippers**.
6 He also takes **insect repellent** because he always gets **stung.**

Studio Grammaire: reflexive verbs

Use the *Studio Grammaire* box to cover reflexive verbs. Point out that they already know the reflexive verb *s'appeler*.

R Give pupils one minute to look at the list of reflexive verbs in the *Studio Grammaire* box. They then close their books. Prompt in English (e.g. 'I do my hair') to elicit the correct reflexive verb in French (e.g. *Je me coiffe*).

6 Écoute et complète le tableau en anglais. (1–5) (Listening L3)

Listening. Pupils copy out the table. They listen to five people saying what they do on holiday and what they take with them, then complete the table with the details in English.

Audioscript Track 53

1 *Quand je vais en vacances, je me baigne dans la mer. Alors, je prends des lunettes de plongée.*
2 *Quand je vais en vacances, je m'ennuie. Donc je prends un chargeur pour ma PlayStation Portable.*
3 *Quand je vais en vacances, je me coiffe tous les soirs. Alors, je prends beaucoup de gel coiffant.*

4 Spécial vacances 3 C'est indispensable!

4 *Quand je vais en vacances, je me fais piquer par les moustiques. Donc je prends une bombe anti-insectes.*
5 *Quand je vais en vacances, je me fais bronzer. Alors, je prends de la crème solaire.*

Answers

	action	takes with him/her
1	swimming (in sea)	swimming goggles
2	gets bored	charger (for Portable PlayStation)
3	does hair (every evening)	hair gel
4	gets stung (by mosquitoes)	insect-repellent spray
5	sunbathes	sun cream

7 En tandem. Ton/Ta camarade dit une lettre. Tu fais une phrase. (Speaking L4)

Speaking. In pairs: pupils take it in turn to give a prompt (from pictures **A–E**) and to respond with a sentence. A sample exchange is given.

8 Copie et complète les phrases qui disparaissent. Utilise tes propres idées. (Writing L4)

Writing. Pupils copy and complete the sentences, using their own ideas. Encourage them to be inventive. Draw their attention to the tip box on using *alors* and *donc* to improve their writing by creating longer sentences.

Plenary

Ask pupils how reflexive verbs are different from other verbs. Elicit the reflexive verbs used in the unit, along with their meanings.

Make up sentences round the class. Explain that each sentence will consist of three parts:

1 *Quand je vais en vacances,*
2 *je* + reflexive verb
3 *alors je prends* + an appropriate item

You could make it competitive by asking the class to stand. If a pupil makes a mistake or can't think of anything to add, he/she is 'out' and sits down. The winner is the last one standing.

Workbook, page 39

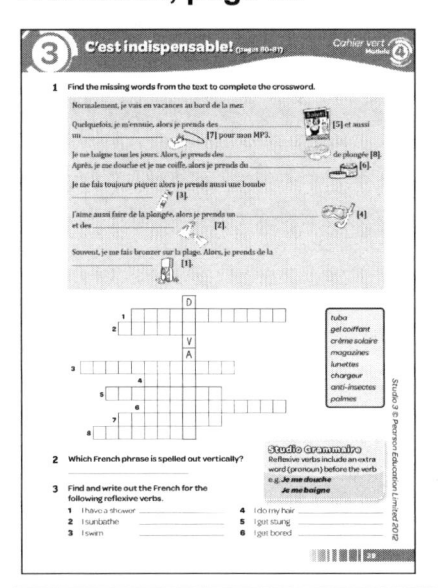

Answers

1 1 crème solaire 2 palmes 3 anti-insectes
   4 tuba 5 magazines 6 gel coiffant
   7 chargeur 8 lunettes

2 des vacances

3 1 Je me douche
   2 Je me fais bronzer
   3 Je me baigne
   4 Je me coiffe
   5 Je me fais piquer
   6 Je m'ennuie

Worksheet 4.3 Learning by heart

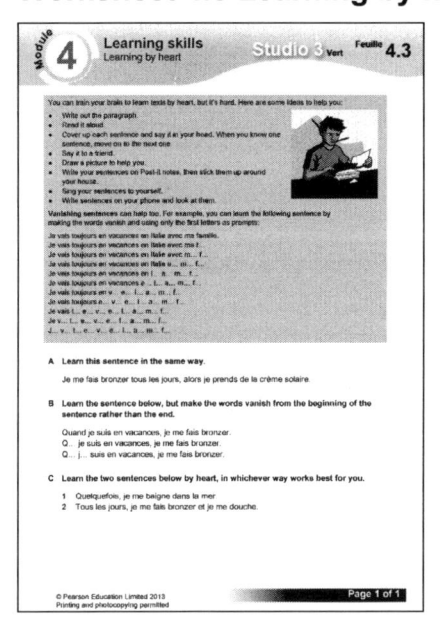

3 C'est indispensable! Spécial vacances 4

Worksheet 4.4 Logic puzzle

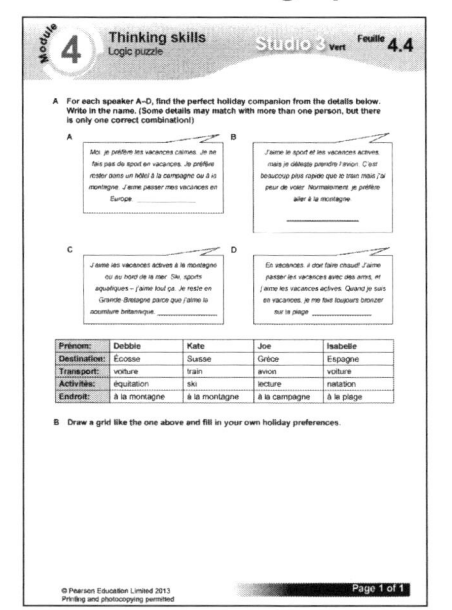

Answers
A A Joe B Kate C Debbie D Isabelle
B (Answers will vary.)

Video

Episode 7: On part

Samira has arranged a mystery holiday for the team, who each reveal what they have decided to pack. Video worksheet 7 can be used in conjunction with this episode.

Answers to video worksheet (ActiveTeach)

1 A – The French summer holidays are longer. A lot of families head for the coast, causing massive traffic jams.

– Guesses should be along these lines: Mehdi – something sporty; Alex – something practical; Marielle – something cool; Samira – something sensible; Hugo – whatever Samira wants!

2 A Tomorrow (*demain*).
 B They are going to work filming reports for StudioFR while on holiday.
 C She'd like to go on safari in Africa.
 D Go fishing.
 E Try extreme sports.
 F A desert island.
 G No, it's a surprise.
 H Nine o'clock the next morning.

3 A Anti-insect spray, binoculars, torch.
 B Hair dryer, adaptor, mp3 player.
 C Fishing gear: rod, straw hat; also camera, matches and clothes.
 D Extreme sports (climbing, horse riding, mountain biking).
 E A quiet beach holiday.
 F Because the holiday she has planned covers everyone's wishes.
 G Marielle, because she doesn't like camping.
 H Sailing and mountain biking (*voile, VTT*).

© Pearson Education Ltd 2013. Copying permitted for purchasing institution only. This material is not copyright free.

(Pupil Book pp. 82–83)

4 Quel désastre!

Learning objectives
- Describing holiday disasters
- Using perfect tense verbs

Programme of Study references
GV1 Tenses (perfect)
LC1 Listening and responding
LC3 Conversation
LC6 Reading comprehension

FCSE links
Unit 3: Holidays and travel (Problems on holiday; Holiday experiences)

Grammar
- the perfect tense

Key language
J'ai oublié mon passeport.
J'ai perdu mon portemonnaie.
J'ai cassé mon appareil photo.
J'ai pris un coup de soleil.
J'ai mangé quelque chose de mauvais.
On a raté l'avion.
Aïe!
Mince!
Oh là là!
C'est pas possible!
Quel désastre!
Quelle horreur!

PLTS
S Self managers

Cross-curricular
English: tense usage
ICT: word-processing

Resources
Audio files:
54_Module4_Unit4_Ex2.mp3
55_Module4_Unit4_Ex4.mp3
56_Module4_Unit4_Ex6.mp3
Workbooks:
Cahier d'exercices Vert, pages 40 & 41
ActiveTeach:
Starter 1 resource
Starter 2 resource
p.082 Grammar
p.082 Grammar practice
p.083 Video 8
p.083 Video worksheet 8
p.083 Grammar skills
p.083 Thinking skills
ActiveLearn:
Listening, Reading Grammar

Starter 1
Aim
To review the perfect tense; To practise applying grammatical patterns

Write up the following. Give pupils three minutes working in pairs to complete the grid.

infinitive	present tense	English	perfect tense	English
oublier			j'ai oublié	I forgot/ I have forgotten
	je casse	I break		
		I eat	j'ai mangé	
rater		I miss		

Check answers. Ask pupils when they would use the present tense and when the perfect tense. Ask how the perfect tense is formed.
(**Answers** (by row): j'oublie, I forget; casser, j'ai cassé, I broke/I have broken; manger, je mange, I ate/I have eaten; je rate, j'ai raté, I missed/I have missed)

1 Trouve la bonne photo pour chaque phrase. (Reading L5)

Reading. Pupils match the sentences and pictures. *quelque chose de mauvais* is glossed for support.

Answers
1 b 2 a 3 f 4 c 5 d 6 e

2 Écoute. Qui parle? Écris le bon prénom de l'exercice 1. (1–6) (Listening L5)

Listening. Pupils listen to six people talking about things that have gone wrong on holiday. They use the text in exercise 1 to identify who is speaking each time.

Audioscript Track 54

1 Oh là là! J'ai perdu mon portemonnaie!
2 Aïe! J'ai mangé quelque chose de mauvais!
3 Quelle horreur! J'ai pris un coup de soleil!
4 pas possible! J'ai oublié mon passeport!
5 Quel désastre! On a raté l'avion!
6 Mince! J'ai cassé mon appareil photo!

Answers
1 Aïcha 2 Enzo 3 Léna 4 Ryan 5 Salomé 6 Benoît

© Pearson Education Ltd 2013. Copying permitted for purchasing institution only. This material is not copyright free.

4 Quel désastre! Spécial vacances

Studio Grammaire: the perfect tense (verbs with *avoir*)

Use the *Studio Grammaire* box to review forming the perfect tense (verbs with *avoir*). There is more information and further practice on Pupil Book p. 93.

R Pupils write out the perfect tense forms of the following verbs:

je danse   je joue   je marche   je passe

3 Écris correctement les phrases. Puis traduis-les en anglais. (Writing L3)

Writing. Pupils write the jumbled sentences out correctly, then translate them into English.

Answers
1. J'ai oublié mon passeport.
   I forgot my passport.
2. J'ai pris un coup de soleil.
   I got sunburnt.
3. J'ai cassé mon appareil photo.
   I broke my camera.
4. On a raté l'avion.
   We missed the plane.
5. J'ai perdu mon portemonnaie.
   I lost my purse.
6. J'ai mangé quelque chose de mauvais.
   I ate something bad.

Starter 2

Aim
To review the perfect tense; To review language for talking about holiday problems

Write up the following, replacing each underlined word with a line. Give pupils three minutes to complete the sentences using the correct past participle. You could make the task more challenging by supplying infinitives as prompts rather than the past participles and telling pupils that they need to create the correct forms.

pris   raté   oublié   mangé   cassé   perdu

1. J'ai <u>oublié</u> mon passeport!
2. J'ai <u>perdu</u> mon portemonnaie!
3. J'ai <u>cassé</u> mon appareil photo!
4. J'ai <u>pris</u> un coup de soleil!
5. J'ai <u>mangé</u> quelque chose de mauvais!
6. On a <u>raté</u> l'avion!

Check answers. Ask pupils to summarise how the perfect tense is formed and when it is used.

Alternative Starter 2:
Use ActiveTeach p.082 Grammar practice to practise the perfect tense.

4 Écoute à nouveau les personnes de l'exercice 2. Tu entends quelle expression? (1–6) (Listening L5)

Listening. Pupils listen again to the exercise 2 recording. They identify the expression of annoyance each speaker uses, choosing from the two options given each time (**a** or **b**).

Audioscript Track 55
See audioscript for exercise 2.

Answers
1 b   2 a   3 a   4 b   5 a   6 a

5 En tandem. Joue au «bip» avec ton/ta camarade. (Speaking L5)

PLTS S

Speaking. In pairs: pupils play a game of 'Bip'. One pupil starts a sentence, but stops before the last word. The second pupil says the whole sentence, completing it with an appropriate word. They take it in turn to start. A sample exchange is given. Draw pupils' attention to the tip box on improving their speaking by including expressions like *Mince!* and *Quelle horreur!* Suggest they add this advice to their Skills Notebook. Encourage them to practise using the expressions at home and with friends, trying as hard as they can to sound like they mean what they say.

6 Écoute et note le problème en anglais. (1–4) (Listening L5)

Listening. Pupils listen to four conversations about holiday problems. For each they note in English the problem mentioned.

Audioscript Track 56

1. – *Salut! T'as passé de bonnes vacances?*
   – *Non! J'ai perdu mon portable!*
   – *T'as perdu ton portable?*
   – *Oui, sur la plage.*
   – *Oh là là!*
2. – *Alors, t'as passé de bonnes vacances?*
   – *Pas du tout. J'ai mangé un mauvais hamburger.*
   – *Un mauvais hamburger! Quelle horreur!*
   – *Ben oui, j'ai vomi toute la nuit!*
3. – *Allô?*
   – *Coucou, c'est moi! T'as passé de bonnes vacances?*
   – *Pas tellement. J'ai cassé ma PlayStation Portable.*
   – *T'as cassé ta PSP? Oh, mince!*

© Pearson Education Ltd 2013. Copying permitted for purchasing institution only. This material is not copyright free.

4 Spécial vacances 4 Quel désastre!

– Oui, c'était un vrai désastre!
4 – Salut. T'as passé de bonnes vacances?
– Ah non. D'abord, on a raté le train …
– Le train?
– Oui, le train pour aller à l'aéroport.
– Oh là là!
– Et puis on a raté l'avion!
– Vous avez aussi raté l'avion? Quel désastre!

Answers
1 *Lost* mobile phone (on beach).
2 Ate a bad burger (and vomited all night).
3 Broke Portable PlayStation.
4 Missed train (to airport) and missed plane.

7 En tandem. Fais une conversation. Choisis parmi les images. (Speaking L5)

Speaking. In pairs: pupils make up a conversation each, choosing the problems to include from the picture prompts. They take it in turn to ask and answer. A sample exchange is given.

8 Lis le texte et les phrases. C'est vrai (V) ou faux (F)? (Reading L5)

Reading. Pupils read the text, then decide whether each sentence is true (writing V) or false (writing F). *son/sa* is glossed for support.

Answers
1 V   2 F   3 F   4 V   5 F   6 V

9 Copie et complète le texte. Utilise les images de l'exercice 7 ou tes propres idées. (Writing L4)

Writing. Pupils copy and complete the gap-fill text, using the pictures from exercise 7 or their own ideas.

Pupils could do the task on computer, making it easier for them to produce a second draft.

Point out how useful the *D'abord, … Ensuite, … Puis … Après, … Et finalement,* … framework is: it could be used with a range of other topics. Encourage them to write it in their Skills Notebook and to use it again in future.

Plenary

Ask the class to summarise how the perfect tense is formed and when it is used. Elicit examples from the unit.

Ask pupils to come up with sentences describing a really bad holiday: challenge them to try and trump each other's problems, by coming up with more and more imaginative and awful problems. Supply any words that they don't know.

Workbook, pages 40 and 41

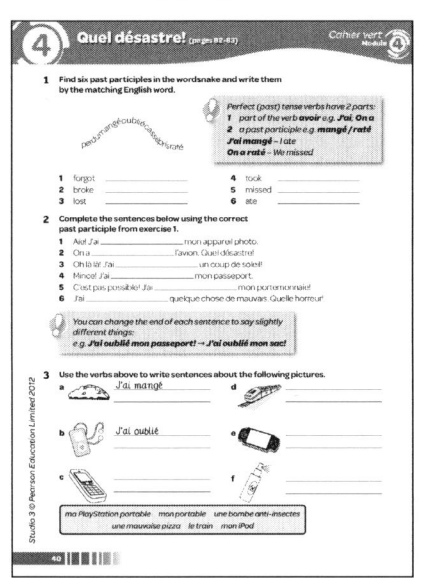

© Pearson Education Ltd 2013. Copying permitted for purchasing institution only. This material is not copyright free.

4 Quel désastre! Spécial vacances **4**

Answers

1 1 oublié 2 cassé 3 perdu 4 pris 5 raté
   6 mangé
2 1 cassé 2 raté 3 pris 4 oublié/perdu
   5 oublié/perdu 6 mangé
3 a J'ai mangé une mauvaise pizza.
   b J'ai oublié/cassé/perdu/pris mon iPod.
   c J'ai perdu/oublié/cassé mon portable.
   d J'ai raté/pris le train.
   e J'ai cassé/perdu/oublié ma PlayStation Portable.
   f J'ai pris une bombe anti-insectes.
4 1 c 2 a 3 d 4 g 5 b 6 e 7 f 8 h
   Pour mes vacances, je suis allé en Grèce avec ma famille. Quel désastre! D'abord, j'ai perdu mon portable. Quelle horreur! Ensuite, j'ai mangé un mauvais hamburger et j'ai vomi! Puis ma mère a cassé son appareil photo! Finalement, mon frère a oublié son passeport à l'hôtel et donc, on a raté l'avion. Quelles vacances horribles!
5 1 Grèce 2 sa famille 3 portable 4 mauvais
   5 cassé 6 son frère 7 raté 8 horribles
6 (Answers will vary.)

Worksheet 4.5 Using the perfect tense

Answers

A 1 J'ai perdu mon portemonnaie.
   2 Il a raté l'avion.
   3 Elle a cassé son portable.
   4 J'ai oublié mon passeport.
   5 On est allés en Espagne.
   6 Tu as mangé des chips.
B 1 est 2 a 3 J'ai 4 a 5 J'ai 6 es
C (Answers will vary.)
D (Answers will vary.)

Worksheet 4.6 Drawing from text

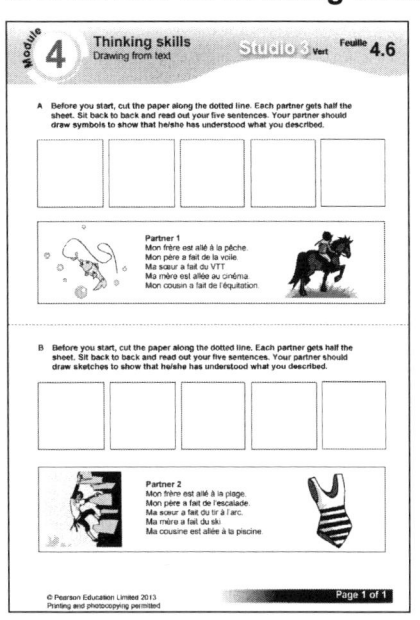

Answers

(Answers will vary.)

Video

Episode 8: Les vacances (1)

The boys begin their holiday with a fishing trip, while the girls discover the wildlife on a nature trail. Video worksheet 8 can be used in conjunction with this episode.

Answers to video worksheet (ActiveTeach)

1 A It's a camping holiday in France.
   – It could be things like fishing, riding, walking, sailing.
   – Mehdi and Hugo would be up for active things, Alex for practical activities, Marielle for partying and Samira would be flexible.
2 A Samira.
   B A walk.
   C Yes – they all respond positively.
3 A water, sky and la nature – nature
   B No, he's bored: he says there's nothing to do.
   C They think it's disgusting.
   D Alex caught a fish so it was a successful trip for him, but Hugo and Mehdi didn't enjoy fishing so the trip wasn't a success for them.
4 A She thinks she's going on safari.
   B An aquatic bird/a water bird.
   C It's magnificent (*magnifique*).
   D They smell it (it's mint) and rub the leaves between their fingers.
   E They are pretending to look for lions.
   F A green frog.

© Pearson Education Ltd 2013. Copying permitted for purchasing institution only. This material is not copyright free.

5 À la base de loisirs

(Pupil Book pp. 84–85)

Learning objectives
- Visiting a tourist attraction
- More practice with the perfect tense

Programme of Study references
GV1 Tenses (perfect)
GV2 Grammatical structures (possessive adjectives)
LC5 Speaking coherently and confidently
LC8 Writing creatively

Grammar
- the perfect tense
- possessive adjectives

Key language
J'ai …
Il/Elle a …
fait du tir à l'arc
fait du trampoline
fait de l'escalade
Je suis …
Il/Elle est …
allé(e) à la pêche

PLTS
C Creative thinkers

Cross-curricular
ICT: internet research

Resources
Audio files:
57_Module4_Unit5_Ex1.mp3
58_Module4_Unit5_Ex3.mp3
Workbooks:
Cahier d'exercices Vert, pages 42 & 43
ActiveTeach:
Starter 1 resource
Starter 2 resource
p.084 Flashcards
p.085 Video 9
p.085 Video worksheet 9
p.085 Class activity
p.085 Reading skills
ActiveLearn:
Listening, Reading
Grammar, Vocabulary

Starter 1
Aim

To review the perfect tense (*je*)

Write up the following. Give pupils three minutes to write out the sentences correctly, unscrambling the verb forms.

1 ssaipJ'aé des vacances horribles.
2 druJ'peai mon passeport.
3 éJ'taria l'avion.
4 gnmaaJ'ié du mauvais poisson.

Check answers. Ask the class to summarise how the perfect tense is formed. (**Answers:** 1 J'ai passé, 2 J'ai perdu, 3 J'ai raté, 4 J'ai mangé.)

Alternative Starter 1:

Use ActiveTeach p.084 Flashcards to introduce vocabulary for holiday activities.

1 Écoute et lis. Mets les images dans l'ordre du texte. (Listening L5)

Listening. Pupils listen to Mathis talking about his trip to a leisure park, and read the text at the same time. They then put the pictures in the order they are mentioned.

Audioscript Track 57

Salut! Je m'appelle Mathis. Le weekend dernier, je suis allé à la Base de Loisirs de Jonzac avec ma famille. D'abord, on a fait de la voile. C'était génial! Ensuite, mon frère a fait du VTT et ma soeur a fait de l'équitation. Mon beau-père est allé à la pêche et ma mère a fait du tir à l'arc. Et moi, j'ai fait de l'escalade! C'était hypercool!

Answers
b, e, f, a, c, d

Studio Grammaire: the perfect tense

Use the *Studio Grammaire* box to review the perfect tense (verbs with *avoir* and *être*). There is more information and further practice on Pupil Book p. 93.

Pupils identify and copy out all the perfect tense verbs in the text in exercise 1.

2 Relis le texte. Qui a fait quoi? Complète le tableau avec les bonnes lettres. (Reading L5)

Reading. Pupils read the exercise 1 text again. They copy and complete the grid, using the letters of the correct pictures from exercise 1.

Answers

Mathis	d
mother	c
stepfather	a
brother	e
sister	f
whole family	b

© Pearson Education Ltd 2013. Copying permitted for purchasing institution only. This material is not copyright free.

5 À la base de loisirs Spécial vacances 4

3 Écoute Clémence. Choisis la bonne réponse. (1–5) (Listening L5)

Listening. Pupils listen to Clémence talking about her trip to a leisure park. They complete each sentence by choosing the correct option from the two supplied (**a** or **b**).

Audioscript Track 58

1
- Allô, oui?
- Salut, Clémence! Tu as passé un bon weekend?
- Ah oui! Je suis allée à la Base de Loisirs de Jonzac avec ma famille.
- Super! Qu'est-ce que tu as fait comme activités?
- J'ai fait du tir à l'arc.
- Du tir à l'arc! Génial!

2
- Et ta soeur, qu'est-ce qu'elle a fait?
- Ma soeur a fait du trampoline.
- Pardon?
- Du trampoline!
- Ah, d'accord!

3
- Et ton demi-frère? Qu'est-ce qu'il a fait?
- Mon demi-frère … Il est allé à la pêche.
- Ah oui, bien sûr, il est allé à la pêche! Il adore ça.

4
- Et tes parents? Qu'est-ce que ton père a fait?
- Alors … Mon père a fait du canoë-kayak.
- D'accord, il a fait du canoë-kayak …

5
- Et ta belle-mère?
- Ma belle-mère? Elle a fait de l'escalade!
- Tu rigoles!
- Non, c'est vrai. Elle a fait de l'escalade!

Answers
1 b   2 b   3 a   4 b   5 a

Starter 2

Aim

To review possessive adjectives; To practise applying grammatical patterns

Write up the following. Give pupils three minutes to translate the English expressions into French, using the models supplied for support.

ma soeur   ma belle-mère
mon père   mon beau-frère

1 my brother   3 my stepfather
2 my mother   4 my stepsister

Check answers, asking pupils how they worked them out. Ask what *ma* and *mon* mean and when you use each form. (**Answers: 1** *mon frère,* **2** *ma mère,* **3** *mon beau-père,* **4** *ma belle-soeur*)

Alternative Starter 2:
Use ActiveTeach p.085 Class activity to practise holiday activities vocabulary.

4 En tandem. Imagine que tu es Thomas ou Clara. Fais une conversation. (Speaking L5)

Speaking. In pairs: pupils make up a conversation each, taking it in turn to ask the questions and to respond as Thomas or Clara, using the picture prompts given. A framework is also supplied.

Studio Grammaire: possessive adjectives

Use the *Studio Grammaire* box to review possessive adjectives (*mon/ma, ton/ta, son/sa*). There is more information and further practice on Pupil Book p. 112.

R Pupils copy and complete a grid for *soeur* and *frère*, using *mon/ma, ton/ta, son/sa*.

5 Écris correctement les phrases. (Writing L3)

Writing. Pupils write out each sentence, separating the words correctly.

Answers
1 J'ai fait de la voile.
2 On a fait du tir à l'arc.
3 Mon frère est allé à la pêche.
4 Ma soeur a fait du VTT.
5 Ma mère a fait de l'escalade.
6 Mon père a fait de l'équitation.

6 Lis et complète le texte avec les mots de la case. (Reading L5)

PLTS C

Reading. Pupils complete the gap-fill text, using the words supplied. Draw pupils' attention to the tip box on using the grammar they know to work out the answers.

Answers
1 du   2 escalade   3 pêche   4 soeur
5 fait   6 génial

© Pearson Education Ltd 2013. Copying permitted for purchasing institution only. This material is not copyright free.

4 Spécial vacances 5 À la base de loisirs

7 Imagine que tu es membre d'une famille célèbre. Décris une visite à la base de loisirs. (Writing L5)

Writing. Pupils imagine that they are a member of a famous family and write a description of their family's visit to the leisure park. Encourage them to be inventive. Read together through the key language box first, eliciting what the language means in English. A sample opening is supplied.

Pupils could look up bases *de loisirs* on the internet and identify extra activities to include in their writing.

8 Mémorise ton texte et fais un exposé oral. (Speaking L5)

Speaking. Pupils memorise the text they wrote in exercise 7 and use it to give a presentation.

Plenary

Ask how the perfect tense is formed and when it is used.

Challenge the class to come up with as many different sentences featuring the perfect tense as they can. Explain that *j'ai fait du VTT* and *elle a fait du VTT* count as two separate examples, so it is in their interest to use as many different subjects (*je, il, elle,* etc.) as they can. If they can make up 12 or more correct sentences, they win; if fewer, you win.

Workbook, pages 42 and 43

Answers

1 climbing; zip-lining; canoeing/kayaking; horse riding

2 1 La Base de Réals
   2 8 years old
   3 No – you have to be with a team of instructors
   4 in a river
   5 in the natural park of the Haut-Languedoc
   6 €149
   7 €50
   8 5

3 1 c 2 f 3 a 4 e 5 b 6 d

4 1 Ma copine Sarah a fait de l'équitation.
   2 J'ai fait de l'escalade.
   3 On a fait du VTT.
   4 'ai fait du tir à l'arc.
   5 Mon copain Max est allé à la pêche.
   6 Mon copain Robert a fait de la voile.

5 (Answers will vary.)

5 À la base de loisirs Spécial vacances 4

Worksheet 4.7 Reading complicated texts

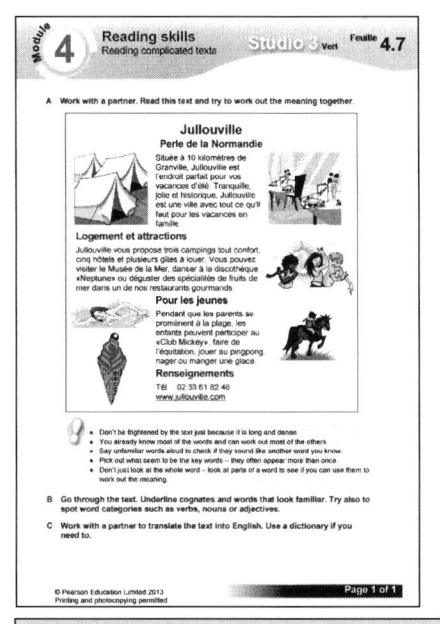

Answers

A (Answers will vary.)

B Cognates and familiar words:
située; kilomètres; vacances d'été; tranquille; jolie; historique; une ville; les vacances; famille; campings; hôtels; visiter le Musée; la Mer; danser à la discothèque; spécialités; restaurants; les jeunes; parents; participer; pingpong

C (Sample translation:)
Jullouville
Pearl of Normandy
Situated 10 kilometres from Granville, Jullouville is the perfect place for your summer holidays. Tranquil, pretty and historic, Jullouville is a town with everything you need for a family holiday.
Accommodation and attractions
Jullouville offers 3 luxury campsites, 5 hotels and several holiday homes to rent. You can visit the Sea Museum, go dancing in the 'Neptune' disco or try the local seafood specialities in one of our gourmet restaurants.
For young people
While parents go for a walk on the beach, children can go to the 'Mickey Club', go horse riding, play ping pong, swim or eat an ice cream.

Video

Episode 9: Les vacances (2)

The team continue their camping trip with a mountain-bike ride and a sailing lesson. Video worksheet 9 can be used in conjunction with this episode.

Answers to video worksheet (ActiveTeach)

1 A – Of the activities Samira promised, we haven't seen sailing and mountain biking yet.
– Mixed. Mehdi was bored; Marielle would have preferred a real safari.

2 A She got sunburnt (*j'ai pris un coup de soleil*).
B Lions!
C A frog and lots of birds.
D He's revolted (because it's fish with marshmallows).
E Mountain biking (*VTT*).

3 A It means that it was a disaster and frustrating.
B Hugo and Samira were going too slowly.
C Sailing. They are all pleased.

4 A Kévin.
B They get the boat ready (get it out of the shed, put the sail up) and put on their lifejackets.
C She is soaked because she fell in the water.

(Pupil Book pp. 86–87)

④ Bilan et Révisions

Bilan

Pupils use this checklist to review language covered in the module, working on it in pairs in class or on their own at home. Encourage them to follow up any areas of weakness they identify. There are Target Setting Sheets included in the Assessment Pack, and an opportunity for pupils to record their own levels and targets on the *J'avance* page in the Workbook, p. 48. You can also use the *Bilan* checklist as an end-of-module plenary option.

Révisions

These revision exercises can be used for assessment purposes or for pupils to practise before tackling the assessment tasks in the Assessment Pack.

Resources
Audio files:
59_Module4_Rev_Ex1.mp3
Workbooks:
Cahier d'exercices Vert, pages 44 & 45

---

1 C'est quelle activité? La réaction est positive ou négative? Complète le tableau. (1–5) (Listening L3)

Listening. Pupils copy out the grid. They listen to five conversations and identify the activity proposed, and whether the reaction to the question is positive or negative each time. They complete the grid with the details in English.

Audioscript Track 59

1 – Est-ce que tu voudrais faire un safari en Afrique?
– Pourquoi pas?
2 – Est-ce que tu voudrais habiter sur une île déserte?
– Quelle horreur!
3 – Est-ce que tu voudrais faire de la plongée sous-marine?
– Ce n'est pas mon truc.
4 – Est-ce que tu voudrais aller au pôle Nord?
– Tu rigoles!
5 – Est-ce que tu voudrais faire des sports extrêmes?
– Ouais! Cool!

Answers

	activity	☺	☹
1	safari in Africa	✓	
2	a desert island		✓
3	scuba diving		✓
4	North Pole		✓
5	extreme sports	✓	

2 En tandem. Fais trois conversations. Utilise les questions et les images. (Speaking L4)

Speaking. In pairs: pupils make up three conversations, using the questions and sets of picture prompts supplied. They take it in turn to ask and answer. A sample exchange is given.

3 Lis le texte. Choisis la bonne réponse aux questions. (Reading L5)

Reading. Pupils read the text, then identify who is being described in each question, using the options supplied.

Answers
1 a 2 c 3 d 4 b 5 e 6 f

4 À la base de loisirs. Écris des phrases. (Writing L3)

Writing. Pupils write sentences about what people did at the leisure park, using the picture prompts supplied.

Answers
1 J'ai fait **du VTT**.
2 J'ai **fait du canoë-kayak**.
3 Mon père a fait **de la voile**.
4 Ma mère a **fait de l'équitation**.
5 Ma soeur **a fait de l'escalade**.
6 Mon frère est allé **à la pêche**.

© Pearson Education Ltd 2013. Copying permitted for purchasing institution only. This material is not copyright free.

Bilan et Révisions Spécial vacances **4**

Workbook, pages 44 and 45

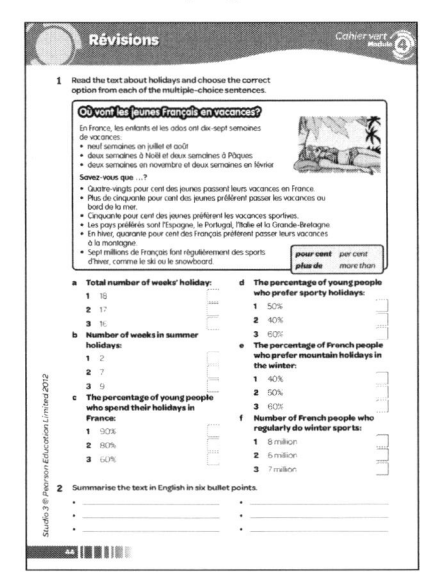

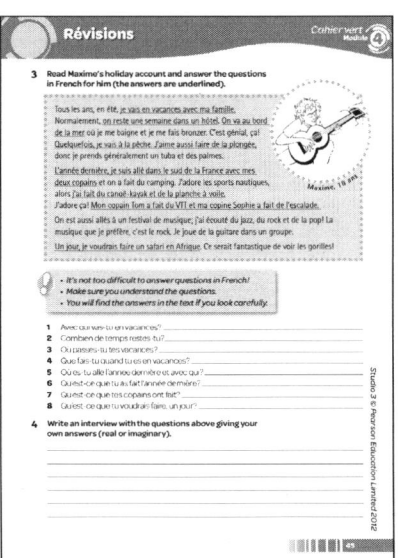

Answers

1 **a** 2 **b** 3 **c** 2 **d** 1 **e** 1 **f** 3

2 (Answers may include:)
- Young people in France have 17 weeks' holiday
- 80% of young people spend their holidays in France
- more than 50% prefer going to the seaside
- 50% prefer sporty holidays
- favourite countries for a holiday are Spain, Portugal, Italy and GB
- 40% of French people prefer mountain holidays in winter
- 7 million French people regularly do winter sports

3
- **a** Je vais en vacances avec ma famille.
- **b** On reste une semaine [optional: dans un hôtel].
- **c** On va au bord de la mer.
- **d** Quelquefois, je vais à la pêche. J'aime aussi faire de la plongée.
- **e** L'année dernière, je suis allé dans le sud de la France avec mes deux copains.
- **f** J'ai fait du canoë-kayak et j'ai aussi fait de la planche à voile.
- **g** Mon copain Tom a fait du VTT et ma copine Sophie a fait de l'escalade.
- **h** Un jour, je voudrais faire un safari en Afrique.

4 (Answers will vary.)

© Pearson Education Ltd 2013. Copying permitted for purchasing institution only. This material is not copyright free.

En plus: Des vacances au collège!

(4)

(Pupil Book pp. 88–89)

Learning objective
- Debating the idea of 'open school' in the holidays

Programme of Study references
LC1 Listening and responding
LC6 Reading comprehension
LC6 Translation into English
LC8 Writing creatively

FCSE links
Unit 2: Education and future plans (School: type of school)

Key language
Review of language from the module

PLTS
E Effective participators

Cross-curricular
ICT: using a presentation package
Citizenship: the role of school in the broader community

Resources
Audio files:
60_Module4_EnPlus_Ex1.mp3
61_Module4_EnPlus_Ex5.mp3
ActiveTeach:
p.089 Assignment 4
p.089 Assignment 4: prep

Starter

PLTS E

Aim
To introduce the topic.
Have a class discussion in English on what pupils do in the summer holidays when they don't go away. Elicit their opinions of the various options.

1 Écoute et lis. Choisis le bon titre en anglais pour le texte. (Listening L4)

Listening. Pupils listen to the feature about holiday activities at a French school, reading the text at the same time. They choose the correct title for the feature from the four options supplied. Draw pupils' attention to the tip box on reading strategies. *gratuity* is glossed for support.

Audioscript Track 60

Tu trouves les vacances scolaires un peu ennuyeuses? En France, on peut aller au collège pendant les grandes vacances!

Beaucoup de collèges restent ouverts en juillet et en août. Dans ces collèges, on peut faire toutes sortes d'activités. Et c'est gratuit!

Par exemple, on peut faire un stage avec les pilotes de l'air, visiter les studios d'une chaîne de télévision, ou enregistrer une chanson avec l'aide de musiciens professionnels!

En plus, on peut aussi faire des révisions pour la rentrée de septembre.

Alors, tu trouves que c'est une bonne idée?

Answer
C – Free holiday activities at school

2 Complète la traduction des phrases du texte. (Reading L4)

Reading. Pupils complete the translation of the sentences from the text, using reading strategies to try and work each one out. They then check their answers in the *Mini-dictionnaire* at the back of the Pupil Book. Draw their attention to the tip box on using context to work out meaning and to *Stratégie 4* on Pupil Book p. 95.

Answers
1 Do you find the school holidays a bit **boring**?
2 Lots of schools stay **open** in July and August.
3 You can do a **course** with pilots.
4 You can visit the studios of a **TV channel**.
5 You can record a **song** with the help of professional musicians.
6 You can also do some revision for the **return to school** in September.

3 Relis les phrases de l'exercice 2. Qu'est-ce que c'est en anglais? (Reading L4)

Reading. Pupils use the sentences in exercise 2 to translate the French phrases listed into English.

Answers
1 the school holidays
2 lots of schools
3 you can
4 pilots
5 record
6 do some revision

© Pearson Education Ltd 2013. Copying permitted for purchasing institution only. This material is not copyright free.

En plus: Des vacances au collège! Spécial vacances **4**

4 Trouve et corrige les cinq erreurs dans le résumé du texte. (Reading L4)

Reading. Pupils find and correct the five mistakes in the English summary of the exercise 1 text.

> **Answer**
>
> Some French schools stay open in the **summer** holidays. You can do all sorts of activities and **it is free**. For example, at one school you can do a **pilot** training course, visit a **TV channel** studio or record a song. You can also do some revision for the return to school in **September**.

5 Écoute. Note dans le tableau: l'activité, l'opinion et la raison. (1–4) (Listening L5)

Listening. Pupils copy out the grid. They listen to the four conversations and complete the grid in English with details of the activity, opinion and reason mentioned by each speaker.

Audioscript Track 61

1 – *Alex, tu as fait des activités au collège pendant les vacances scolaires …*
 – *Oui, c'est ça.*
 – *Qu'est-ce que tu as fait, comme activités?*
 – *Alors, … On a visité les studios d'une chaîne de télévision.*
 – *C'était comment?*
 – *C'était génial.*
 – *Ah bon? Pourquoi?*
 – *Parce que j'ai rencontré un de mes acteurs préférés.*

2 – *Et toi, Noëmie? Qu'est-ce que tu as fait comme activités au collège?*
 – *Moi, j'ai enregistré une chanson avec l'aide de musiciens professionnels!*
 – *Tu as aimé ça?*
 – *Ah oui, c'était super!*
 – *Pourquoi?*
 – *Parce que j'adore chanter! Un jour, je veux être chanteuse professionnelle.*

3 – *Salut, Malik. Qu'est-ce que tu as fait comme activités?*
 – *On a fait des révisions pour la rentrée. On a fait des révisions d'anglais, de français et de maths.*
 – *Des révisions? C'était intéressant?*
 – *Ah non, c'était ennuyeux.*
 – *Pourquoi c'était ennuyeux?*
 – *Parce que je déteste l'anglais, le français et les maths!*

4 – *Et finalement, Morgane. Qu'est-ce que tu as fait comme activités au collège?*
 – *J'ai fait un stage avec des pilotes de l'air.*
 – *Un stage avec des pilotes! Et c'était comment?*
 – *Alors, … c'était sympa.*
 – *C'était sympa? Alors, pourquoi c'était sympa?*

 – *Ben … Parce qu'ils étaient sympas, les pilotes.*
 – *Ils étaient beaux, aussi?*
 – *Ah oui, ils étaient beaux!*

Answers

	activity	😊 ☹	why?
1	b	😊	met one of his favourite actors
2	c	😊	loves singing/wants to be a professional singer one day
3	d	☹	hates English, French and maths
4	a	😊	the pilots were nice (and good-looking!)

6 En tandem. Imagine que tu as fait des activités au collège de l'exercice 1. Fais une conversation. (Speaking L5)

Speaking. In pairs: pupils imagine that they have done the school activities listed in exercise 1 and make up a conversation about it. A framework is supplied.

7 Imagine que ton collège va rester ouvert pendant les vacances. Écris un programme d'activités pour une semaine. (Writing L4)

Writing. Pupils imagine that their school is going to stay open during the holidays and write a programme of activities for one week. A sample opening is given.

Pupils could design this as a poster, adding pictures and using colour to sell the programme. This could be done on computer using a DTP package.

8 Imagine que tu as suivi le programme d'activités de ton collège. Écris un paragraphe. (Writing L5)

Writing. Pupils imagine that they followed the programme of activities at their school and write a paragraph about their experience. Draw pupils' attention to the tip box on improving their writing. A framework and a key language box are supplied.

Plenary

Ask some pupils to read aloud the programme of activities they wrote for exercise 7. Take a class vote by a show of hands on the most appealing programme.

© Pearson Education Ltd 2013. Copying permitted for purchasing institution only. This material is not copyright free.

4 Spécial vacances En plus: Des vacances au collège!

Worksheet 4.8 Le centre de vacances. Assignment 4: speaking

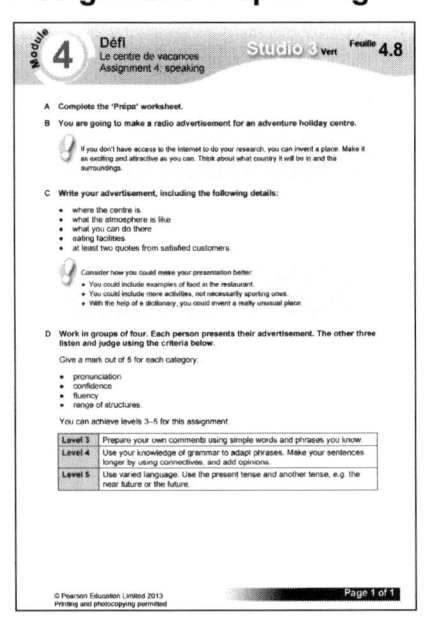

Answers

A 1 Blasimon is situated 100 kilometres from Bordeaux, in the south-west of France.

2 The activity centre welcomes individuals, families and (groups of) friends.

3 Sports activities available are climbing, archery, swimming, mini-golf, mountain biking, horse riding, windsurfing and waterskiing.

4 In the evening, you can eat in the restaurant.

5 Solange visited Blasimon with her two children.

6 Marc thought it was great.

B (Answers will vary.)

C (Answers will vary.)

Worksheet 4.9 Le centre de vacances: Prépa

© Pearson Education Ltd 2013. Copying permitted for purchasing institution only. This material is not copyright free.

(Pupil Book pp. 90–91)

4 J'écris

The challenge
- Writing a 100-word blog entry on your dream holiday

Overview
Explain how this section works.
- Pupils read the context and what they need to do to complete the challenge.
- They then read the list of suggested details to include. Explain that they should use this both to help structure their content and as a checklist as part of their final preparations.
- Explain that the exercises which follow in this section are structured to help them prepare for the extended writing task.
- Before starting, pupils read the POSM feature: this will help them to improve their performance. Encourage them to use this approach routinely in writing tasks.

Programme of Study references
GV3 Developing vocabulary
GV4 Accuracy (grammar; spelling; punctuation)
LC4 Expressing ideas (writing)
LC8 Writing creatively

1 Copy and complete these sentences, using suitable words from the umbrella. There are three 'red herrings'.

Pupils copy and complete the sentences, using the words supplied. The umbrella also contains three distractors.

Answers
1 Normalement, je passe mes vacances **au bord de la mer**.
2 Je vais en vacances avec ma **famille**.
3 Je reste **une semaine**.
4 Je fais de la **voile**.
5 Je me fais bronzer sur la **plage**.

2 Rewrite the sentences in exercise 1 to describe your own holidays. They don't have to be true!

Pupils rewrite the sentences in exercise 1 to describe their own holidays. They can invent the details if they wish.

3 Look at what Zoë takes on holiday and complete her list.

Pupils write Zoë's holiday packing list using the picture prompt.

Answers
de la crème solaire
du gel coiffant
un chargeur pour mon/son mp3
des lunettes de plongée
une bombe anti-insectes

4 Copy and complete each of these sentences with one of the items from Zoë's packing list.

Pupils copy and complete the sentences with appropriate items. Draw pupils' attention to the tip box on using *alors* and *donc* to create longer, more impressive sentences.

Answers
1 Je me baigne dans la mer, alors je prends **des lunettes de plongée**.
2 Je me douche et je me coiffe, donc je prends **du gel coiffant**.
3 J'écoute de la musique, alors je prends **un chargeur pour mon mp3**.
4 Je me fais bronzer, donc je prends **de la crème solaire**.
5 Je me fais piquer par des insectes, alors je prends **une bombe anti-insectes**.

5 Write out these sentences about what Samir did on his dream holiday and choose the correct picture for each one.

Pupils write out the sentences correctly and then match each sentence to the correct picture.

Answers
1 J'ai fait de la plongée. (c)
2 J'ai fait de l'équitation. (d)
3 J'ai fait de la planche à voile. (a)
4 Je suis allé à la pêche. (f)
5 J'ai mangé au restaurant. (b)
6 J'ai dansé toute la soirée. (e)

© Pearson Education Ltd 2013. Copying permitted for purchasing institution only. This material is not copyright free.

4 Spécial vacances J'écris

6 Use the words below to translate the following time expressions into French. Then add one of them to each of the sentences in exercise 5.

Pupils translate the English time expressions into French, using the words supplied. They then develop the sentences they wrote for exercise 5 by adding one of the time expressions to each of them. Draw pupils' attention to the tip box on how they can improve their writing by including time expressions like these.

Answers
1 lundi matin
2 mercredi après-midi
3 vendredi soir
4 samedi matin
5 hier soir

7 Write a sentence for your blog about something you would like to do one day. Look back at pages 78–79 for ideas.

Pupils write a sentence for their blog about something they would like to do one day, using Pupil Book pp. 78–79 for ideas.

8 Now write the blog from your dream holiday destination. Use your answers to the exercises to help you. Write four separate paragraphs, using the structure on the right.

Pupils write their blog in four paragraphs, using the language they have developed in the exercises. A framework is supplied. They might also find it useful to look again at the tips on Pupil Book p. 128.

9 Check what you have written for accuracy using the checklist at the bottom of page 25 and redraft your writing if necessary.

Pupils check their work, using the checklist at the bottom of Pupil Book p. 25. They then write a second draft if necessary, correcting any errors.

Studio Grammaire

(Pupil Book pp. 92–93)

The *Studio Grammaire* section provides a more detailed summary of the key grammar covered in the module, along with further exercises to practise these points. The activities on ActiveTeach pages 92 and 93 are repeated from elsewhere in the module.

Grammar topics
- asking questions using question words
- *je voudrais* + infinitive
- the perfect tense
- using the perfect tense to say what other people did

Asking questions using question words

1 Rewrite these questions using inversion. The words in bold are the ones you need to invert.

Pupils rewrite the questions using inversion. The words to be inverted are shown in bold.

> **Answers**
> 1 Où passes-tu tes vacances?
> 2 Avec qui vas-tu à Paris?
> 3 Combien de temps restes-tu en France?
> 4 vas-tu en France?
> 5 À quelle heure arrives-tu?

2 Rewrite these questions using *est-ce que*. The English translation is there to help you.

Pupils rewrite the inversion questions using *est-ce que*. The questions are translated into English for support.

> **Answers**
> 1 Où est-ce que tu habites?
> 2 Combien de temps est-ce que tu passes en France?
> 3 Avec qui est-ce que tu vas au cinéma?
> 4 Comment est-ce que tu vas au collège?
> 5 À quelle heure est-ce que tu commences le matin?

je voudrais + infinitive

3 Write five sentences to help Rémi say what he would like to do one day. Use an infinitive from the first bubble and choose a sentence ending from the second bubble that makes sense.

Pupils write five sentences, each using an infinitive and an appropriate sentence ending from those supplied.

> **Answers**
> Je voudrais aller à New York.
> Je voudrais faire du snowboard.
> Je voudrais habiter dans une grande maison.
> Je voudrais avoir une petite amie.
> Je voudrais être footballeur professionnel.

The perfect tense

4 Copy and complete the blog using the perfect tense. Remember that perfect tense verbs have two parts! Use each past participle given below once.

Pupils copy and complete the text with the correct form of *avoir* or *être* and the past participles supplied.

> **Answers**
> Je suis allé en colo au bord de la mer. J'ai fait de la plongée et j'**ai fait** de la voile. C'était génial! Mais un jour, je **suis allé** à la pêche et j'**ai pris** un coup de soleil. Quelle horreur! Puis j'**ai perdu/ai cassé** mon appareil photo et j'**ai perdu/ai cassé** mon portable. Finalement, j'**ai oublié** mon passeport et j'**ai raté** l'avion. Quel désastre!

Using the perfect tense to say what other people did

5 Copy out the sentences, choosing the correct part of *avoir* or *être*. Then translate the sentences.

Pupils write out the sentences, choosing the correct verb form from the two options given each time. They then translate the completed sentences into English.

> **Answers**
> 1 Je **suis** allé en France avec ma famille.
>   I went to France with my family.
> 2 J'**ai** fait de la plongée sous-marine.
>   I went scuba diving.
> 3 Tu **as** mangé quelque chose de mauvais.
>   You ate something bad.
> 4 Chloë **a** perdu son portemonnaie.
>   Chloë lost her purse.
> 5 Ma soeur est **allée** à la plage.
>   My sister went to the beach.
> 6 On est **allés** à Paris.
>   We went to Paris.
> 7 On **a** raté l'avion.
>   We missed the plane.
> 8 Le père de Samuel **est** allé en Espagne.
>   Samuel's father went to Spain.
> 9 **As**-tu cassé ton portable?
>   Have you broken/Did you break your mobile phone?
> 10 Je n'**ai** pas fait de la voile.
>   I didn't go sailing.

© Pearson Education Ltd 2013. Copying permitted for purchasing institution only. This material is not copyright free.

4 À toi

(Pupil Book pp. 122–123)

Self-access reading and writing

A Reinforcement

1 Lis les listes et regarde les images. Qu'est-ce que Rémi et Zoë ont oublié? (Reading L2)

Reading. Pupils read the lists and look at the pictures to identify what Rémi and Zoë have forgotten to pack.

> **Answers**
> **Rémi:** des palmes
> **Zoë:** de la crème solaire

2 Imagine que tu passes tes vacances dans une des destinations ci-dessous. Qu'est-ce que tu prends avec toi? (Writing L3)

Writing. Pupils imagine that they are spending their holidays at one of the destinations listed. They adapt and complete the sentence opening supplied by giving details of what they take with them. Draw their attention to the tip box on using a dictionary to look up new items they want to mention.

3 Lis les textes et réponds aux questions pour chaque personne. (Reading L4)

Reading. Pupils read the texts and answer all of the questions for Solène, Alban and Jérémy. The answer openings are supplied.

> **Answers**
> **Solène:**
> 1 Je passe mes vacances **au bord de la mer.**
> 2 Je vais en vacances avec **mes parents et mon frère.**
> 3 reste **quinze jours.**
> 4 **Je me baigne** (dans la mer) et (quelquefois) je fais de la plongée sous-marine.
> **Alban:**
> 1 Je passe mes vacances en colo, **à la montagne.**
> 2 Je vais en vacances avec **mes copains de classe.**
> 3 Je reste **dix jours.**
> 4 **Je fais de l'escalade ou du canoë-kayak.**
> **Jérémy:**
> 1 Je passe mes vacances **à la campagne.**
> 2 Je vais en vacances avec **mes grands-parents.**
> 3 Je reste **trois semaines.**
> 4 **Je vais à la pêche** (avec mon grand-père) et (l'après-midi) je fais de l'équitation.

B Extension

1 Trouve les paires de mots qui riment. (Reading L2)

Reading. Pupils find the pairs of words that rhyme.

> **Answers**
> en vacances – Marie-France
> de l'équitation – Simon
> du ski – Élodie
> au bord de la mer – mon frère
> en colo – Hugo
> du tir à l'arc – Jean-Marc
> de la plongée sous-marine – Justine
> du VTT – Chloé
> du canoë-kayak – Jean-Jacques
> à la base de loisirs – Samir

2 Écris un rap au sujet des vacances. Utilise tes réponses à l'exercice 1. (Writing L5)

Writing. Pupils use their answers to exercise 1 to write a rap about holidays. A sample opening is supplied. Draw pupils' attention to the tip box on how to say where they went and what they did.

3 Lis le texte. Utilise un dictionnaire, si nécessaire. Puis réponds aux questions par «oui» ou «non». (Reading L4)

Reading. Pupils read the text and answer the questions, using *oui* or *non*. They can use a dictionary.

> **Answer**
> 1 non 2 oui 3 non 4 oui 5 oui 6 non 7 oui

4 Imagine que tu as passé une semaine à la colo Ma Belle Corse. Qu'est-ce que tu as fait? C'était comment? Écris un paragraphe. (Writing L5)

Writing. Pupils imagine that they spent a week at *Ma Belle Corse* holiday camp and write a paragraph saying what they did and what it was like. A sample opening is supplied.

© Pearson Education Ltd 2013. Copying permitted for purchasing institution only. This material is not copyright free.

(Pupil Book pp. 96–115)

Module 5: Moi dans le monde

Unit & Learning objectives	Programme of Study references	Key language	Grammar and other language features
1 Mes droits (pp. 98–99) Discussing what you are allowed to do Using *j'ai le droit de* + infinitive	**GV2** Grammatical structures (*j'ai le droit de* + infinitive) **LC3** Conversation **LC6** Reading comprehension **LC4** Expressing ideas (writing)	*J'ai le droit …* *Je n'ai pas le droit …* *d'aller au MacDo avec mes copains* *de regarder la télé dans ma chambre* *de sortir seul(e)* etc.	**G** *avoir le droit de* + infinitive
2 Mes priorités (pp. 100–101) Explaining what's important to you Using mon, ma and mes	**GV2** Grammatical structures (*mon/ma/mes*) **GV3** Developing vocabulary **LC1** Listening and responding **LC3** Conversation	*Mes priorités sont …* *le foot* *la musique* *ma famille* *mes amis* etc. *Je n'aime pas du tout …* *le racisme* *la pauvreté dans le monde.* *la violence* etc.	**G** possessive adjectives – developing writing skills
3 Tu aimes le shopping? (pp. 102–103) Talking about things you buy Using three tenses together	**GV1** Tenses (present, perfect and near future) **LC1** Listening and responding **LC4** Expressing ideas (writing) **LC5** Accurate pronunciation and intonation	*J'achète…* *J'ai acheté…* *Je vais acheter…* *des jeux vidéo et des DVD* *des produits du commerce équitable* *des produits d'occasion* etc. *en général* *hier* *la semaine prochaine* etc.	**G** using three tenses together – developing speaking skills
4 Le bonheur, c'est … (pp. 104–105) Describing what makes you happy Using infinitives to mean '–ing'	**GV2** Grammatical structures (using infinitives to mean '–ing') **LC1** Listening and responding **LC6** Reading comprehension **LC6** Translation into English	*Pour moi, le bonheur, c'est…* *d'être en famille* *de danser* *de faire les magasins* *de jouer au foot* *de partir en vacances* etc.	**G** *c'est de* + the infinitive – developing writing skills

© Pearson Education Ltd 2013. Copying permitted for purchasing institution only. This material is not copyright free.

5 Moi dans le monde

Unit & Learning objectives	Programme of Study references	Key language	Grammar and other language features
Bilan et Révisions (pp. 106–107) Pupils' checklist and practice exercises			
En plus: Les jeunes contre l'injustice (pp. 108–109) Learning about human rights issues	**LC3** Conversation **LC4** Expressing ideas (writing) **LC6** Reading comprehension **LC8** Writing creatively	Review of language from the module	– developing reading strategies
Je parle (pp. 110–111) Extended speaking practice	**GV1** Tenses (past, present and future) **LC4** Expressing ideas (speaking) **LC5** Speaking coherently and confidently	Review of language from the module	– developing speaking skills – checking your work
Studio Grammaire (pp. 112–113) Detailed grammar summary and practice exercises			**G** avoir **G** possessive adjectives **G** using a variety of structures **G** using different time frames: which tense to use?
À toi (pp. 124–125) Self-access reading and writing at two levels			

© Pearson Education Ltd 2013. Copying permitted for purchasing institution only. This material is not copyright free.

1 Mes droits

(5)

(Pupil Book pp. 98–99)

Learning objectives
- Discussing what you are allowed to do
- Using *j'ai le droit de* + infinitive

Programme of Study references
GV2 Grammatical structures (*j'ai le droit de* + infinitive)
LC3 Conversation
LC6 Reading comprehension
LC4 Expressing ideas (writing)

FCSE links
Unit 1: Relationships, family and friends (Good and bad relations; Issues; Taking sides)

Grammar
- *avoir le droit de* + infinitive

Key language
J'ai le droit …
Je n'ai pas le droit …
d'aller au MacDo avec mes copains
d'aller sur des forums
d'aller sur Facebook
de jouer à des jeux vidéo le soir
de regarder la télé dans ma chambre
de sortir avec mes copains le weekend
de sortir seul(e)
de surfer sur Internet une heure par jour

PLTS
T Team workers

Cross-curricular
ICT: using a presentation package
PSHE: personal well-being

Resources
Audio files:
62_Module5_Unit1_Ex1.mp3
63_Module5_Unit1_Ex2.mp3
Workbooks:
Cahier d'exercices Vert, page 49
ActiveTeach:
Starter 1 resource
Starter 2 resource
p.098 Flashcards
p.098 Grammar
p.098 Grammar practice
p.099 Video 10
p.099 Video worksheet 10
p.098 Thinking skills
ActiveLearn:
Listening, Reading

Starter 1
Aim
To review infinitives

Photocopy the wordsearch below – one copy for each pair of pupils. Explain that it contains 12 infinitives. Ask pupils what endings infinitives have, then write up *–er*, *–ir* and *–re* for reference.

Give pairs four minutes to circle and list as many infinitives as they can.

a	ê	t	r	e	m	r	b
c	d	r	e	l	t	a	o
h	a	a	g	n	a	t	i
e	n	v	a	l	l	e	r
t	s	o	r	t	i	r	e
e	e	i	d	e	w	p	i
r	r	r	e	s	s	a	c
f	a	i	r	e	u	o	j

Ask pupils to swap and check the list of another pair. Reward the pair who have found the most correct answers.
(**Answers:** horizontally: *être, aller, sortir, casser, faire, jouer* vertically: *acheter, danser, avoir, regarder, rater, boire*)

Alternative Starter 1:
Use ActiveTeach p.098 Flashcards to introduce language for saying what you're allowed to do.

1 Écoute et écris la bonne lettre. (1–8)
(Listening L4)

Listening. Pupils listen to eight teenagers talking about what they are allowed/not allowed to do by their parents. For each they note the letter of the correct picture.

Audioscript Track 62

1 *Moi, j'ai le droit de sortir seule.*
2 *Moi, j'ai le droit d'aller au MacDo avec mes copains.*
3 *J'ai le droit de surfer sur Internet une heure par jour.*
4 *Je n'ai pas le droit d'aller sur Facebook.*
5 *Je n'ai pas le droit de jouer à des jeux vidéo le soir.*
6 *Moi, j'ai le droit de sortir avec mes copains le weekend.*
7 *J'ai le droit de regarder la télé dans ma chambre.*
8 *Je n'ai pas le droit d'aller sur des forums.*

Answers
1 b **2** c **3** d **4** g **5** f **6** a **7** e **8** h

© Pearson Education Ltd 2013. Copying permitted for purchasing institution only. This material is not copyright free.

5 Moi dans le monde 1 Mes droits

Studio Grammaire: *avoir le droit de* + infinitive

Use the *Studio Grammaire* box to review *avoir le droit de* + infinitive and the verb *avoir* (present tense singular). There is more information and further practice on Pupil Book p. 112.

2 Écoute. Copie et complète le tableau en anglais. (1–4) (Listening L4)

Listening. Pupils copy out the grid. They listen to four teenagers talking about what they are allowed/not allowed to do by their parents and complete the grid with the details in English.

Audioscript Track 63

1 – Tu as le droit de sortir seule, Amara?
– Moi, j'ai le droit de sortir seule, mais je n'ai pas le droit d'aller sur Facebook.
2 – Tu as le droit d'aller au MacDo avec tes copains, Alexis?
– Oui, j'ai le droit d'aller au MacDo avec mes copains, mais je n'ai pas le droit d'aller sur des forums.
3 – Tu as le droit de sortir avec tes copains le weekend, Jonathan?
– Moi, j'ai le droit de sortir avec mes copains le weekend, mais je n'ai pas le droit de jouer à des jeux vidéo le soir.
4 – Tu as le droit de surfer sur Internet, Simon?
– J'ai le droit de surfer sur Internet une heure par jour maximum, mais je n'ai pas le droit de regarder la télé dans ma chambre.

Answers

	is allowed to …	is not allowed to …
1 Amara	go out by herself	go on Facebook
2 Alexis	go to McDonald's with her friends	go on forums
3 Jonathan	go out with friends at the weekend	play video games in the evening
4 Simon	surf the net one hour per day (maximum)	watch TV in his room

3 En tandem. Fais trois dialogues. Change les mots soulignés. (Speaking L4)

PLTS T

Speaking. In pairs: pupils make up three dialogues using the word and picture prompts, by changing the underlined text in the model. They take it in turn to ask and answer.

Starter 2

Aim

To review language for expressing what you are allowed to do

Write up the following. Give pupils two minutes to identify what they are allowed to do.

J'ai le droit de/d' …

1 sortir avec mes copains le weekend
2 jouer à des jeux vidéo le soir
3 aller au MacDo avec mes copains
4 sortir seul(e)
5 aller sur des forums
6 aller sur Facebook
7 regarder la télé dans ma chambre
8 surfer sur Internet une heure par jour

Find out how many pupils have each right by asking for a show of hands. Ask pupils to explain in English why they don't have some of the rights and whether they think the restrictions are justified.

Alternative Starter 2:

Use ActiveTeach p.098 Grammar practice to review and practise expressions with *avoir*.

4 Écris correctement les questions. (Writing L4)

Writing. Pupils write out each jumbled question correctly.

Answers

1 Tu as le droit de sortir avec tes copains le weekend?
2 Tu as le droit de surfer sur Internet tous les soirs?
3 Tu as le droit d'aller au MacDo avec tes copains?
4 Tu as le droit de jouer à des jeux vidéo le soir?
5 Tu as le droit de sortir seul?
6 Tu as le droit d'aller sur Facebook?

R The pupils work in pairs, asking and answering the questions for themselves.

5 Fais un sondage en classe. Pose les questions de l'exercice 4 à cinq personnes. (Speaking L4)

Speaking. Pupils carry out a class survey, asking five people the questions in exercise 4.

R Pupils could compile their results on computer using a presentation package.

© Pearson Education Ltd 2013. Copying permitted for purchasing institution only. This material is not copyright free.

1 Mes droits Moi dans le monde

6 Lis le texte. Trouve l'équivalent des expressions en anglais dans le texte. (Reading L4)

Reading. Pupils read the text, then find in it the French versions of the English expressions listed. *ni* is glossed for support.

Answers
1 Mes parents me traitent comme un enfant.
2 Je suis responsable et assez indépendant.
3 Ce n'est pas juste.
4 Essaie de respecter la décision de tes parents.
5 un mauvais bulletin scolaire
6 Ce n'est pas la peine!

7 Relis le texte. C'est vrai (V) ou faux (F)? (Reading L4)

Reading. Pupils read the exercise 6 text again, then decide whether each sentence is true (writing V) or false (writing F).

Answers
1 V 2 V 3 F 4 F 5 V

8 Écris une lettre à Sylvie pour expliquer tes problèmes. (Writing L4)

Writing. Pupils write a letter to Sylvie explaining their own problems. Encourage them to be inventive. A framework is supplied.

Plenary
Ask what form of the verb is used after *J'ai le droit de …*, eliciting examples of the infinitive.

Challenge the class to remember all of the rights discussed in this unit, prompting in English as necessary.

Ask a few pupils to read out their letters to Sylvie. Ask the rest of the class to respond with advice from Sylvie in English.

Workbook, page 49

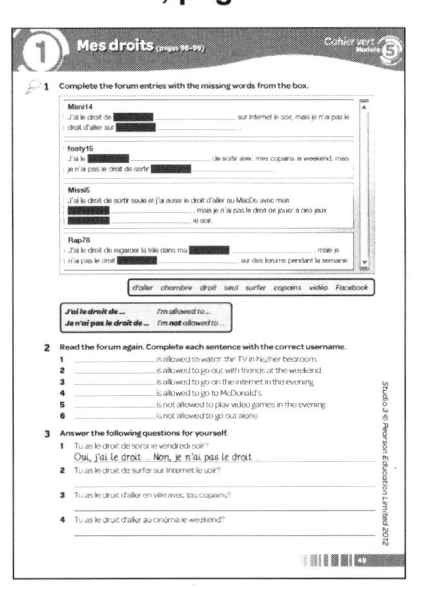

Answers
1 *Mimi 14:* J'ai le droit de **surfer** sur Internet le soir mais je n'ai pas le droit d'aller sur **Facebook**.
Footy15: J'ai le **droit** de sortir avec mes copains pendant le weekend mais je n'ai pas le droit de sortir **seul**.
Missi5: J'ai le droit de sortir seule et j'ai aussi le droit d'aller au MacDo avec mes **copains**, mais je n'ai pas le droit de jouer à des jeux **vidéo** le soir.
Rap78: J'ai le droit de regarder la télé dans ma **chambre** mais je n'ai pas le droit **d'aller** sur des forums pendant la semaine.

2 1 Rap78 2 Footy15 3 Mimi14 4 Missi5
   5 Missi5 6 Footy15

3 (Answers will vary.)

© Pearson Education Ltd 2013. Copying permitted for purchasing institution only. This material is not copyright free.

5 Moi dans le monde 1 Mes droits

Worksheet 5.1 Unravelling texts

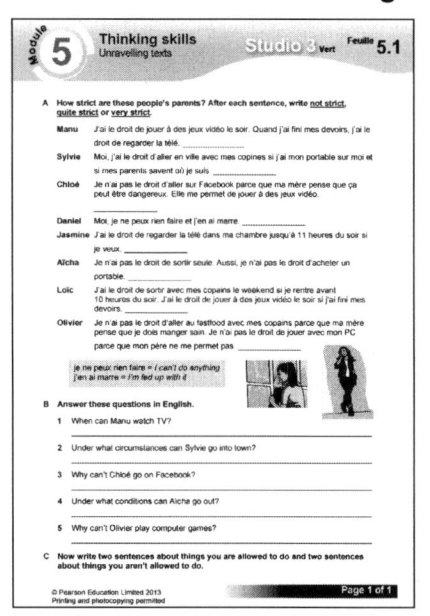

Answers

A Manu: not strict
   Sylvie: quite strict
   Chloé: quite strict
   Daniel: very strict
   Jasmine: not strict
   Aïcha: very strict
   Loïc: quite strict
   Olivier: very strict

B 1 When he has finished his homework.
   2 If she has her mobile with her and her parents know where she is.
   3 Her mother thinks it can be dangerous.
   4 Only if she's not alone.
   5 His father doesn't allow it.

C (Answers will vary.)

Video

Episode 10: Mes droits

The team remember the time when they carried out a survey of local adolescents, to discover what they were allowed to do in their free time. Video worksheet 10 can be used in conjunction with this episode.

Answers to video worksheet (ActiveTeach)

1 A Suggestions may include: going out; having friends round; staying up until a certain time; using phones and computers, etc.

2 A It's great.
  B Skimming stones on the water.
  C Marielle says she can sunbathe (*je peux bronzer*) and Samira says she can eat ice cream three times a day (*je peux manger des glaces trois fois par jour*).

3 A She's allowed to go out with her friends at the weekend but not in the evening.
  B She thinks that's normal.
  C Hugo.
  D Watch TV.
  E No. One girl refuses to be interviewed.
  F She isn't allowed to have a mobile phone.
  G They think her parents shouldn't be so protective (*ses parents ont tort de la protéger comme ça!*).

4 A A group of young people.
  B McDonald's.
  C Play video games.
  D Laughing with friends.
  E Go for a cola with her.

5 A She means he is the 'love of [her] life'.
  B Have an ice cream.

© Pearson Education Ltd 2013. Copying permitted for purchasing institution only. This material is not copyright free.

(Pupil Book pp. 100–101)

⑤ 2 Mes priorités

Learning objectives
- Explaining what's important to you
- Using *mon*, *ma* and *mes*

Programme of Study references
GV2 Grammatical structures (*mon/ma/mes*)
GV3 Developing vocabulary
LC1 Listening and responding
LC3 Conversation

FCSE links
Unit 7: Local area and environment (Preferences; Environment; Recycling)

Grammar
- possessive adjectives

Key language
Mes priorités sont ...
le foot
la musique
la santé
l'argent
mon chien
ma famille
mes amis
mes études
Je n'aime pas du tout ...
le racisme
la cruauté envers les animaux
la pauvreté dans le monde
la violence
l'état de la planète

PLTS
E Effective participators

Cross-curricular
ICT: internet research
PSHE: diverse values in society; personal well-being

Resources
Audio files:
64_Module5_Unit2_Ex1.mp3
65_Module5_Unit2_Ex6.mp3
Workbooks:
Cahier d'exercices Vert, page 50
ActiveTeach:
Starter 2 resource
p.100 Flashcards (a)
p.100 Flashcards (b)
p.100 Grammar
p.100 Grammar practice
ActiveLearn:
Listening, Reading
Grammar, Vocabulary

Starter 1
Aim
To predict vocabulary in a new topic
Tell the class that this unit is about the priorities of young people: what is important to them and what they are concerned about. Ask pupils what kind of language they think will come up. Explain that predicting is a useful strategy in language learning as it puts learners in a stronger position to work out new words in context.

Alternative Starter 1:
Use ActiveTeach p.100 Flashcards (a) to introduce language for talking about what's important to you and ActiveTeach p.100 Flashcards (b) to introduce language for talking about what concerns you.

1 Qui est-ce? Écoute et écris le bon prénom. (1–4) (Listening L4)
Listening. Pupils listen to four teenagers talking about the priorities in their lives and use the pictures to identify who is speaking each time.

Audioscript Track 64
1 – Quelles sont tes priorités dans la vie?
 – Mes priorités sont d'abord ma famille, ensuite mes amis et puis aussi mon chien. Je n'aime pas du tout la cruauté envers les animaux. J'ai horreur de ça.
2 – Quelles sont tes priorités dans la vie?
 – Mes priorités sont d'abord l'argent et ensuite, mes études. Je n'aime pas du tout l'état de la planète. Ça m'inquiète.
3 – Quelles sont tes priorités dans la vie?
 – Mes priorités sont le foot, et puis le foot et ... ah oui, le foot! Je n'aime pas du tout ni la violence, ni le racisme.
4 – Quelles sont tes priorités dans la vie?
 – Mes priorités sont d'abord la santé et puis la musique. Je n'aime pas du tout la pauvreté dans le monde. Je trouve ça injuste.

Answers
1 Zahra 2 Lucas 3 Karima 4 Manu

Studio Grammaire: possessive adjectives
Use the *Studio Grammaire* box to review possessive adjectives (*mon/ma/mes, ton/ta/tes*). There is more information and further practice on Pupil Book p. 112.

Pupils work in pairs to make different phrases from those in the *Studio Grammaire*

© Pearson Education Ltd 2013. Copying permitted for purchasing institution only. This material is not copyright free.

5 Moi dans le monde 2 Mes priorités

box, using these possessive adjectives and a different appropriate noun each time.
mon ... ma ... mes ...
ton ... ta ... tes ...

2 Copie les titres. Fais une liste de tes priorités dans la vie. (Writing L4)

Writing. Pupils copy out the headings (*Mes priorités sont/Je n'aime pas du tout*) then list under them their own priorities and what they object to. Draw pupils' attention to the tip box on using a dictionary to make their response as personal as they can. Suggest they add this advice to their Skills Notebook.

3 En tandem. Fais trois dialogues. (Speaking L4)

Speaking. In pairs: pupils make up three dialogues using the picture prompts. A framework is supplied. They take it in turn to ask and answer.

> **Starter 2**
> **Aim**
> To review language for talking about priorities and issues of concern
> Write up the following, replacing the scored-through text with a line each time. Give pupils three minutes to copy and complete the phrases.
>
> | *Mes priorités sont ...* | *Je n'aime pas du tout ...* |
> |---|---|
> | ~~les animaux~~. | l'état de la ~~planète~~. |
> | ~~mes~~ amis. | la ~~pauvreté~~ dans le ~~monde~~. |
> | l'~~argent~~. | la ~~violence~~. |
> | le ~~sport~~. | le ~~racisme~~. |
> | la ~~musique~~. | la ~~cruauté~~ envers les animaux. |
>
> Check answers.
> **Alternative Starter 2:**
> Use ActiveTeach p.100 Grammar practice to review and practise possessive adjectives.

4 Lis le texte. Quelles photos ne sont pas mentionnées? (Reading L5)

Reading. Pupils read the text, then note the letters of the pictures which are not mentioned in it. Some vocabulary is glossed for support.

> **Answers**
> e, g

The pupils work in pairs, asking and answering the questions for themselves.

5 Relis le texte et choisis le bon mot pour compléter chaque phrase. (Reading L5)

Reading. Pupils read the exercise 4 text again, then complete each sentence by choosing the correct option from the two given.

> **Answers**
> 1 Les priorités de Chloé sont d'abord sa famille, ensuite ses amis et puis **les animaux**.
> 2 Elle n'aime pas du tout la cruauté envers **les animaux**.
> 3 Elle est membre **du WWF**.
> 4 Sa famille a adopté **un ours polaire**.
> 5 On fait le «Pandathlon» pour **collecter de l'argent**.
> 6 Chloé pense que travailler au WWF serait **super**.

Pupils could look up the French WWF site and find out in French the words for five more endangered animals. Encourage them to research and use information like this to personalise their own speaking and writing.

6 Écoute Loïc. Complète le texte en anglais. (Listening L4)

Listening. Pupils listen to Loïc talking about his priorities and the things he objects to. They then complete the gap-fill text in English. *les droits de l'enfant* is glossed for support.

> **Audioscript Track 65**
>
> Je m'appelle Loïc et mes priorités dans la vie sont: d'abord, mes amis, ensuite le foot et puis mes études.
>
> Je n'aime pas du tout la pauvreté dans le monde. Je déteste ça, alors j'ai décidé de devenir membre de l'UNICEF qui protège les droits de l'enfant partout dans le monde.

> **Answers**
> 1 friends 2 football 3 his studies
> 4 world poverty 5 world

7 Imagine que tu es Khadija ou Olivier. Écris un paragraphe sur tes priorités dans la vie et ce que tu n'aimes pas. (Writing L4–5)

Writing. Pupils imagine that they are Khadija or Olivier and write a paragraph on their priorities and what they object to, using the prompts. A framework is supplied. Remind pupils to include extra details that will help distinguish their answers from other people's.

© Pearson Education Ltd 2013. Copying permitted for purchasing institution only. This material is not copyright free.

2 Mes priorités Moi dans le monde

Plenary

PLTS E

Ask pupils to read aloud sentences from the texts they wrote in exercise 7. Ask the rest of the class to give constructive feedback on the accuracy of the French. Reward the sentences which include an extra detail.

Workbook, page 50

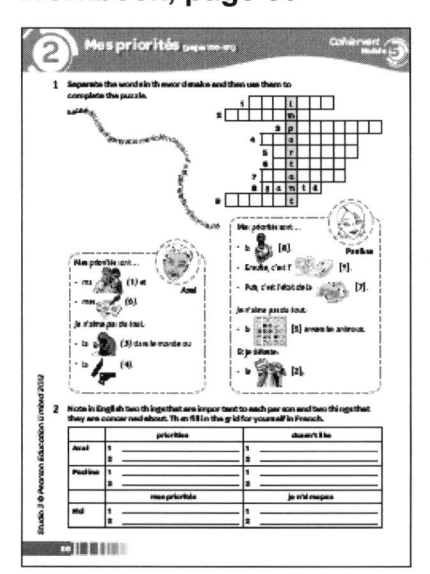

Answers

1 1 famille 2 racisme 3 pauvreté 4 violence 5 cruauté 6 études 7 planète 8 santé 9 argent

2

	priorities	doesn't like
Axel	1 family 2 studies	1 poverty 2 violence
Pauline	1 health 2 money/state of planet	1 cruelty to animals 2 racism
	mes priorités	je n'aime pas
Moi	(Answers will vary.)	(Answers will vary.)

3 Tu aimes le shopping?

(5)

(Pupil Book pp. 102–103)

Learning objectives
- Talking about things you buy
- Using three tenses together

Programme of Study references
GV1 Tenses (present, perfect and near future)
LC1 Listening and responding
LC4 Expressing ideas (writing)
LC5 Accurate pronunciation and intonation

FCSE links
Unit 7: Local area and environment (Preferences)

Grammar
- using three tenses together

Key language
J'achète …
J'ai acheté …
Je vais acheter …
des jeux vidéo et des DVD
des vêtements ou des chaussures
des produits du commerce équitable
des produits d'occasion
des produits écolos
des produits que j'aime
en général
hier
le weekend dernier
la semaine dernière
demain
le weekend prochain
la semaine prochaine

PLTS
R Reflective learners

Cross-curricular
PSHE: social aspects of financial issues

Resources
Audio files:
66_Module5_Unit3_Ex1.mp3
67_Module5_Unit3_Ex3.mp3
68_Module5_Unit3_Ex5.mp3
Workbooks:
Cahier d'exercices Vert, page 51
ActiveTeach:
Starter 1 resource
Starter 2 resource
p.103 Grammar
p.103 Grammar practice
p.103 Class activity
p.103 Grammar skills
p.103 Learning skills
p.103 Thinking skills
ActiveLearn:
Listening, Reading
Grammar, Vocabulary

Starter 1

Aim

To use reading strategies

Write up the following. Give pupils three minutes working in pairs to match the French and English.

1 des produits écolos
2 des jeux vidéo et des DVD
3 des produits du commerce équitable
4 des vêtements ou des chaussures
5 des produits d'occasion
6 des produits que j'aime

a video games and DVDs
b clothes or shoes
c fair-trade products
d second-hand products
e products that I like
f 'green' products

Check answers, asking pupils which reading strategies they used to work them out (previous knowledge, grammar knowledge, cognates, process of elimination, etc.).
(**Answers:** 1 f, 2 a, 3 c, 4 b, 5 d, 6 e)

1 Écoute et écris la bonne lettre. (1–6)
(Listening L4)

Listening. Pupils listen to six teenagers talking about what they buy when they go shopping. For each they write the letter of the correct picture. Some vocabulary is glossed for support.

Audioscript Track 66

1 – *Quand tu fais du shopping, qu'est-ce que tu achètes?*
  – *J'achète des vêtements ou des chaussures.*
2 – *Quand tu fais du shopping, qu'est-ce que tu achètes?*
  – *J'achète des produits écolos.*
3 – *Quand tu fais du shopping, qu'est-ce que tu achètes?*
  – *J'achète des produits que j'aime.*
4 – *Quand tu fais du shopping, qu'est-ce que tu achètes?*
  – *J'achète des jeux vidéo et des DVD.*
5 – *Quand tu fais du shopping, qu'est-ce que tu achètes?*
  – *J'achète des produits du commerce équitable.*
6 – *Quand tu fais du shopping, qu'est-ce que tu achètes?*
  – *J'achète des produits d'occasion.*

Answers
1 f 2 a 3 d 4 c 5 b 6 e

2 En tandem. Joue! Fais la plus longue phrase possible! (Speaking L4)

Speaking. In pairs: pupils play a game. They take it in turn to ask and answer the question *Quand tu fais du shopping, qu'est-ce que tu achètes?* When they reply, they try to make the longest sentence they can. A sample exchange is given. Draw

© Pearson Education Ltd 2013. Copying permitted for purchasing institution only. This material is not copyright free.

3 Tu aimes le shopping? Moi dans le monde **5**

pupils' attention to the tip box on pronouncing the question.

3 Écoute. Copie et complète le tableau en anglais. (1–3) (Listening L4)

Listening. Pupils copy out the grid. Remind them of the meanings of *souvent* and *quelquefois*, which are glossed for support. They listen to three teenagers talking about what they buy when they go shopping and complete the grid with the details in English.

Audioscript Track 67

1 – *Rémi, quand tu fais du shopping, qu'est-ce que tu achètes?*
   – *Moi, j'achète souvent des jeux vidéo et des DVD et quelquefois, j'achète des produits écolos.*
2 – *Aïcha, quand tu fais du shopping, qu'est-ce que tu achètes?*
   – *Moi, j'achète souvent des vêtements ou des chaussures et quelquefois, j'achète des produits d'occasion.*
3 – *Gabriel, quand tu fais du shopping, qu'est-ce que tu achètes?*
   – *Moi, j'achète souvent des produits du commerce équitable et quelquefois, j'achète des produits que j'aime.*

Answers

	often buys …	sometimes buys …
1 Rémi	video games and DVDs	green products
2 Aïcha	clothes or shoes	second-hand products
3 Gabriel	fair-trade products	products that he likes

4 Écris les phrases. (Writing L4)

Writing. Pupils use the picture prompts and time expressions to write sentences.

Answers

1 *J'achète souvent des produits écolos et quelquefois, j'achète des produits d'occasion.*
2 *J'achète souvent des vêtements ou des chaussures et quelquefois, j'achète des jeux vidéo et des DVD.*
3 *J'achète souvent des produits du commerce équitable et quelquefois, j'achète des produits que j'aime.*

Starter 2

Aim

To distinguish between tenses

Write up the following, omitting the underline (used to indicate the answers). Give pupils three minutes to work out the odd one out in each grouping.

1 *elle a acheté   je suis allée   je vais manger   on a raté*
2 *tu vas aller   je bois   je vais acheter   on va regarder*
3 *on sort   il casse   j'achète   j'ai acheté*

Check answers, asking pupils to explain their choices (in each group there is one verb in a different tense). Also accept plausible alternatives. Ask pupils to identify the tense of all the verbs used and to translate each verb into English.

Alternative Starter 2:

Use ActiveTeach p.103 Class activity to practise talking about shopping using three tenses, or p.103 Grammar practice to practise using three tenses.

5 Écoute et lis les textes (1–4). (Listening L6)

Listening. Pupils listen to four teenagers talking about their shopping habits, and read the texts at the same time. Some vocabulary is glossed for support.

Audioscript Track 68

1 **Adrien**
En général, j'achète des produits que j'aime. J'aime faire mon choix. C'est important pour moi. Hier, par exemple, j'ai acheté du crédit pour mon portable. La semaine prochaine, je vais acheter un mp3. Génial!

2 **Samir**
J'aime faire du shopping parce que j'adore la mode. En général, j'achète des vêtements d'occasion. Le weekend dernier, j'ai acheté un tee-shirt d'occasion et demain, je vais acheter des chaussures.

3 **Lola**
En général, j'achète des produits écolos parce que l'environnement, c'est une de mes priorités. Le weekend dernier, j'ai acheté un sac fabriqué avec des canettes de boissons gazeuses recyclées. C'est cool! La semaine prochaine, je vais acheter du papier recyclé.

4 **Fifi**
En général, je n'achète pas beaucoup de choses. Je recycle et je réutilise les choses. Le weekend dernier, je n'ai rien acheté et la semaine prochaine, je ne vais rien acheter!

© Pearson Education Ltd 2013. Copying permitted for purchasing institution only. This material is not copyright free.

5 Moi dans le monde 3 Tu aimes le shopping?

R Pupils identify and write the possessive forms in the text, labelling them with the correct gender, e.g. *mon choix* – masculine.

Studio Grammaire: using three tenses

Use the *Studio Grammaire* box to cover using three tenses in the same piece of work: the present, perfect and near future tenses. There is more information and further practice on Pupil Book p. 113

6 Relis les textes. Copie le tableau. Qui achète quoi? Écris les lettres dans la bonne colonne. (Reading L6)

Reading. Pupils read the exercise 5 texts again. They copy out the grid and complete it by writing the letter of each picture in the correct column. Draw pupils' attention to the tip box on identifying tenses.

Answers

	has bought	usually buys	is going to buy
1 Adrien	h	f	b
2 Samir	a	j	d
3 Lola	c	i	e
4 Fifi	g	g	g

+ Pupils choose a person from exercise 6 and use the information in the grid to write three sentences in the 3rd person about that person's purchases, using the perfect, present and near future tenses appropriately. You could also introduce and practise simple question forms in different tenses, e.g. *Qu'est-ce que tu as acheté le weekend dernier? Qu'est-ce que tu vas acheter le weekend prochain?*

7 Écris un paragraphe sur tes achats. (Writing L6)

Writing. Pupils write a paragraph on their own shopping habits. A list of features to include is supplied, along with a framework..

Plenary

PLTS R

Ask pupils which tense they find most difficult to use, eliciting details of whether it is how the tense is formed or when to use it that causes the difficulties. Tell them to look back through the unit and note down examples of sentences featuring the tense (including time expressions).

They should try to memorise these, asking a friend or family member to test them. Explain that this will give them a very clear model in their head when they come to use the tense in their speaking or writing.

Agree with the class a different action for each of the tenses (e.g. perfect = face the back of the class, present = put your hands on your head, future = move arms as though doing breast stroke). Read out sentences about different purchases, using *j'achète, j'ai acheté* and *je vais acheter* in random order: pupils respond with the correct action.

Continue the game, this time asking pupils to take it in turn to give the instructions.

Workbook, page 51

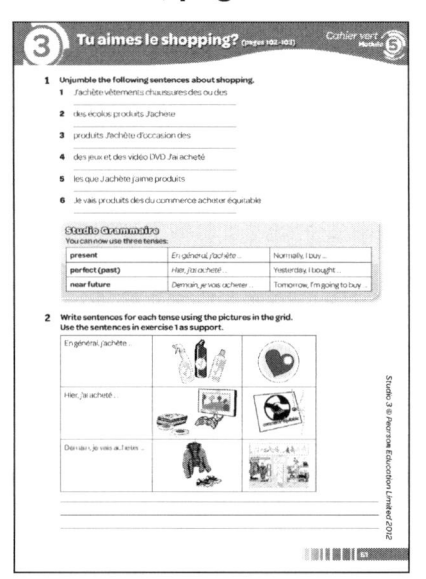

Answers

1 1 J'achète des vêtements ou des chaussures.

  2 J'achète des produits écolos.

  3 J'achète des produits d'occasion.

  4 J'ai acheté des jeux vidéo et des DVD.

  5 'achète les produits que j'aime.

  6 Je vais acheter des produits du commerce équitable.

2 En général, j'achète des produits écolos et les produits que j'aime.
Hier, j'ai acheté des jeux vidéo et des DVD. J'ai aussi acheté des produits du commerce équitable. Demain, je vais acheter des vêtements et des chaussures. Je vais aussi acheter des produits/ vêtements d'occasion.

© Pearson Education Ltd 2013. Copying permitted for purchasing institution only. This material is not copyright free.

3 Tu aimes le shopping? Moi dans le monde 5

Worksheet 5.2 Using three tenses

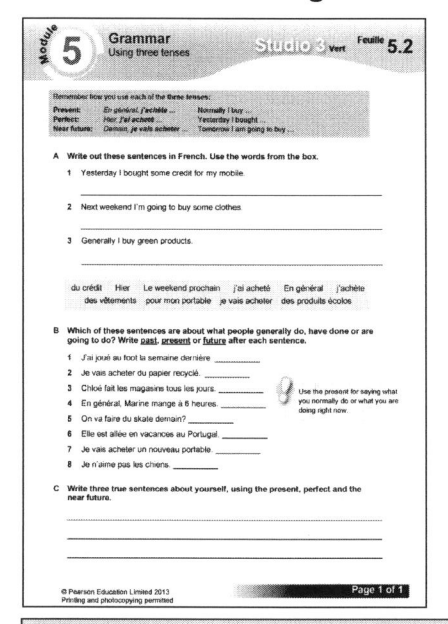

Answers

A 1 Hier, j'ai acheté du crédit pour mon portable.

2 Le weekend prochain, je vais acheter des vêtements.

3 En général, j'achète des produits écolos.

B 1 past **2** future **3** present **4** present
5 future **6** past **7** future **8** present

C (Answers will vary.)

Worksheet 5.3 Interpreting texts

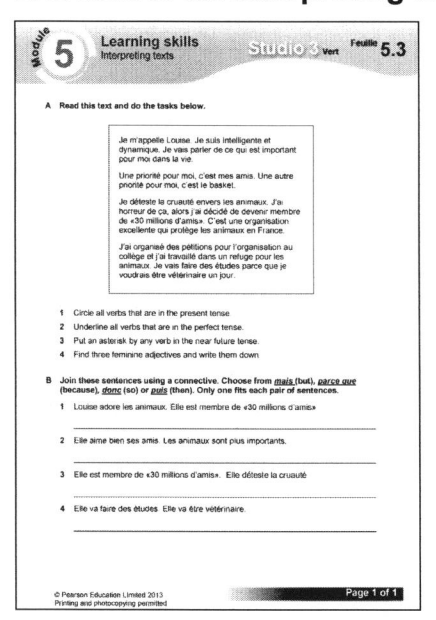

Answers

A 1–3

Je m'appelle Louise. Je suis intelligente et dynamique. Je vais parler* de ce qui est important pour moi dans la vie.
Une priorité pour moi, c'est mes amis. Une autre priorité pour moi, c'est le basket.
Je déteste la cruauté envers les animaux. J'ai horreur de ça, alors j'ai décidé de devenir membre de «30 millions d'amis». C'est une organisation excellente qui protège les animaux en France.
J'ai organisé des pétitions pour l'organisation au collège et j'ai travaillé dans un refuge pour les animaux. Je vais faire* des études parce que je voudrais être vétérinaire un jour.

4 The three feminine adjectives are *intelligente*, *dynamique* and *excellente*.

B 1 Louise adore les animaux, **donc** elle est member de «30 millions d'amis».

2 Elle aime bien ses amis **mais** les animaux sont plus importants.

3 Elle est membre de « 30 millions d'amis » **parce qu'**elle déteste la cruauté.

4 Elle va faire des études, **puis** elle va être vétérinaire.

Worksheet 5.4 Fact or opinion?

Answers

A 1 F **2** F **3** O **4** O **5** O **6** O **7** F **8** O
9 F **10** F

B 3 déteste, affreux **4** à mon avis
5 je n'aime pas **6** c'est fou **8** à mon avis

C (Answers will vary.)

© Pearson Education Ltd 2013. Copying permitted for purchasing institution only. This material is not copyright free.

(Pupil Book pp. 104–105)

5 4 Le bonheur, c'est …

Learning objectives
- Describing what makes you happy
- Using infinitives to mean '–ing'

Programme of Study references
GV2 Grammatical structures (using infinitives to mean '–ing')
LC1 Listening and responding
LC6 Reading comprehension
LC6 Translation into English

Grammar
- *c'est de* + the infinitive

Key language
Qu'est-ce que c'est pour toi, le bonheur?
Pour moi, le bonheur, c'est …
d'aller à la pêche
d'être avec mon chien
d'être en famille
de danser
de faire les magasins
de jouer au foot
de manger de la pizza
de partir en vacances
de retrouver mes copains

PLTS
C Creative thinkers

Cross-curricular
PSHE: personal well-being

Resources
Audio files:
69_Module5_Unit4_Ex2.mp3
70_Module5_Unit4_Ex5.mp3
Workbooks:
Cahier d'exercices Vert, pages 52 & 53
ActiveTeach:
p.104 Flashcards
p.105 Video 11
p.105 Video worksheet 11
p.105 Class activity
p.105 Learning skills
p.105 Grammar skills
ActiveLearn:
Listening, Reading

Starter 1

Aim

To introduce the topic

Ask the class what would make them happier. Note their ideas in English on the board and take a class vote on which is the most popular.

Alternative Starter 1:

Use ActiveTeach p.104 Flashcards to introduce language for talking about what makes you happy.

1 Lis et trouve la bonne photo pour chaque personne. (Reading L2)

Reading. Pupils read the sentence from each person and match it to the correct picture.

Answers
Éric – c   Margaux – f   Farid – e   Cécile – b
Arthur – a   Léa – d

2 Écoute. Qui parle? Écris le bon prénom de l'exercice 1. (1–6) (Listening L2)

Listening. Pupils listen to the six people from exercise 1 talking about what happiness is for them and identify the speaker each time.

Audioscript Track 69

1 *Pour moi, le bonheur, c'est d'être avec mon chien.*
2 *Pour moi, le bonheur, c'est de faire les magasins!*
3 *Pour moi, le bonheur, c'est de retrouver mes copains en ville.*
4 *Pour moi, le bonheur, c'est de partir en vacances.*
5 *Pour moi, le bonheur, c'est de jouer au foot.*
6 *Pour moi, le bonheur, c'est d'être en famille.*

Studio Grammaire: *c'est de* + the infinitive

Use the *Studio Grammaire* box to cover *c'est de* + the infinitive (= '–ing').

Answers
1 Arthur   2 Margaux   3 Éric   4 Léa   5 Farid
6 Cécile

R Pupils work in pairs to write two more sentences using *c'est de* + the infinitive.

3 En tandem. Joue au «bip» de mémoire! Utilise les phrases de l'exercice 1. (Speaking L3)

Speaking. In pairs: pupils play a game of 'Bip'. The first pupil says one of the sentences from exercise 1, stopping before the last word; the second pupil says the whole sentence, supplying the missing word. They take it in turn to go first. A sample exchange is given.

4 Écris cinq phrases sur le bonheur. Utilise les mots à droite. (Writing L3)

Writing. Pupils write five sentences about what happiness is, using the words supplied.

© Pearson Education Ltd 2013. Copying permitted for purchasing institution only. This material is not copyright free.

4 Le bonheur, c'est … Moi dans le monde 5

Answers

Pour moi, le bonheur, c'est de manger de la pizza.
Pour moi, le bonheur, c'est de jouer sur ma PlayStation.
Pour moi, le bonheur, c'est de danser.
Pour moi, le bonheur, c'est d'écouter du R&B.
Pour moi, le bonheur, c'est de faire du skate.

Starter 2

Aim

To review language for talking about what makes you happy

Write up the following. Give pupils three minutes to complete the sentence in three different ways.

Pour moi, le bonheur, c'est …

Hear answers.

Alternative Starter 2:

Use ActiveTeach p.105 Class activity to practise language from the module.

5 Écoute et complète le tableau. (1–6)
(Listening L4)

Listening. Pupils copy out the grid. They listen to six conversations about happiness and complete the grid with the details, writing in English what makes each speaker happy and identifying the letter of the correct reason.

Audioscript Track 70

1 – Salut. Qu'est-ce que c'est pour toi, le bonheur?
– Pour moi, le bonheur, c'est de jouer au foot.
– Pourquoi?
– Ben … Parce que c'est mon sport préféré!
2 – Et toi? Qu'est-ce que c'est pour toi, le bonheur?
– Pour moi, le bonheur, c'est de partir en vacances.
– Pourquoi?
– Parce que j'adore le soleil!
– D'accord, merci.
3 – Qu'est-ce que c'est pour toi, le bonheur?
– Pour moi, le bonheur, c'est d'être avec mon chien.
– Pourquoi?
– Ben … Parce que c'est mon meilleur ami.
4 – Et toi? Qu'est-ce que c'est pour toi, le bonheur?
– Pour moi, le bonheur, c'est de faire les magasins!
– Pourquoi?
– Parce que j'adore acheter des vêtements!
5 – Tu es d'accord? Qu'est-ce que c'est pour toi, le bonheur?

– Pour moi, le bonheur, c'est de retrouver mes copains en ville.
– Pourquoi?
– Parce qu'on s'amuse bien ensemble.
6 – Et finalement. Qu'est-ce que c'est pour toi, le bonheur?
– Alors, pour moi, le bonheur, c'est d'être en famille.
– Pourquoi?
– Parce que je m'entends bien avec mes parents et mon frère.
– C'est bien, ça.

Answers

	what makes him/her happy?	reason
1	playing football	c
2	going on holiday	a
3	being with his dog	e
4	shopping	d
5	meeting up with friends in town	b
6	being with family	f

Pupils work in pairs. Using the completed grid, they take it in turn to say in French what makes each person happy.

6 Traduis les raisons de l'exercice 5 en anglais. Utilise un dictionnaire, si nécessaire. (Reading L3)

Reading. Pupils translate the reasons listed in exercise 5 into English, using a dictionary if necessary.

Answers

a … because I love the sunshine.
b … because we have fun/have a laugh together.
c … because it's my favourite sport.
d … because I love buying clothes.
e … because he's my best friend.
f … because I get on well with my parents and my brother.

7 Lis le texte et réponds aux questions. (Reading L5)

Reading. Pupils read the text and answer the questions in English.

Answers

1 Canada.
2 When he was nine.
3 Every week.
4 Because it's very fast.
5 It's dangerous – you have to wear protective clothing.

© Pearson Education Ltd 2013. Copying permitted for purchasing institution only. This material is not copyright free.

5 Moi dans le monde 4 Le bonheur, c'est …

8 Qu'est-ce que c'est pour toi, le bonheur? En secret: écris une phrase et donne une raison. (Writing L3)

PLTS C

Writing. Pupils write a sentence on a scrap of paper saying what happiness is to them and giving a reason. They should not tell or show anyone what they have written. Collect in the papers.

Draw pupils' attention to the tip box on improving their writing by including reasons and by using the language they know from previous modules. Suggest they add this advice to their Skills Notebook.

9 Ton/Ta prof te donne la réponse d'un(e) de tes camarades. Lis la réponse à voix haute. La classe devine qui c'est. (Speaking L3)

Speaking. Shuffle and hand out the papers from exercise 8, so that no one knows whose paper he/she has. Pupils take it in turn to read out the sentence they have. The rest of the class tries to guess who wrote it. A sample exchange is given.

Plenary

Create a 'happiness chain' together. Start the chain off, by saying e.g. *Pour moi, le bonheur, c'est de danser dans la cuisine*. A pupil repeats the list so far, then a different pupil adds an item, e.g. *… et de sortir avec mes copains*. Continue in this way, trying to make the chain as long as possible. Reward pupils who come up with a new/amusing idea.

Workbook, pages 52 and 53

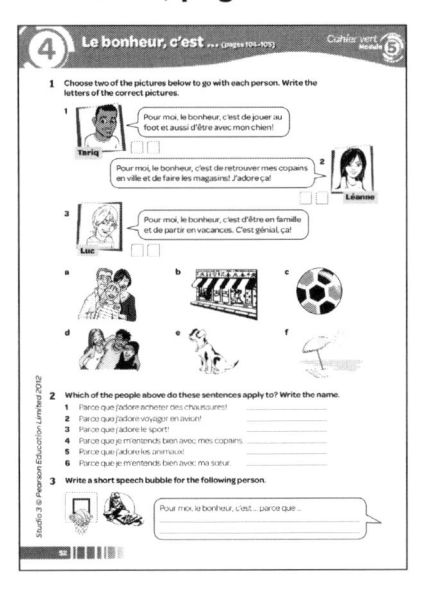

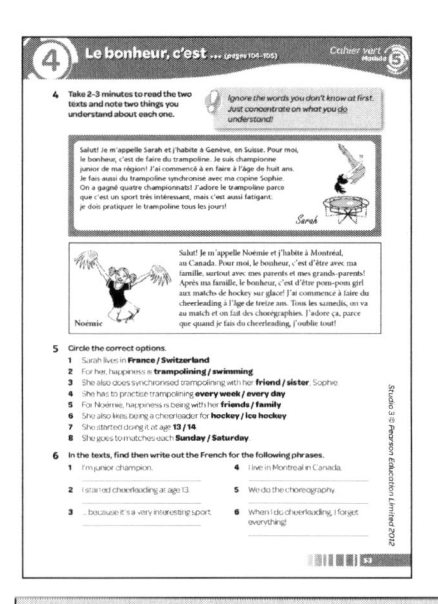

Answers

1   1 c, e   2 b, d   3 a, f

2   1 Léanne   2 Luc   3 Tariq   4 Léanne
    5 Tariq   6 Luc

3   (Example answer:)
    Pour moi, le bonheur, c'est de jouer au basket parce que j'adore le sport et j'aime aussi être en forme! J'adore aussi faire du shopping/faire les magasins parce que la mode, ça m'intéresse … C'est génial!

4   (Answers will vary.)

5   1 Switzerland   2 trampolining   3 friend
    4 every day   5 family   6 ice hockey
    7 13   8 Saturday

6   1 Je suis championne junior.
    2 J'ai commencé à faire du cheerleading à l'âge de treize ans.
    3 … parce que c'est un sport très intéressant.
    4 J'habite à Montréal, au Canada.
    5 On fait des chorégraphies.
    6 Quand je fais du cheerleading, j'oublie tout!

4 Le bonheur, c'est ... Moi dans le monde

Worksheet 5.5 Recognising patterns

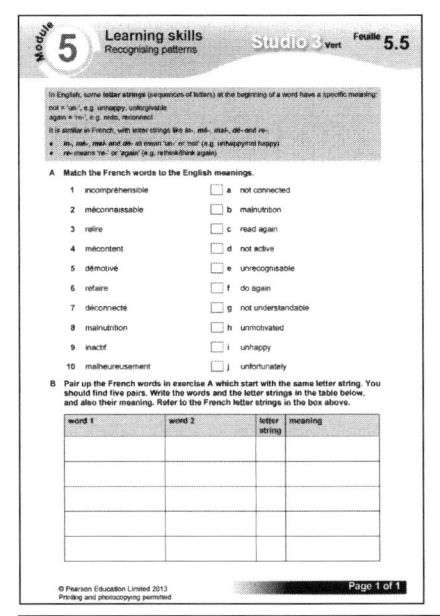

Answers

A 1 g 2 e 3 c 4 i 5 h 6 f 7 a 8 b
  9 d 10 j

B

word 1	word 2	letter string	meaning
incompréhensible	inactif	in	un-, not
méconnaissable	mécontent	mé	un-, not
relire	refaire	re	re-,
démotivé	déconnecté	dé	again
malnutrition	malheureusement	mal	un-, not

Worksheet 5.6 Infinitives

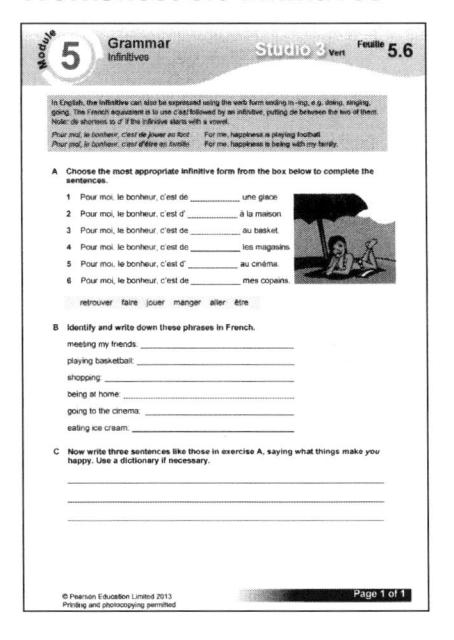

Answers

A 1 manger 2 être 3 jouer 4 faire
  5 aller 6 retrouver

B meeting my friends: retrouver mes copains
  playing basketball: jouer au basket
  shopping: faire les magasins
  being at home: être à la maison
  going to the cinema: aller au cinéma
  eating ice cream: manger une glace

C (Answers will vary.)

Video

Episode 11: Le bonheur

The team look back at some special moments from the filming of StudioFR, as they talk about the things that make them happy. Video worksheet 11 can be used in conjunction with this episode.

Answers to video worksheet (ActiveTeach)

1 A Mehdi might choose the judo video. Marielle would like the one where she met Guillaume. Alex would like the fishing one.

  B Probably something like: Alex: technical things; Mehdi: sport; Marielle: fashion and fronting the videos; Samira and Hugo: friendship.

2 A Hugo is hungry and Marielle is thirsty.

  B Going fishing.

  C The fish he has caught.

  D StudioFR.

3 A Marielle enjoyed the video report on the fire brigade, probably because she got picked up by the fireman.

  B Alex liked the fashion sketch – 'despite myself' (*malgré moi*) he says, probably because it was his moment in the limelight.

  C The crêpe restaurant and the chocolate cake.

  D Being chosen to join the team.

  E 'Superman'.

  F Friends for life.

© Pearson Education Ltd 2013. Copying permitted for purchasing institution only. This material is not copyright free.

Bilan et Révisions

(Pupil Book pp. 106–107)

Bilan

Pupils use this checklist to review language covered in the module, working on it in pairs in class or on their own at home. Encourage them to follow up any areas of weakness they identify. There are Target Setting Sheets included in the Assessment Pack, and an opportunity for pupils to record their own levels and targets on the *J'avance* page in the Workbook, p. 61. You can also use the *Bilan* checklist as an end-of-module plenary option.

Révisions

These revision exercises can be used for assessment purposes or for pupils to practise before tackling the assessment tasks in the Assessment Pack.

Resources
Audio files:
71_Module5_Rev_Ex1.mp3
Workbooks:
Cahier d'exercices Vert, pages 54 & 55

1 Écoute et complète le tableau. (1–4)
(Listening L3)

Listening. Pupils copy out the grid. They listen to four conversations in which teenagers talk about what their parents allow them/don't allow them to do, then complete the grid using the letters of the correct pictures.

Audioscript Track 71

1 – Tu as le droit de sortir seule?
   – Non, je n'ai pas le droit de sortir seule, mais j'ai le droit de sortir avec mes copains le weekend.
2 – Tu as le droit de jouer à des jeux vidéo le soir?
   – Oui, j'ai le droit de jouer à des jeux vidéo le soir, mais je n'ai pas le droit d'aller sur des forums.
3 – Tu as le droit d'aller sur Facebook?
   – Non, je n'ai pas le droit d'aller sur Facebook, mais j'ai le droit de surfer sur Internet une heure par jour maximum.
4 – Tu as le droit de regarder la télé dans ta chambre?
   – Oui, j'ai le droit de regarder la télé dans ma chambre, mais je n'ai pas le droit d'aller au MacDo avec mes copains.

Answers

	is allowed to …	is not allowed to …
1	g	e
2	f	c
3	a	h
4	b	d

2 En tandem. Fais une conversation. Utilise les questions suivantes.
(Speaking L4)

Speaking. In pairs: pupils make up a conversation using the questions supplied. They take it in turn to ask and answer. A sample exchange is given.

3 Lis le texte et complète les phrases en anglais. (Reading L5)

Reading. Pupils read the text and complete the sentences in English.

Answers
1 Every weekend, Baptiste **goes shopping**.
2 Sometimes, he buys second-hand **video games** or **DVDs**.
3 At the supermarket, he buys 'green' products, because **the environment is one of his priorities/he is worried about the environment**.
4 He doesn't often buy **clothes**.
5 Last weekend, he bought **(a pair of) shoes**.
6 Next weekend, he is going to buy **credit for his mobile**.

4 Écris des phrases sur le bonheur pour trois célébrités ou personnages.
(Writing L3)

Writing. Pupils choose three celebrities or famous characters and write sentences about what happiness means to them. An example is given.

Bilan et Révisions Moi dans le monde 5

Workbook, pages 54 and 55

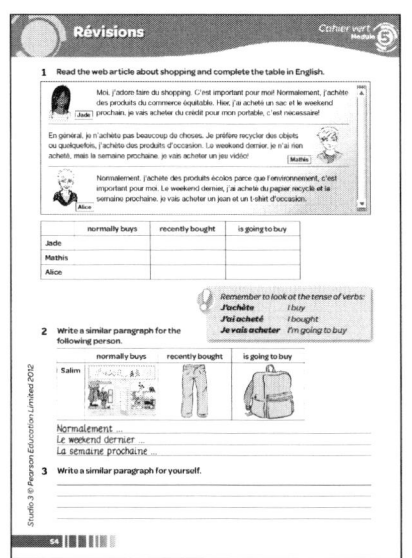

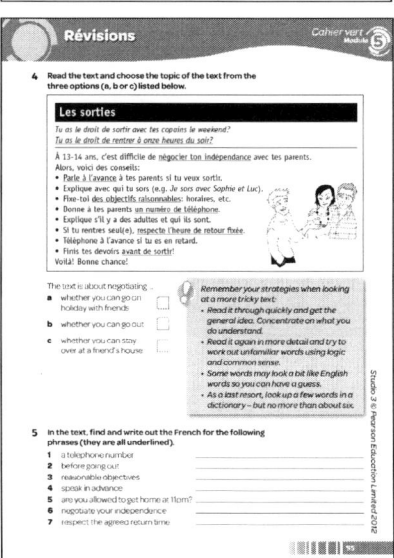

Answers

1

	normally buys	recently bought	is going to buy
Jade	fair-trade products	bag	credit for mobile
Mathis	second-hand products	nothing recycled	video game
Alice	green products	paper	jeans + second-hand T-shirt

2 (Example answer:)
Normalement, j'achète des produits d'occasion parce que l'environnement, c'est important pour moi. Le weekend dernier, j'ai acheté un jean et la semaine prochaine, je vais acheter un sac pour le collège.

3 (Answers will vary.)

4 b whether you can go out

5 1 un numéro de téléphone

2 avant de sortir

3 des objectifs raisonnables

4 parle à l'avance

5 Tu as le droit de rentrer à onze heures du soir?

6 négocier ton indépendance

7 respecte l'heure de retour fixée

En plus: Les jeunes contre l'injustice

(5)

(Pupil Book pp. 108–109)

Learning objective
- Learning about human rights issues

Programme of Study references
LC3 Conversation
LC4 Expressing ideas (writing)
LC6 Reading comprehension
LC8 Writing creatively

Key language
Review of language from the module

PLTS
I Independent enquires

Cross-curricular
ICT: internet research; using a presentation package

Resources
Audio files:
72_Module5_EnPlus_Ex1.mp3
73_Module5_EnPlus_Ex6.mp3
ActiveTeach:
p.109 Assignment 5
p.109 Assignment 5: Prep

Starter

Aim

To introduce the topic

Ask the class what powers they think children have to change the world, as an introduction to the story about Craig Kielburger.

1 Écoute et lis. (Listening L5)

Listening. Pupils listen to the feature on the history of Enfants Entraide, an organisation that promotes children's rights throughout the world, founded by Craig Kielburger when he was 12 years old. They read the text at the same time. Some vocabulary is glossed for support. Draw pupils' attention to the tip box on the reading strategy of starting by looking for words you know when facing a challenging text.

Audioscript Track 72

En 1995, à l'âge de douze ans, Craig Kielburger a fondé Enfants Entraide. La mission d'Enfants Entraide est de lutter contre le travail des enfants.

Craig Kielburger habite à Toronto. Un jour, il a vu dans le journal la photo d'un garçon de son âge: Iqbal Masih. Craig a lu l'histoire tragique d'Iqbal.

Iqbal est né au Pakistan. À l'âge de quatre ans, il a été vendu comme esclave par ses parents. Il a été forcé à fabriquer des tapis.

Après six ans, Iqbal s'est évadé. Il a voyagé partout dans le monde, pour lutter contre le travail des enfants. Mais il a été assassiné à l'âge de douze ans, par «la mafia des tapis».

Choqué par l'histoire d'Iqbal, Craig a décidé de faire quelque chose. Il a décidé de fonder Enfants Entraide. Aujourd'hui, un million de jeunes profitent des programmes d'éducation et de développement d'Enfants Entraide.

2 Fais correspondre les expressions françaises et anglaises. Utilise un dictionnaire. (Reading L5)

Reading. Pupils match the French and English expressions, using a dictionary.

Answers
1 f 2 g 3 e 4 b 5 d 6 a 7 c

3 Relis le texte et choisis la bonne réponse. (Reading L5)

Reading. Pupils read the text in exercise 1 again and complete each sentence by choosing the correct option from the two given each time.

Answers
1 12 ans 2 Enfants Entraide 3 Toronto
4 Iqbal Masih 5 au Pakistan

4 Complète les phrases suivantes. Utilise tes réponses aux exercices 2 et 3. (Reading L5)

Reading. Pupils complete the gap-fill sentences in English, using their answers to exercises 2 and 3.

Answers
1 Craig Kielburger founded **Enfants Entraide** at the age of **12**.
2 The mission of Enfants Entraide is to **fight against** child labour.
3 Craig read about the story of Iqbal Masih in **the newspaper**.
4 At four years old, Iqbal was **sold as a slave** by his parents.
5 He was forced to **make carpets**.
6 After six years, Iqbal **escaped**.
7 He travelled **all over the world** to fight against child labour.
8 When he was 12 years old, Iqbal **was murdered (by the 'carpet mafia')**.

© Pearson Education Ltd 2013. Copying permitted for purchasing institution only. This material is not copyright free.

En plus: Les jeunes contre l'injustice Moi dans le monde **5**

5 Trouve la deuxième partie de chaque question et copie les questions. (Writing L4)

Writing. Pupils match the question halves, writing out the completed questions.

Answers

See audioscript for exercise 6: pupils listen to the exercise 6 recording to check their answers.

6 Écoute et vérifie. (1–5) (Listening L5)

Listening. Pupils listen and check their answers to exercise 5.

Audioscript Track 73

1 À quel âge as-tu fondé Enfants Entraide?
2 Quelle est la mission d'Enfants Entraide?
3 Où as-tu lu l'histoire d'Iqbal Masih?
4 À quel âge est-ce qu'il a été assassiné?
5 Combien de jeunes profitent des programmes d'Enfants Entraide?

Answers

See audioscript.

7 En tandem. Invente une interview avec Craig Kielburger. Utilise les questions de l'exercice 5. (Speaking L5)

Speaking. In pairs: pupils make up an interview with Craig Kielburger, taking it in turn to be Craig and the interviewer. They use the questions they prepared in exercise 5. A sample exchange is given. Draw pupils' attention to the tip box on changing the verb forms from 3rd to 1st person when answering questions 1 and 3.

8 Cherche sur Internet des images et des informations sur Craig Kielburger, Enfants Entraide et Iqbal Masih. (Reading L5)

PLTS

Reading. Pupils search on the internet for pictures and information about Craig Kielburger, Enfants Entraide and Iqbal Masih. Tell them that this is in preparation for designing a poster in exercise 9, to help them focus their searches.

9 Dessine un poster sur le sujet suivant: «On n'est jamais trop jeune pour changer le monde.» Utilise les résultats de tes recherches. (Writing L3–5)

Writing. Pupils design a poster on the topic 'You are never too young to change the world', using the findings from their research in exercise 8 and including pictures.

Pupils could design the poster on computer using a DTP package.

Plenary

Conclude the topic with a class discussion on what could be done to help children in countries where child labour is common.

Worksheet 5.7 Le bonheur. Assignment 5: writing

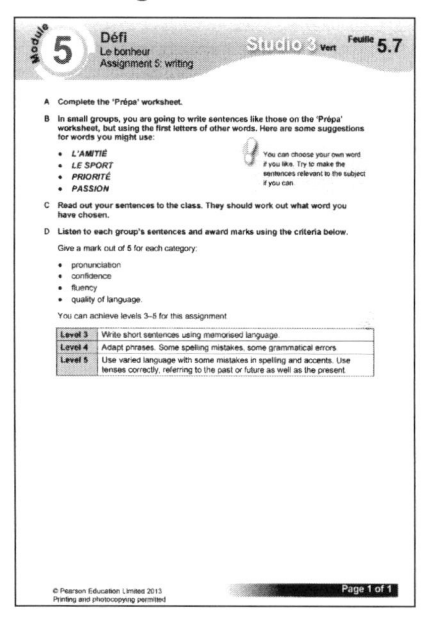

© Pearson Education Ltd 2013. Copying permitted for purchasing institution only. This material is not copyright free.

5 Moi dans le monde En plus: Les jeunes contre l'injustice

Worksheet 5.8 Le bonheur: Prépa

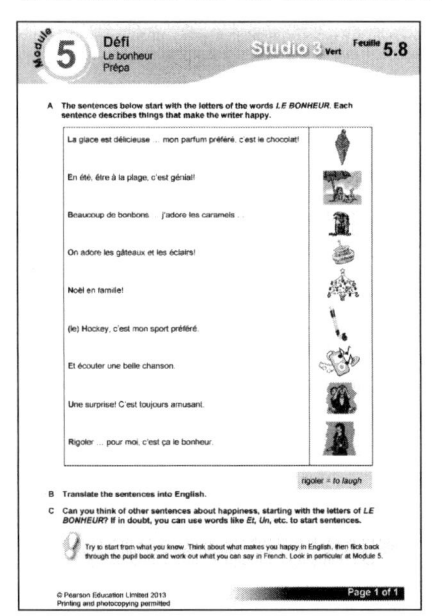

Answers

B Ice cream is delicious ... my favourite flavour is chocolate!

It's wonderful to be on the beach in summer!

Lots of sweets ... I love caramels ...

We love cakes and éclairs!

Christmas with the family!

Hockey is my favourite sport.

And listening to a beautiful song.

A surprise! That's always fun.

Laughing ... for me, that's what happiness is.

C (Answers will vary.)

(Pupil Book pp. 110–111)

5 Je parle

The challenge
- Giving a short video presentation about yourself to convince a French reality TV producer you are right for his show

Overview
Explain how this section works.
- Pupils read the context and what they need to do to complete the challenge.
- They then read the list of suggested details to include. Explain that they should use this both to help structure their content and as a checklist as part of their final preparations.
- Explain that the exercises which follow in this section are structured to help them prepare for their presentation.
- Before starting, pupils read the POSM feature: this will help them to improve their performance. Encourage them to use this approach routinely in speaking tasks.

Programme of Study references
GV1 Tenses (past, present and future)
LC4 Expressing ideas (speaking)
LC5 Speaking coherently and confidently

Resources
Audio files:
74_Module5_Jeparle_Ex8.mp3

1 Find the personal details in this word snake. Write down your own personal details.

Pupils write out Éric's personal introduction, which is hidden in the word snake. They then use this as a model to write out their own personal introduction.

Answers
Je m'appelle Éric. J'ai quinze ans et j'habite à Boulogne, dans le nord de la France. J'y habite depuis dix ans.

2 Unjumble these people's priorities in life.

Pupils write out correctly the jumbled words for people's priorities in life.

Answers
1 mes amis 2 ma famille 3 mes animaux
4 mon chien 5 la musique 6 le football

3 Complete this sentence, giving three of your own priorities.

Pupils complete the sentence to give details of their own priorities.

4 Decode the things that make people happy. Then write one sentence about what makes you happy.

Pupils work out what the sentences say, then write a sentence of their own saying what makes them happy.

Answers
1 Pour moi, le bonheur, c'est d'être en famille.
2 Pour moi, le bonheur, c'est d'être avec mon chien.
3 Pour moi, le bonheur, c'est de faire les magasins!
4 Pour moi, le bonheur, c'est de jouer au foot.
5 Pour moi, le bonheur, c'est de partir en vacances.
6 Pour moi, le bonheur, c'est de retrouver mes copains.

5 Find five opinions in this heart. Choose one to use in your presentation to say why something makes you happy.

Pupils write out the five opinions in the word snakes. They choose one to use in their presentation to say why something makes them happy.

Answers
J'aime ça, c'est bien.
Je trouve ça génial.
Je trouve ça super.
C'est ma passion.
J'adore ça.

6 Match up the things people don't like to the illustrations. Write a sentence you will use in your presentation.

Pupils match the sentences with the pictures, then write a sentence about something they object to that they can use in their own presentation.

Answers
1 d 2 b 3 a 4 c 5 e

© Pearson Education Ltd 2013. Copying permitted for purchasing institution only. This material is not copyright free.

5 Moi dans le monde Je parle

7 Write these sentences in the near future tense the right way round. Then write a similar sentence for your presentation.

Pupils write out correctly the sentences featuring the near future tense. They then use these as a model to write a sentence for their own presentation.

> **Answers**
> 1 Un jour, je vais aller en Guadeloupe. Ça va être génial.
> 2 Un jour, je vais faire le tour du monde. Ça va être super.
> 3 Un jour, je vais aller aux États-Unis. Ça va être cool.
> 4 Un jour, je vais être pilote. Ça va être intéressant.
> 5 Un jour, je vais aller au Sénégal. Ça va être top.

8 Listen to Jamel's presentation. Fill in the gaps.

Pupils listen to Jamel's presentation and complete the gap-fill version of the text, using the words supplied.

> **Audioscript Track 74**
>
> *Coucou! Je m'appelle Jamel. J'ai quinze ans et j'habite à Toulouse, dans le sud-ouest de la France. J'y habite depuis dix ans.*
>
> *Mes priorités dans la vie sont mes amis, ma famille et mon chat. Pour moi, le vrai bonheur, c'est de jouer au foot. C'est top.*
>
> *Je n'aime pas du tout le racisme. J'ai horreur de ça. Un jour, je vais aller aux États-Unis où je vais faire un camp de football. Ça va être cool.*

> **Answers**
> 1 J'ai 2 depuis 3 et 4 bonheur 5 pas du tout
> 6 faire

9 Now draft your own presentation for the challenge. Check that what you have written is accurate and makes sense. Use the vocabulary and phrases you've collected in the previous exercises.

Pupils now write their presentation in full, using the language they have developed in the exercises in this section. They check their work to make sure it is logical and accurate.

Draw pupils' attention to the tip box on writing out their presentation in full or in note form, and the importance of including different tenses. They might also find it useful to look again at the tips on Pupil Book p. 128.

10 Now memorise your presentation and rehearse it!

Pupils memorise and practise their presentation.

Pupils then give their presentation. They should ask their audience to give feedback and use this to identify areas for improvement in extended speaking tasks they do in Key Stage 4.

(Pupil Book pp. 112–113)

Studio Grammaire 5

The *Studio Grammaire* section provides a more detailed summary of the key grammar covered in the module, along with further exercises to practise these points. The interactive activities on ActiveTeach pp.112 and 113 are repeated from elsewhere in the module.

Grammar topics
- *avoir*
- possessive adjectives
- using a variety of structures
- using different time frames: which tense to use?

Resources
Workbooks:
Cahier d'exercices Vert, pages 56 & 57

avoir

1 Follow the lines to find the translations for these expressions.

Pupils follow the lines to match the French and English expressions.

Answers
1 avoir chaud — to be hot
2 avoir froid — to be cold
3 avoir peur — to be frightened
4 avoir raison — to be right
5 avoir tort — to be wrong
6 avoir l'occasion de — to have the opportunity to
7 avoir horreur de — to hate
8 avoir le droit de — to be allowed to

2 Write out the sentences with the correct form of *avoir*. Translate the sentences into English.

Pupils complete the gap-fill sentences with the correct form of *avoir*. They then translate the sentences into English.

Answers
1 J'ai chaud.
   I'm hot.
2 Tu as froid?
   Are you cold?
3 J'ai horreur des légumes.
   I hate vegetables.
4 Elle a peur des vampires.
   She is frightened of vampires.
5 Tu as tort!
   You're wrong!
6 Il a raison.
   He is right.
7 Tu as le droit de sortir seul?
   Are you allowed to go out by yourself?
8 On a l'occasion de visiter l'Espagne.
   We have the opportunity to visit/go to Spain.

Possessive adjectives

3 Copy the sentences, using the correct possessive adjective.

Pupils copy and complete each sentence, choosing the correct possessive adjective from the three options given.

Answers
1 Je regarde les photos de **mes** copains.
2 Je prends **ma** caméra et **mon** micro et je filme les gens.
3 **Ma** mère pense que parler une autre langue, c'est important.
4 Il aime **son** boulot parce que c'est motivant.
5 Qui est **ton** chanteur préféré?
6 **Sa** soeur s'appelle Nathalie.

Using a variety of structures

4 Write these sentences correctly using the English translations to help you.

Pupils write out each jumbled sentence correctly, using the English translations supplied for support.

Answers
1 Je vais aller à la fac.
2 Je veux travailler dans un autre pays.
3 Je voudrais habiter à l'étranger.
4 Je n'aime pas surfer sur Internet.
5 Je dois faire mes devoirs tous les soirs.

Using different time frames: Which tense to use?

5 Which tense is needed in each gap? Write PR for present, PER for perfect or F for future. Use the time expressions and context to help you decide.

Pupils work out which tense is required to fill each gap in the text, writing PR for present, PER for perfect and F for future.

Answers
1 PR 2 PR 3 PR 4 PER 5 PER 6 PER
7 F 8 F

© Pearson Education Ltd 2013. Copying permitted for purchasing institution only. This material is not copyright free.

5 Moi dans le monde Studio Grammaire

6 Fill in each gap in exercise 5, using a verb from the list that makes sense.

Pupils complete the gap-fill text in exercise 5, using the verbs supplied.

Answers
1 vais 2 mange 3 joue 4 suis allée
5 ai écouté 6 ai fait 7 vais aller 8 vais chanter

7 Look carefully at the context and put the verbs in brackets into the correct tense.

Pupils complete the text, replacing the infinitive prompts with the appropriate verb in the correct tense. Remind them to use time expressions to help them work out which tense is required..

Answers
1 vais 2 aime 3 ai fait 4 vais aller
5 va voyager 6 vais prendre 7 a
8 vais prendre

Workbook, pages 56 and 57

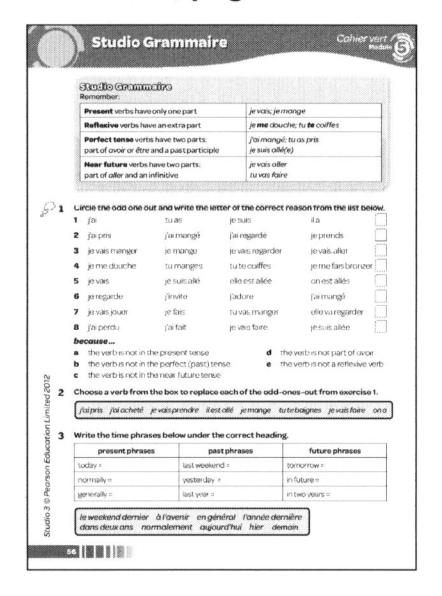

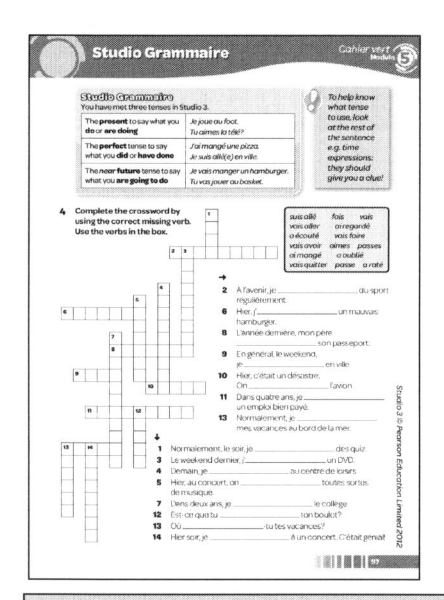

Answers
1 1 je suis, d 2 je prends, b 3 je mange, c
   4 tu manges, e 5 je vais, b 6 j'ai mangé, a
   7 je fais, c 8 je vais faire, b

2 1 on a 2 j'ai acheté or j'ai pris
   3 je vais prendre or je vais faire
   4 tu te baignes 5 il est allé 6 je mange
   7 je vais prendre or je vais faire
   8 j'ai pris or j'ai acheté

3

present phrases	past phrases	future phrases
today = aujourd'hui	last weekend = le weekend dernier	tomorrow = demain
normally = normalement	yesterday = hier	in future = à l'avenir
generally = en général	last year = l'année dernière	in two years = dans deux ans

4

→	↓
2 vais faire	1 fais
6 ai mangé	3 ai regardé
8 a oublié	4 vais aller
9 vais	5 a écouté
10 a raté	7 vais quitter
11 vais avoir	12 aimes
13 passe	13 passes
14 suis allé	

© Pearson Education Ltd 2013. Copying permitted for purchasing institution only. This material is not copyright free.

(Pupil Book pp. 124–125)

5 À toi

Self-access reading and writing

A Reinforcement

1 Lis et complète les phrases avec les mots d'en bas. Puis écris la lettre de la bonne photo. (Reading L2)

Reading. Pupils complete the gap-fill sentences using the words supplied. They then match each sentence to the correct picture.

Answers

1 J'ai le droit de regarder la télé dans ma **chambre**. (b)
2 Je n'ai pas le droit d'aller sur **Facebook**. (d)
3 J'ai le droit d'aller au **MacDo** avec mes copains. (e)
4 Je n'ai pas le droit de jouer à des **jeux vidéo** le soir. (c)
5 J'ai le droit de sortir avec mes copains pendant le **weekend**. (a)

2 Lis l'exemple. Puis écris des phrases pour Marion, Yoni et toi! Utilise les photos de l'exercice 1. (Writing L4)

Writing. Pupils write sentences for Marion and Yoni, using the information in the table, then write about themselves in a similar way. A sample is supplied.

Answers

Marion: J'ai le droit de sortir avec mes copains le weekend, mais je n'ai pas le droit de jouer à des jeux vidéo le soir et je n'ai pas le droit d'aller sur Facebook. Ce n'est pas juste!
Yoni: J'ai le droit de regarder la télé dans ma chambre et j'ai le droit de jouer à des jeux vidéo le soir. Mais je n'ai pas le droit d'aller au MacDo. Ce n'est pas juste!

3 Associe les deux parties de chaque phrase et copie les phrases complètes. Utilise un dictionnaire, si nécessaire. (Reading L3)

Reading. Pupils match the sentence halves, then copy out the complete sentences.

Answers

1 Pour moi, le bonheur, c'est d'écouter du hip-hop, parce que ça me donne envie de danser.
2 Pour moi, le bonheur, c'est d'aller au cinéma, parce que je suis fan de films d'horreur.
3 Pour moi, le bonheur, c'est de faire du judo, parce que j'aime beaucoup les arts martiaux.
4 Pour moi, le bonheur, c'est de regarder X-Factor, parce que c'est mon émission de télé préférée.
5 Pour moi, le bonheur, c'est de sortir avec ma petite copine, parce qu'elle est très sympa.
6 Pour moi, le bonheur c'est de faire de l'équitation, parce que j'adore les chevaux.

B Extension

1 Lis les textes et réponds aux questions. Écris le bon prénom. (Reading L6)

Reading. Pupils read the texts, then answer the English questions by identifying the person being described in each one.

Answers

1 Yasmine 2 Lucie 3 Éva 4 Lucie
5 Yasmine 6 Éva

2 Trouve un copain/une copine britannique pour chaque Français(e). (Reading L4)

Reading. Pupils find a British friend for each French person by matching their interests.

Answers

Mélissa – Lewis
Najim – Jade
Éloïse – Katia
Abel – Amy
Irina – Matthew

3 Écris des e-mails à trouvedesamis.fr pour Ludo, Malika et toi. (Writing L4)

Writing. Pupils write emails to trouvedesamis.fr for Ludo and Malika, using the information in the table. They then write about themselves in a similar way.

Answers

Ludo: *Mes priorités sont* (d'abord) *la musique* et (puis) *le foot. Je n'aime pas du tout* la pauvreté dans le monde.
Malika: Mes priorités sont (d'abord) ma famille et (puis) mes études. Je n'aime pas du tout le racisme.

© Pearson Education Ltd 2013. Copying permitted for purchasing institution only. This material is not copyright free.